THE EVER-CHANGING ORGANIZATION

♥

Creating the Capacity for
Continuous Change,
Learning and Improvement

ADVANCE PRAISE

With this book, providing leadership just got easier for those executives and managers looking to create 'change seeking or friendly' organizations. The level of thought given by the authors in the form of tools, approaches, methods and practices will serve to guide you and your team well through your own change journey. I especially believe their focus of looking at the organization as a 'living system' will enhance your own decision making process.

—**Wesley C. Cantrell**, president and CEO,
Lanier Worldwide

Is your organization capable of continuous change? Pieters and Young have made an important contribution by making a compelling argument for continuous change in a turbulent world and by providing an excellent framework for answering this question about your own organization as well as the tools for developing this essential capability. They provide you with a means for rising above the clutter of fads and fashions that populate the management landscape.

—**Michael Beer**, Cahners-Rabb Professor of Business Administration,
Harvard Business School

Gerry Pieters and Doyle Young's book is a powerful and provocative approach to building the 'better model' for the absorption and transference of knowledge. If you are a true believer in the concept of continuous learning and wish to build the better learning organization, this book is a must read. I recommend it highly.

—**William L. Miller**, senior V.P.,
Corporate Director of the Employee Development Group,
The Money Store

Drawing on their impressive experience as managers and consultants, Pieters and Young offer a carefully written elaboration of their own Ever-Changing Organization (ECO) model that serves as an invaluable 'how-to' on building 'high capacity for change' organizations. Their book is a treasure trove of tested and thought-provoking assessment tools shown to be powerful aids in affecting successful change.

—**Reuben T. Harris**, professor and chairman,
Department of Systems Management, Naval Postgraduate School

The Ever-Changing Organization is a compelling approach for building the organization of the future that delivers successful results. I know because I've worked with Pieters for nearly 30 years and he is superb with ideas and getting people to adopt them.

—**Charles C. Harwood**, author and retired CEO, U.S. Philips Semiconductors

THE
EVER-CHANGING
ORGANIZATION

Creating the Capacity for Continuous Change, Learning and Improvement

by

Gerald R. Pieters, Ph.D.
Doyle W. Young

S^t_L

St. Lucie Press

Boca Raton London New York Washington, D.C.

Library of Congress Cataloging-in-Publication Data

Pieters, Gerald R.
   The ever-changing organization : creating the capacity for
continuous change, learning, and improvement / Gerald R. Pieters and
Doyle W. Young.
      p.   cm.
   Includes bibliographical references and index.
   ISBN 1-57444-262-7 (alk. paper)
   1. Organizational change.   2. Organizational learning.   I. Young,
Doyle W.   II. Title.
HD58.8.P525   1999
658.4'06--dc21

99-30449
CIP

Preface

Change! Everyone's talking and writing about it — piecemeal. We have talked with large numbers of people about this book, including potential publishers. Many say we don't need another book on change. They believe that there are too many already and they all say essentially the same thing. Well, we happen to disagree and that's why we wrote this book. In addition, we have discussed the concept of the book with a wide range of people in organizations who feel strongly that such a book is sorely needed. Most are associated with organizations that are already in trouble because they lack the capabilities of an Ever-Changing Organization, and they don't yet realize it.

We ask you, the reader, to read this book carefully and thoughtfully. Suspend any tendency to dismiss the writing and the model of the Ever-Changing Organization as "the same old thing." It's not! And if you are an executive or an aspiring executive, this book is for you. The rate of change you face is greater than you have ever faced before and will only become greater. You are remiss in your duty to yourself, your career, and your organization if you do not prepare for the challenges brought on by accelerating change.

Our discussions and work together began in 1994. As we talked it became obvious to us that virtually all books dealing with change ended up focusing on one of two areas. Many look almost exclusively at the leader of change and his or her influence on the success or failure of change efforts. Others describe processes for planning and managing change with focus on reengineering or a specific change event and its implementation. Yet, the issue is not just the leader. Nor is the issue to manage a specific, one-time change. These are parts of the needs an organization has, but are incomplete in their scope.

What we couldn't find then, and still cannot find, was an overall model of organizations as living systems facing rapid and accelerating change. We felt a strong need for such a model to give focus to (1) the capacity for change an organization requires and (2) the issues that must be addressed to create increased change capacity in an increasingly unstable world. These are critical issues. Most organizations are already unable to cope with the pace of change they must manage. And the problem will only get worse.

The model of the Ever-Changing Organization (ECO) presented in this book has evolved to its current form through several stages. Earlier versions of the model were oversimplified. They were too much like other work on change. The present version of the ECO model views the organization as a living system and addresses an organization's required change capability along with the issues that determine existing capacity. It provides a framework for increasing the capacity for change, learning, and improvement. New change initiatives need not involve pursuit of the latest management fad or to become the "program of the month" we have observed so often.

The ECO framework provides a rational guide for selecting as well as rejecting new initiatives for change. The model is easy for the reader and the people of his or her organization to understand. Changes that are consistent with needs identified by using the model fit and make sense. Those that do not are rejected. Decisions made on this basis provide all with the sense that management knows what the organization is doing and where it is going even in these increasingly turbulent times. Support for their efforts is greater.

Our combined business experience represents over 50 years of work involving some 400 organizations around the world. Many of the examples in the book come from hands-on experience with people in these organizations from the executive suite to the first line. Our jobs have ranged from positions as business owners, to key executives and managers, and to internal and external consultants and researchers. The conceptual aspects of the model were developed from educational experiences, our reading of others' ideas and theories, and from models we synthesized in support of our own consulting work. Other ideas were developed specifically for the book from interviews with executives and conversations with consulting colleagues. All were involved with organizations coping with rapid change.

We believe, as did the eminent social psychologist Kurt Lewin, that "there is nothing more practical than good theory." We have attempted to integrate hands-on experience with theoretical models to produce a very practical framework for thinking and analysis about organizations facing rapid and increasing change. We have developed specific materials to use in applications of the ECO model. Many of these are tools and methods for diagnosis and action planning. The ECO model can be used by anyone willing to invest in learning and adapting it to the unique needs of his organization. Some will find that there is a long journey ahead. Others will find comfort in the fact that much has already been done that addresses their organization's needs for ECO capability. No matter where you are, or how far you have to go, the model and materials in the book will guide you.

The Ever-Changing Organization model is something we consider a "work in progress." What the book describes is the thinking that has developed in our first four years of work. We truly believe that we cannot allow that work to stop and still be true to what we espouse. Much remains to be learned about creating ECO capacity. Significantly more learning will be needed in the future as even more rapid change descends on all of us. To support that ongoing learning and continuing development of the ECO model, we have created The EverChange Institute. The challenge of the Institute is to continue the study of the issues that influence need and ECO capacity. Bringing people together to exchange experiences, whether successful or not, or to share and develop ideas will allow the model to continue to evolve. Sponsoring research on the features of the ever-changing environment and the influential components of the ECO model will add to our knowledge base. Consulting and training support services to organizations needing to increase their capacity for change, learning, and improvement are also available through the Ever-Change Institute.

Any reader who has interest in the work of the Institute or is in need of its services can contact us at The EverChange Institute, 3478 Buskirk Ave., #1031, Pleasant Hill, CA 94523 or by phone at (925)746-7165. Individually, we can be reached by email at gpieterssr@aol.com (Gerry Pieters) or EvrChnge@pacbell.net (Doyle Young). Or you can contact us through our web site at www.EverChange.com. We are interested in building alliances, receiving input regarding organizations' experiences with change, sharing ideas about the model, and doing whatever else might advance our understanding of the Ever-Changing Organization and its needs.

Abraham Lincoln once said, "A smart man is always getting himself out of situations that a wise man never gets himself into in the first place." It is our hope and intention that careful reading and use of this book will make you a wiser person. We want you to be a person who will never have to get out of the situation of potential failure because you have not created the capacity for change, learning, and improvement your organization needs, i.e., you have not engaged in the ongoing work of "becoming" an Ever-Changing Organization.

Gerald R. Pieters
Doyle W. Young

About the Authors

Gerald R. Pieters, M.A., Ph.D., is Chairman of the EverChange Institute and President of The Quality Improvement Company. He received his master's and Ph.D. degrees from Southern Illinois University in Carbondale. His concentration was in the field of industrial psychology and organizational behavior. In the mid-1970's he attended Columbia University's first Advanced Program in Organization Development and Human Resource Management for experienced practitioners in the field. His 30 years of experience includes over 14 years as an external consultant and 16 in internal consulting and management positions. He began his career with Corning Glass Works. He then moved to Signetics Corporations (now Philips Semiconductor) in the microelectronics business where he served as a member of the senior management team and V.P. of Management and Organization Development.

He cofounded The Quality Improvement Company with Charles Harwood in 1985. For over 14 years that company has provided consultation, training, on-the-job tools, and workbooks to clients implementing organization-wide quality and continuous improvement processes. He has written extensive materials for clients and has designed highly successful workshops and learning experiences for people at all levels of an organization. More than 100 organizations around the world, over 200 management teams, and in excess of 50,000 people have used the materials and services of the company. In 1996 he cofounded the EverChange Institute with his coauthor, Doyle W. Young. The Institute is focused on supporting diagnostic and implementation processes for the ECO-building efforts of client organizations. It is also designed to support research and ongoing learning about the needs and characteristics of organizations facing ongoing and accelerating change.

Dr. Pieters has authored many articles and has been a frequent presenter at business and professional conferences. His affiliations include the national and San Francisco Bay area Organization Development Networks and the American Society for Quality. He has also taught organizational behavior and managerial psychology courses at Elmira College (New York) and San Jose State University (California).

Dr. Pieters' current interests are focused on building ECO capacity. In particular he is concerned with the use and abuse of control processes and their effects on change capacity and on development of valid and predictive methods for diagnosis and assessment of organizational capacity for change, learning, and improvement.

Doyle W. Young, M.B.A., is cofounder and President of the EverChange Institute (ECI), a joint venture of On-Site Plus and The Quality Improvement Company. He is also managing partner of On-Site Plus, a consulting firm he founded in 1984 that offers clients over 400 areas of learning and improvement through a nation-wide network of over 350 consultants and subject matter experts.

Mr. Young's work experience has included a position as acting COO and corporate V.P. of Lesher Communications, Inc., a $100 million broadcast media company and newspaper publisher. In 1982 and 1983 he was President of Northwest Management Associates, an independent affiliate of the American Management Association. He has been director of AMA's Regional San Francisco Management Center and also director of marketing for Zenger-Miller, a subsidiary of Times-Mirror Publishing now known as Achieve Global.

As founder and managing director of On-Site Plus, Mr. Young markets and manages the firm's service offerings to organizations seeking advice and counsel in many areas. These include training workshops, developing corporate learning centers, continuous learning and improvement, competency development, executive coaching and development, change processes, instructional systems development, professional skills development, management development, and the use of new technologies for learning and development.

Mr. Young is a frequent speaker and writer for professional publications and business conferences. He holds an undergraduate degree in industrial psychology and an M.B.A. in management. Currently he is an Adjunct Professor of business at the graduate school of Golden Gate University specializing in business management.

Acknowledgments

Writing a book is more work than either of us realized. Many hours of discussion and planning are required. Ideas that shape the materials and the framework for the book are developed and tested over the course of years with friends, colleagues, and clients.

In the early days of developing the ECO model, members of the professional staff of The Quality Improvement Company were great sounding boards who pushed our thinking. Thanks to Terry Neri, Faye August, Larry Seeger, Tony Sweet, and Dave Cherin.

Other consultants and colleagues who reviewed drafts of material and commented on our work included Kevin Wheeler, Jeanne Cherbeneau, Beverly Scott, Tamra Fleming, Bill Miller, Keith Myers, Donna Stoneham, Lee Garner, Dean Michelson, Jim Bandrowski, Warren Wilhelm, and Marc Taylor. Thanks to all for their time, stories, and insights. They have enriched our understanding and contributed in ways they might not realize.

Executives and managers of client organizations have also shared ideas on the issues of continuous change, learning and improvement and examples from their experience that have given substance to the book. Thanks to Mike Hackworth, Don Liddie, Bob Mollerstuen, Lionel Kirton, Dick Watkin, Norm Gottschalk, Ray Looney, Tom Ryan, Larry Parker, Earl Wright, Bill Siart, and many others. We've learned from all of you.

Our research for the book included a number of substantial interviews with CEOs and top level executives. We thank them for their valuable time and for sharing insights from the perspective of those at the top of organizations having to learn to cope with constant change. Among those interviewed are Dennis Snyder, Steve Jensen, Wesley Cantrell, James C. Morgan,

Bill Miller, Jeffrey Miller, Dr. Asad Madni, Eric Herr, Tony Ridder, Bob Ingle, Kathy Yates, Mary Jean Connors, Nate Oubre, Wanda Lee, Pat Spainhour, Dave Olsen, and Robert Miller. We appreciate their time and willingness to let us use materials from their interviews. A few others prefer to remain anonymous yet provided material that has been used in the book. They know who they are and we thank them also.

Pat Roberson of CRC Press (parent of St. Lucie Press) has provided help and guidance as we have prepared the manuscript. Drew Gierman, Publisher of St. Lucie Press, has encouraged us from the time we met. We thank them for their support.

Betty Jacobsen is appreciated for her devoted efforts at transcribing and editing the interview tapes. Danna Bell provided invaluable assistance with scheduling and countless other details needed to complete the book in a somewhat organized fashion. Connie Herman spent hundreds of hours overseeing the development of a web site and application process for consultants — her work will become more important to those trying to reach us and share their interest in ECO. And, finally, thanks to Judy Rôsie for her effort and creativity in preparing the artwork for the figures.

Doyle Young's Personal Acknowledgments

There are many acknowledgments due when a work represents over 50 years of combined experience and a lifetime of work. For my coauthor's role, I would like to say that I came to deeply appreciate his "at-the-fingertips" command of his experience and its application to our work together. Like our model, ours was a synergy that went beyond the sum of the parts. I especially wish to acknowledge his unfailing integrity and healthy skepticism to keep pressing for data (or "where is the beef?") and demanding clarity on how ideas being developed related to our goal of helping organizations build the capabilities of an Ever-Changing Organization.

Other important influences include my friend Carlyle Johnson, who taught me much and has been unfailing in his chiding to always go deeper. Other leaders who were mentors and helped make this book possible are Frank Dellunde, who gave me my start and was always a great source of support; Norm Curtis, who encouraged me to use my gifts to serve others; and Larry Carney, my first boss, who was also the first to push me to recognize the power of business as an expression of personal faith.

Gerry Pieters' Personal Acknowledgments

Michael Beer was my first manager in the business world and has been my friend and mentor ever since. His confidence and intense creative stimulation started me on a successful career and made this book possible. Chuck Harwood is my close friend, prior boss, former partner, and business mentor. He has taught me more about the world of business than anyone I have encountered, beginning with the admonition to "talk manager talk" instead of hiding behind professional jargon. Our countless hours of discussion and debate have shaped many of the ideas in the book. Chuck has continually forced me to look at the practical application and implications of my work for helping managers improve results. Thanks are not enough to express my appreciation for his help and support.

The "core faculty" and participants of the original Advanced Program in Organization Development and Human Resource Management at Columbia University have had great influence on my development. Included specifically are Warner Burke, Noel Tichy, and David Nadler along with the other faculty of the program. They taught me the importance of articulating the model guiding one's actions as a writer or consultant. Models and assumptions guide one's focus in selecting relevant data from the overwhelming mass of data available. That thinking has guided the development of the ECO model. I fervently hope that our model will also guide executives as they make decisions and set direction for increasing capabilities as an ECO.

I sincerely appreciate the intensity and dogged determination of my coauthor, Doyle Young, as we have invested nearly five years together in developing the model and the book. Without his energy and support there are times I may have decided to end the journey.

My younger son, Steve Pieters, began pressing me to write a book over fifteen years ago. He has never let up and has offered encouragement and support throughout the entire process. My other children, Kimberly Mac-Fadyen and Gerry, Jr. have also offered ongoing support and encouragement, even when the press of work on the book interfered with other plans. My mother, Ida Pieters, has been a life-long inspiration, never letting me back off and always urging me on. Her love and devotion is a mother's true and unconditional love.

And, finally, my loving wife and lifelong encourager, Peggy, has provided incredible support throughout my education and career, often at her own expense. She has stood firm through thick and thin, sacrificing her personal time and needs in ways that have made it possible for me to focus on my work and on the book. I can't thank or love her enough for her enormous love and support.

Contents

Dedications

Doyle Young:
To Letia and Scott who always make it worthwhile.

Gerry Pieters:
To Peg and Mom,
Kim, Gerry, Jr. and Steve:
You're what keeps me going.

1 Introduction to the Ever-Changing Organization

F or many years we have heard the expression "There's nothing more certain than death and taxes!" It now seems prudent to add the idea of the certainty of change to that expression. Even the IRS, the agency that deals with our taxes throughout our life and after our death, is being threatened with fundamental change in the tax code they administer as well as with congressional action to force modification of approaches based on fear and intimidation of the taxpayer. Who would've thought?

I. Leaders and the Ever-Changing Organization

If ongoing change is a certainty, it behooves the leaders of organizations to examine how they are designed and managed to cope with change — explore the extent to which the organization must become more capable of dealing with change — become aware of the conditions in the organization that support or inhibit change. The model of the Ever-Changing Organization (ECO) in this book is designed to help leaders do just that.

Organizations vary dramatically in their capacity for continuous change, learning, and improvement. Many books on the subject of change place their primary emphasis on the role of the leader or on processes for managing a particular change activity. This book goes beyond how individual change activities are managed. It goes beyond the role of the leader. In this book we are concerned with the characteristics of the overall design of organizations that build capacity for change. In particular, with more change happening all the time, we are concerned with situations in which growth in capacity for change, learning, and improvement lags the increase in the rate of change the organization must handle.

A key premise of the book is that most organizations, no matter how they are currently put together, must increase their capacity for change to avoid getting out of sync with the accelerating change in their outside world. Gaps are growing between the way the organization is currently set up to cope with change and the rates of change that will be experienced in the predictably near future. Understanding what defines an ECO, how to assess the current and future needs of an organization for functioning as an ECO, and how to plan and implement the changes necessary to move towards becoming an ECO are the primary focuses of this book.

II. A Snapshop Look at ECO Need and Status

Setting an organization on a course to develop greater capability as an Ever-Changing Organization involves a substantial commitment. Executives need to approach such a decision with a "gut-level" comfort that it makes sense for their organization. This book has been written to help executives come to grips with their needs for becoming an ECO and determining what it will take to get there. Reading the entire book is an important part of that process. Reading the entire book also requires a commitment of precious time and we hope that you will decide to make that investment. To start you on the journey, we developed a tool to help the reader get an up-front "gut-feel" for the ECO model and how it relates to their organization. An overview of the ECO model is presented in this chapter and a graphic representation of the components of the model is displayed in Figure 1.1. Substantial detail about the model and its major components is covered in the other chapters of the book.

Where the organization needs to be as an ECO is derived from a look at the organization's current and projected environment. As the environment becomes more complex and uncertain, the need for ECO capabilities increases substantially. Existing levels of ECO capacity are estimated based on the "snapshot" of the other ECO components, i.e., the stabilizing base for coping with increasing turbulence in the environment, how the organization is managing for change, and its processes for continuous improvement and continuous learning. Increasing capacity in these areas aligns the organization

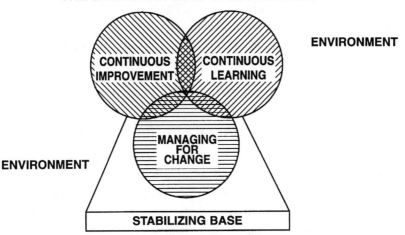

THE EVERCHANGING ORGANIZATION

Figure 1.1   Model of the Ever-Changing Organization as a system. Key components are the external environment, a stabilizing base, and the organization's managing FOR change, continuous improvement and continuous learning processes.

more closely with the ECO capacity required in highly uncertain environments. The results of the snapshot diagnosis provide a quick and dirty estimate of need and a general idea of what it would take to move the organization to where it needs to be.

The "snapshot diagnosis" follows, but we offer a few words of caution before proceeding with this brief look ahead. The snapshot involves responding to a single scale regarding complex subjects. The results should be viewed only as a general indicator of where the organization is at the present time. The snapshot, especially before the entire book has been read, can easily be distorted by focus on only one or two aspects of the ECO components. There is also a tendency to respond to each scale with what we want to believe rather than on the basis of what actually exists in the organization. To avoid the latter, the snapshot diagnosis of each ECO component asks you to list facts and observable data that support your rating. The more factual you are the more useful the picture developed from the snapshot as an indicator of needs and status.

Please do not consider the snapshot a substitute for a full ECO diagnosis. The full-blown process described in the chapter on implementation involves detailed analysis of each of the ECO components. It stresses examining actual behaviors, documents, and operating practices. These form a factual basis for a more complete and valid diagnosis. The full process lends more comfort for the decision to proceed and provides more specific guidance for setting direction and prioritizing initiatives. Buy-in to decisions based on the full diagnosis will be greater for management and those who need to support them.

Snapshots of Key Components of the ECO Model

Review the description of each of the components of the Ever-Changing Organization model. Then respond on the extent scale (circle the appropriate point on the scale) to describe how you believe your organization or environment fits the description provided. The existence of ECO capability increases as your organization is more like the description provided for each component. In the space for supporting data list specific, observable behaviors, processes, structures, and ways of operating that you have considered in reaching your conclusion. Be as objective as possible in making your choices, i.e., base them on facts and what really happens vs. what would be good or you would like to believe happens.

Using the Results of Your Snapshot Analysis

First, review the overall scale point you selected to describe your organization's environment. The more to the right your response, the higher the level of change and uncertainty you are faced with, and the greater your need for higher level ECO status.

Next, examine your snapshot answers regarding the ECO components. Consider the extent to which they are more towards the left than your description of your business environment. The greater the gap, the more likely that your organization is out of alignment with the change capability it needs. And the more likely it is that you will benefit from the more thorough assessment process described in this book.

If you describe your organization as more to the right on the ECO component scales than your description of your environment, it is still important to consider the issue of whether or not a thorough assessment would be helpful. Being too far to the right could mean that you are too flexibly designed and without sufficient structure and control for the environment you live in.

Environmental Snapshot

Our organization's external environment is subject to substantially more change and uncertainty than that of other organizations. Technological changes force us to be proactive to remain competitive. The need to introduce products or services with advanced technological capabilities has increased. New products or services have shortened life cycles. Customer needs and competitive actions require more rapid and timely development of greater numbers of new products and services.

Customer demands for improvements in areas such as quality, pricing, timeliness of delivery, and ease of use continue to grow. The competitive situation is changing rapidly with advances in technology or new approaches to supporting customer needs. Rapid expansion of opportunities in existing markets or via globalization adds to the complexity of decisions regarding market strategies, allocation of resources, and strategies for competing in unfamiliar cultures.

The growing complexity of the environment creates demands for people with more specialized skills and knowledge and increases the difficulty of achieving coordinated efforts among them. Access to accurate information about the environment and getting feedback regarding the impact of our decisions has become more difficult. Growing concern with the effects of our actions on the environment has raised new issues demanding our attention and resources.

Place a "C" on the scale below to indicate the extent to which the writing above describes the nature of your current environment and an "F" for the extent to which it describes the environment you anticipate in the predictable "future."

	_____		_____		_____		_____	
Very Limited	Limited Extent	Some Extent	Great Extent	Very Great
Extent				Extent

Supporting data for current environment (be as factual as possible):

Supporting data for future environment (be as factual as possible):

Stabilizing Base Snapshot

We have articulated a set of positive values. All members of the organization know these values and their implications for acceptable as well as unacceptable behavior. The values are accompanied by a clear and compelling vision of where the organization is going. The vision is shared and discussed so that everyone understands its meaning and implications for their personal behavior. Measurement systems help track progress towards our vision and development of behavior consistent with our values.

We have deliberately designed our systems, structures, and infrastructure to create the flexibility needed for continuous learning, improvement, and change. Open sharing of information allows everyone to act in the best interests of the organization. Operating practices are tested to assure that they are built on the belief that people can be trusted and not designed to thwart the many because of inappropriate actions of the few. There is a stable base of people who know and are committed to the organization. Clear goals guide the organization. Each person has clear direction that is linked to the organizational direction. All are empowered to act as they see necessary without fear of retribution.

There is a balanced orientation to the needs of all stakeholders, including members of the organization, customers, suppliers, the communities we live in, governmental and regulatory agencies, and the owners of the organization. This balance acknowledges the need for short-term results and continuing performance to high standards but in ways that also preserve our shared values.

The impact of these practices creates stabilizing forces in our increasingly changeable environment. They prevent rigidity and paralysis that inhibit action, but also minimize actions that would create even more destabilizing conditions.

To what extent does the stabilizing base of your organization match the description of the stabilizing base of a fully developed ECO above:

|_____|_____|_____|_____|
Very Limited   Limited Extent   Some Extent   Great Extent   Very Great
Extent   Extent

List specific facts supporting your rating:

Managing FOR Change Snapshot

"Focus on the customer" is more than a trite phrase. Assessing customer needs is critical to decision making with respect to product and service development. Customer feedback on performance and service is used to assess trends and to take proactive steps for improvement. Along with customer sensing, other environmental sensing activities support proactive behavior. Surprises that detract from planned activities and consume valuable energy are minimized or avoided.

Change is approached from a systems perspective, considering all key components of the system in change, including its environment. Steps are taken to assure that all of the interconnected pieces of the system are aligned to prevent inconsistencies and confusion. Change is known to produce predictable dynamics. Those involved with changes understand the dynamics and use them to improve change efforts. Plans for change are designed to optimize acceptance, maximize readiness, and assure success.

Instead of being at the mercy of others and having to react to changes introduced or imposed by them, change is seen as a positive strategic weapon. Planning and strategy development processes examine ways to force others to react and allow continuing forward movement by our organization as the leader. Change is viewed as an ally, not as an adversary.

Policies, procedures, and control processes are designed assuming that self-control is more powerful than external control. They are designed to make change easy, eliminate the wasted effort of continuing approvals, encourage individual initiative, and support innovation. Work is designed to include change, learning, and improvement as part of the responsibility of each individual and team. Trained change agents and facilitators, including supervisors, support managing FOR change.

To what extent does your organization manage FOR change in ways that match the description above of the managing FOR change practices of a fully developed ECO?

|_____|_____|_____|_____|
Very Limited   Limited Extent   Some Extent   Great Extent   Very Great
Extent   Extent

List specific facts supporting your rating:

Continuous Improvement Snapshot

Continuous improvement is an organization-wide process, managed from the top. Management direction for continuous improvement is clear to all and communicated via goals and time frames for expected results. Ongoing communication of progress and recognition and celebration of successes is common.

The challenge of continuous improvement is part of each person's job and is focused on understanding and achieving "what's possible," often via benchmarking, vs. meeting the competition or being "good enough." Everyone knows that his work is part of a process and that those who provide input to him are suppliers while those who receive his work output are customers. Expectations and requirements are clarified up front. Performance to requirements is measured objectively and feedback provides data that makes improvement possible.

A common language of quality and continuous improvement reduces communication breakdowns and maximizes focus on appropriate issues, especially the importance of customers and of meeting their requirements. All improvements, small or large and from any area of work, are encouraged. We assume that improvement is always possible. Improvement efforts include the elimination of obstacles to change and the search for innovation in work processes.

Systematic problem-solving and process improvement methods are used by all. These processes use observable facts and data. Structures and time are provided to make the work of improvement legitimate. People are empowered to identify and pursue improvement opportunities and to initiate changes that emerge. Focus of improvement efforts is on prevention of failures and not on more and better inspection.

To what extent does your organization address continuous improvement in ways that match the description above of the continuous improvement practices of a fully developed ECO?

|_____|_____|_____|_____|
Very Limited   Limited Extent   Some Extent   Great Extent   Very Great
   Extent   Extent

List specific facts supporting your rating:

Continuous Learning Snapshot

Continuous learning is a key task of the organization and a responsibility of each individual. Financial support is provided and viewed as an investment as opposed to a discretionary expense. Life/career-long learning support processes are in place. Competency requirements for advancement opportunities have been analyzed and are made available. Vehicles are provided to help people evaluate their needs and plan for development of needed competencies. Methods are in place for peer and supervisory support for learning, such as mentoring/coaching processes or special assignments. Flexible processes make access to developmental opportunities easy.

Learning from the experiences of the organization is assured through systematic critiques and debriefings. Key tasks are considered incomplete until learning is extracted and captured for improving future performance. All are provided tools that teach them "how to learn" for themselves and the organization. Lessons learned become part of an organizational memory and vehicles are in place for collecting, archiving, and retrieving learning from individual as well as organizational memories.

Tools are available for identifying and testing the assumptions behind individual and organizational behaviors. Making assumptions implicit allows changing them or the behaviors that they produce. Successes and failures are analyzed to identify patterns of behavior and processes associated with the results obtained. Processes to build on success patterns and prevent recurring failures are built from the analyses.

To what extent does your organization address continuous learning in ways that match the description above of the continuous learning practices of a fully developed ECO?

|_____|_____|_____|_____|_____|
Very Limited   Limited Extent   Some Extent   Great Extent   Very Great
  Extent   Extent

List specific facts supporting your rating:

Where you describe a good alignment of your environmental demands for change and your organization's ECO level, there may be little you need to do at this point. However, even with apparently good alignment, there are reasons to consider the complete diagnostic process. First, the results of the full assessment will be more complete and valid. Second, if the premise is correct that the current onslaught of change will continue and accelerate, the full diagnostic process will identify those areas where anticipatory changes today will give the greatest movement towards the ECO level you will need in the future. You may decide to go ahead for either or both of these reasons.

III. Change Keeps Coming and We're Not Prepared

Most people in organizations will have no trouble agreeing with the idea that continuing change has become a certainty. They also accept the likelihood that they will be faced with more rapid change in the future. Yet an examination of the design of most organizations will also reveal that they are poorly prepared to cope with the onslaught of change except in energy-consuming, fire-fighting, and reactive or retroactive ways.

The experiences of the many companies who became involved in quality and continuous improvement processes in the past 20 years confirm this lack of preparation. Finding that the costs of failure often exceeded the income of the organization was a very sobering fact. Learning that most people in organizations spend 40% or more of their time coping with failures or their effects was also frightening. Yet the executives of these organizations, when asked how they spend their time, often complain that they are so busy fire-fighting that they have little or no time for proactive pursuits that would allow them to get out of this insidious mode of operation.

But the history of these and most other organizations and the experience of those who run them has resulted in the design of operating practices and structures oriented to protecting permanence and stability and not for change. And the fact that more and more change is upon us has generally not resulted in reexamination and redesign of these practices and structures to make change easier and the organization more proactive and responsive.

Among the reasons we build organizations for permanence and stability is that our actions are based on a number of questionable, if not fundamentally wrong, assumptions. And the approaches we take to change based on these assumptions are generally self-fulfilling. Take, for example, the frequently expressed belief regarding people's basic feelings about change. A very commonly heard phrase in our experience is that "people naturally resist change."

If this is what we believe about the people of our organizations, we approach change as if making it happen will be a battle. We announce a change and marshal the forces at our disposal to compel it to happen. We establish rules and controls and tell people what will happen, often without their involvement. We expect the process to be time consuming, costly, and messy — and we are right! Not because "people naturally resist all change," but because "people naturally resist imposed change and change that they do not understand or have reason to fear."

Not only are we operating on the assumption that people naturally resist change, we also assume that all change is the same and will be responded to in the same manner. Yet an exceptionally large percentage of people we encounter recognize that a positive understanding of "what's in it for me," or WIIFM, can be a major influence on the issue of resistance and might even produce a condition in which people seek change. Consider, for example, the enormous amount of energy invested by people in organizations who are given the opportunity to problem solve to eliminate defects and errors from their work or to analyze and examine ways to improve their work processes. That energy does not come from people who are naturally resistant to change. It comes from people who seek change that not only benefits them but also benefits their team, their organization, and their customers. And the work involved in making the changes happen is fun!

But another set of faulty assumptions often influences an organization's approach to change. The people of the organization are presumed to be uninvolved in the success of the organization. They are thought to have little or nothing to contribute to improvement. Therefore, it is not a part of every person's job to propose or implement changes for improvement. For some reason, management in these situations assumes that their people are fundamentally different from themselves in their commitment to the organization or ability to contribute. Miles[1] noted that managers prefer to manage others in a different way from how they believe they should be managed. Managers would prefer that their leaders believed in them and their capabilities and used them as committed human resources. However, they prefer to treat their own people as less involved and committed and needing to be closely guided and controlled. The self-fulfilling nature of these preferences is reflected in workforces that are alienated and uninvolved. This is not because that is the way they really are but because they have learned to operate that way as a result of how they are treated and what is expected of them. Yet these same people generally dedicate and invest at least 50% of the waking hours of their working days in their organizations. Many managers will deny that the assumption that people don't care and are incapable of contributing influences their behavior. Yet their actions are built on these or similar implicit assumptions and the managers fail to recognize that their assumptions have been self-fulfilling. Assuming that people do not care or are less capable of making contributions than their managers severely limits the organization's ability to increase capacity for change, learning, and improvement.

Under the assumptions above, organizations frequently resort to the "need to know" concept on communications issues. Assumptions are made for people about what they need to know and are able to understand and use. Instead of providing all of the data that might be of use to people in doing their work effectively or to make changes to improve performance, the data is either deliberately withheld or simply "controlled" by others. An example of this occurred in a consulting engagement we were involved in a number of years ago. A production area manager was asked to identify the data he used on a daily basis to plan and manage his department. He was then asked what he would do without the data. His response was that he would be unable to operate. When then asked how his people could manage without similar data for their work, he acknowledged that they had to be as handcuffed as he would be without the data he needed. They would be unable to identify issues and make changes that would improve performance except via management direction. Assumptions about people's need-to-know had resulted in rationed data. Without the data there were very few contributions from employees and change was difficult. This type of assumption needs to be purged from organizations where increased capacity for change, learning, and improvement is required.

Unless we can change our thinking about people, about change, and about ourselves we will be locked into current ways of operating. We will be unable to grow our capacity for change to meet current or future needs. Those who can make this adjustment will succeed and grow. Those who cannot adjust will fall behind and may fail.

Figure 1.2   Orientation to change scale. Assessments locate the organization at some position on the scale. Where the organization needs to be is primarily influenced by the uncertainty of the business environment.

IV. Organizational Orientation to Change

When organizations are examined closely for the behaviors, systems, and structures that impact their capacity for change, they fall somewhere on the continuum in Figure 1.2 in terms of their **overall** orientation to change. These features of the organization's design reflect the assumptions of those who created them. They send clear messages to the members of the organization and its stakeholders about the change orientation and expectations of management. Further, we contend that it is a valid assumption that people's response to those messages is rational. It is consistent with their perceptions of what is expected and valued. As a result, the organization's position on the orientation to change continuum has direct influence on the ability of the organization to anticipate, cope with, or manage the demands for change with which it is faced. And failure to meet those demands is a prescription for eventual failure.

To reach a conclusion about where an organization falls on the continuum many questions must be asked. The organization's policies and procedures must be reviewed and their underlying values and assumptions identified. Business processes and the constraints under which they operate are explored. Executives, managers, and other members of the organization are interviewed and observed to understand their behaviors and the underlying assumptions and values they act upon in relating to change.

People selected and trained for the task, as described later in this book, will have rated many scales in the diagnostic process. It is likely that the organization will fall at different points on a number of the scales. Yet there is also a great likelihood that patterns of behavior will have been discerned. Those patterns will suggest an overall rating which summarizes the outcomes of the diagnosis. That rating, when compared with the level of ECO capacity required by the nature of the organization's environment, indicates the need or urgency for developing additional ECO strength.

The following paragraphs are overall descriptions of the nature of an organization's orientation to change at the various points of the scale.

A. Change Averse

On the far left of the continuum are organizations whose orientation is "change averse." Change is something to be avoided and prevented. Change is perceived as disruptive — as something that takes people's focus from their real jobs. Energy is devoted to keeping things the way they are. Management is reluctant to initiate changes. Continuous improvement and learning processes are not developed. People are not involved or empowered to make changes and improvements. Top down, institutional control predominates with decisions reserved for the highest levels only. Customers, with the changes they are perceived to force on the organization, are considered a necessary evil and competitors are the enemy. "If it ain't broke, don't fix it" is the guiding direction about change.

B. Change Resistant

"Change-resistant" organizations have long lists of reasons why changes are a bad idea and will fail. They prefer stability and permanence and want to avoid the messiness associated with change. Decisions to change are delayed, sometimes until there is no choice. People are expected to do what they have been asked or told to do and not to look for and propose changes. Their jobs are seen, at this point on the continuum, as simply "doing." Issues with customers, suppliers, or other external agencies are responded to when the demands are great enough to get attention at the highest levels. Learning is left to the individual. When change does occur it is inevitably at the initiation of top management or in response to some externally imposed requirement that cannot be argued away. Top down control of decisions and complex, multilevel approvals are required for change and other actions, even those that have been previously accepted.

C. Change Managing

At the midpoint of the continuum, organizations acknowledge the ongoing nature of change. Stability and permanence are preferred, but these organizations accept change as part of their world and are prepared to adapt to the forces for change. When the forces for change are seen as necessary or imposed by external requirements where resistance is not useful or could be counterproductive, the organization works to manage the change process. Not much is done to anticipate required change, but when faced with the need these organizations do what is necessary. They recognize that the process of change can be managed to make it more successful as well as less disruptive and time consuming. The greater effectiveness of planned change is viewed as worth the investment. Some level of decision making and spending authority regarding change is given to middle levels of the organization but probably not below. People are informed about change decisions and sometimes participate in the process of planning the changes. Opportunities for involvement in continuous improvement and continuous learning become part of the organization's processes. People are trained in the needed skills for learning and improvement. Customers are viewed as critical to the organization's success and processes are designed to stay in touch with customers and their needs. The organization shares its needs and plans with its suppliers. Anticipation of change gains importance as a strategy for minimizing fire fighting and the excessive waste of energy consumed by the need to play "catch-up."

D. Change Friendly

From this point on the continuum, and to the right, organizations implement or redesign systems and processes to make change easier. Barriers to change and improvement are identified and removed. People throughout the organization are provided skills, tools, and time for participation in continuous learning and improvement activities. Mapping of key business processes becomes a major tool for facilitating change. People are empowered in their individual jobs and in their work units to identify and eliminate the sources of defects and to find ways to improve work processes, e.g., reduce cycle times, eliminate non-value-added activities, reduce waste and rework, and so on. Vehicles are put in place to make it easy for customers to do business with the organization or to get problems solved. People who help make these processes work are valued and recognized. Customers' future needs are identified and integrated into the product and service strategy of the organization. Future direction is also shared with suppliers and their support gained for helping the organization achieve its plans. Each person learns that they are suppliers to those who receive their work (their customers) and the customers of those whose input they receive (their suppliers) as well of being "doers" of their own work tasks. They are expected to manage those horizontal relationships and to be involved in ongoing learning and improvement of their performance.

E. Change Seeking

"Change seeking" organizations value change and fear failure to change. They believe that "to stand still is to regress and the beginning of dying." Continuous improvement and continuous learning are more than phrases, they are values that are integrated into the organization. Lifelong learning at the individual and organizational levels is espoused and supported by the organization's policies and systems as well as by its financial backing. Extensive processes are designed for sensing and anticipating the external world in all respects. Customer communication and focus is an obsession. Competitive intelligence is pursued aggressively. Technological changes are examined constantly for opportunities to create new products and services. Potential actions of external agencies are monitored vigorously. These actions are for the purpose of creating change — leading and not being forced to follow. Change seekers define the competitive agenda. They strive to satisfy customers' needs before others are able to. People are viewed as the organization's most critical assets. This belief is reflected in the way they are developed and how their capabilities are used. Clear statements of the organization's vision and values and an understanding of their implications guide each person's behavior. Self-management and control is understood to be much more powerful than external control, and well-skilled and informed people are assumed to be able to make appropriate choices for changes for themselves and the organization.

F. Implications of Orientation to Change

The intent of the orientation to change continuum is to be descriptive, not evaluative. Where an organization falls on the continuum is neither inherently good nor bad. Where issues arise for an organization derives from whether the orientation to change is functional or dysfunctional, i.e., whether or not the orientation towards change helps the organization in the context of its business and environment. And, of course, the concern today is greater as a result of the accelerated rates of change being experienced.

In more stable environments there will generally be less need for a strong change orientation. And, to the extent that the management of the organization has made reasoned choices in this area, being more resistant or less change friendly can serve the organization positively. Yet, even historically more stable environments have become less stable and demanding of greater receptivity to change, both internally and externally. Consider, for example, pressures for changes in human resources processes such as family leave, recognition of same sex partnerships for benefits, or the requirements of ADA (the Americans with Disabilities Act). Being change averse or resistant on these issues can result in fines, retrofits, or loss of business.

Look also at the changes in technology and the opportunities presented. Failure to acquire and use the technology may not be fatal in the short run, but long delays are likely to put businesses at a competitive disadvantage. Geoffrey Moore, in his book *Crossing the Chasm: Marketing and Selling Technology Products to Mainstream Customers*,[2] describes a scale from innovators and early adapters of technology to laggards, who resist new technology until it approaches the end of its life cycle. Moore's concern is with development of marketing and selling strategies, i.e., whom to sell to and when. Our concern is more with the issue of whether people are making decisions to buy early or late based primarily on their orientation to change and whether that orientation serves the organization well or poorly. In the present world, change averse or change resistant choices in adapting new technology, whether selected explicitly or implicitly, are generally becoming more dysfunctional.

V. Assumptions, Behaviors, Consequences, and Change Orientation

In the mid-1970s, while working in the highly uncertain environment of the semiconductor industry, Pieters[3] developed the ABC model for helping managers understand and solve problems that would often persist despite their repeated efforts to eliminate them. He had become frustrated with attempts

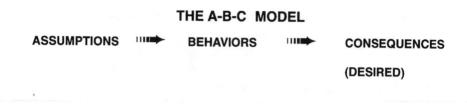

Figure 1.3 The Assumptions–Behaviors–Consequences (A–B–C) Model. Exposing faulty assumptions opens up options for new behaviors in pursuit of desired consequences and results.

to use McGregor's "Theory X" and "Theory Y"[4] as a consulting tool in these situations. McGregor described two sets of assumptions that drive the behavior of many managers. The first set of assumptions, labeled "Theory X," was more limiting and viewed people as uninvolved in their work. The managerial behavior they produce tends to be directive, controlling, and manager centered. "Theory Y," on the other hand, is a more positive set of assumptions that views work as natural and the achievement of results as satisfying to people. These assumptions produce behaviors that are more participative, caring, and goal oriented. Unfortunately, many managers reject one or more of the assumptions specified by McGregor as descriptive of their personal beliefs. Based on this they dismiss the entire model as applying to them. They conclude that theory X is too autocratic or theory Y too "touchy-feely" to represent the assumptions influencing their behavior.

A. The ABC Model

Fundamentally, the ABC model (Figure 1.3) says that **A**ssumptions drive our **B**ehaviors as we pursue **C**onsequences of importance to us. When the Experienced consequences of our behavior are different from the Desired consequences, we try other behaviors to get the results we want. But the success of our attempts to change will only be likely if our underlying assumptions are valid. If not, they will guide us to select other behaviors that also fail to produce the desired results. Under these conditions we need somehow to change our underlying assumptions. But our underlying assumptions are usually implicit and not available for examination. A tool is needed to help surface explicit assumptions and beliefs. The ABC model is such a tool.

Several premises form the basis for the ABC model, as follows:

1. People's behavior is purposeful and goal directed, not random.
2. Behind all behavior is a set of assumptions the individual makes about (a) him/herself, (b) other people, and (c) the cause-effect relationship between his/her behavior and the desired effects of that behavior.
3. Most often our assumptions are implicit and, therefore, not available to be tested.
4. Assumptions can be inferred and made explicit. Doing so requires that both the observable behaviors of the person and their desired consequences are also made explicit.
5. Behaviors based on valid/useful theory and assumptions lead to the desired consequences. Likewise, behaviors based on invalid assumptions will not produce desired consequences.
6. The ability to successfully change behavior that is not producing desired results requires that the underlying assumptions also be changed.
7. People's behavior is rational to them. If what people do fails to meet what we expect, we should examine what in our behavior makes their actions rational to them.

When underlying assumptions are made explicit using the ABC model, questionable assumptions generally stand out like a sore thumb. They can then be challenged and alternative, more viable assumptions developed. Managers are able to buy into the new assumptions as more appropriate without feeling threatened. A new range of behaviors becomes available to them. The likelihood that the manager will implement the new behaviors increases along with the probability of realizing the intended results. The new behavior is based on explicitly articulated and more valid assumptions.

The ABC model has been used in many situations to assist managers who needed to change their behavior because the results being achieved were unacceptable. Examples of typical situations are:

■ **President and CEO.** The problem was the failure of his executive team to control rising numbers of unfilled personnel requisitions in a period of impending recession despite frequent admonitions to do so. The president announced he was taking control and adding himself to the approval process for all replacements or additions. The ABC analysis highlighted implicit, but untenable, assumptions about the locus of control in difficult times. Failure to achieve desired results was predicted to continue. A new process was designed leaving control of requisitions to a negotiated level in the hands of the executives. The desired results were achieved with this new process.

- **Sales VP.** The executive wanted to focus field sales managers on broader business results than simply meeting volume targets. Goals in all areas of concern were set and performance reviewed regularly. The ABC analysis identified a compensation plan based only on volume and the assumption that the managers would pay more attention to what the executive talked about and measured than they would to the issue of how they were paid. Restatement of that assumption lead to changes in the compensation plan and improved performance to established goals.

- **Top management team.** The team recognized that previous ways of dealing with business recessions were ineffective and had not produced the results they wanted. Faulty assumptions about the employees of the organization were identified and changed using the ABC model. New methods for controlling and reducing people cost were developed that greatly improved the effectiveness of the results achieved in the next period of recession.

- **Top management team.** Team members were frustrated with each other and their people for making "casual commitments" and not meeting them. The ABC analysis highlighted implicit assumptions behind management's behavior that made casual commitments the rational thing to do, i.e., we ask people for commitments based on how soon can it possibly be done. Revised assumptions led to realistic commitments focused on when something was really needed.

Without the insights from the ABC analysis, the changes involved and the improvements in results would have been unlikely. And, when confronted with a similar situation, the manager(s) involved would have reverted to the same behaviors or would have attempted new approaches likely to be unsuccessful because they would continue to be driven by inappropriate assumptions. The ABC model is a simple but powerful tool for change.

This book has been written to help organizations change to match the demands of the world in which they exist, now and into the future. As you will see, the ABC model is fundamental to the assessment of the organization's orientation to change and status as an ECO. Analysis based on the model provides important insights into the changes required for increasing the organization's capability as an ECO.

Change will continue. Organizations designed for permanence and stability, and without the capabilities of the Ever-Changing Organization, will struggle and may not survive. Too much of their energy will be diverted to react to changes they cannot avoid and away from the purposes of the organization. The combined use of the ECO model and the tools presented here provides organizations with a way to become aligned with the realities of their current environment and to build in the capacity for change that will assure their survival.

In the rest of the introductory section of this book, a summary description of the overall ECO model and its primary components is presented. A brief discussion of a process for conducting a thorough and highly valid diagnosis of any organization's current position as an ECO completes the chapter.

VI. The Ever-Changing Organization Model

A. Basis for the ECO Model

We were led to develop the "Ever-Changing Organization" (ECO) model by a number of forces in our own worlds. Primary among these factors was our frustration, and the frustration we have encountered in so many organizations, with the limitations of the ongoing parade of "new" ideas and models, none of which have produced the overall promise they were supposed to possess. In organization after organization we encounter confusion and even anger at the profusion of "programs of the month." Most of these are based on what is the most recent book to excite people and the adoption of a program based on that book until the process fails or fades away and the next thing comes along.

Look at the range of ideas that have been presented in the past 15 to 20 years or so. Go "in search of excellence" or "thrive on chaos" or any of a series of thrusts presented by Tom Peters since the mid-1980s. Pursue quality and continuous improvement and pick a guru like Deming, or Juran, or Crosby, or others. And while you're at it, qualify for ISO 9000 registration or compete for the Deming Prize or the Baldrige Award or any of a multitude of other quality awards. Acquire the disciplines of a learning organization. Adopt the habits of highly effective people. Become process focused. Reengineer your business processes or — oops, sorry — forgot that organizations are made up of people, so let's try the next offering. Focus on cycle time as the overall issue to conquer, or learn "stewardship," or focus on building leaders, or managing change, or customer satisfaction and retention, and on and on.

Our analysis is that each of these thrusts has within it much that is good, of potential benefit to organizations, and, in fact, has been used productively by some organizations. But we also find that each is incomplete and, in and of itself, inadequate for the overall task faced by people who run organizations. Yet each flourishes and then fades, having had its moment in the sun and having offered an oversimplified solution that played to the needs of management for a quick and easy fix to their very complex problems.

B. Organizations as Systems

Among the shortcomings of the approaches above is one we consider fatal for dealing with the challenges associated with accelerating change. And that is that each of these approaches looks at a piece of the puzzle but fails to look at the overall picture of the organization as a system, itself a component of even larger systems.

For any system to survive, its components must each be designed and aligned to achieve the purposes of the system. And since the components are all interrelated, they must also be aligned with each other and with the environment of the larger system(s) of which the organization is a part. Change in individual parts of the system impacts the other parts. Impacted parts must also be realigned with the changes taking place to maintain the system's integrity. The approaches that have been "hot" and "programs of the month" for so many organizations have generally addressed the design and effectiveness of an important component of an organizational system, whether that be leadership, quality, customers, or whatever. Even those that include the idea of systems thinking in their writing do not adequately address the issue of the fit and alignment of what strategies they present with the other parts of the system.

Most, for example, simply ignore key aspects of the environment of the organization. Others, in particular those that relate to change, stress the organization's leader(s) and their behavior almost to the exclusion of the many other key components of the system. Or they treat change management as an individual event and address how to manage a specific change without addressing the greater context of the other components of the organizational system that exert so much influence on the success of all change efforts.

C. Systems Model of the Ever-Changing Organization

Figure 1.1 is a graphic representation of the ECO model. It identifies the five key components of the ECO as an organizational system, including the environment within which it must function. The five components, each composed of additional subcomponents, contain issues that an organization must address effectively and align if it is to survive and thrive in an ever-changing world. Following is a description of the major components of the ECO model. Each will be described much more fully in a chapter devoted to it but a brief overview of each at this point will help create a context for reading about each of the parts of the overall model.

1. Environment

Understanding and being in touch with the environment of any organization is critical to being able to function as an ever-changing organization. Many of the forces for change an organization experiences arise in the external environment. These come from customers, suppliers, competitors, technological advances, globalization of businesses and the demands of different cultures, regulations established by governmental agencies at all levels, and so on. Being out of touch with any or all of these forces often results in the kind of negative and imposed change that diverts energy and forces the hated firefighting mode on organizations while others move forward.

Comprehending the environment and its direction is required for organizations that aim to lead. Without this knowledge it is impossible to align business strategies and the design of the internal organization with the requirements for change from outside. As environments become more and more uncertain, more effort must be placed on understanding the environment and on creating internal capabilities to anticipate and align with the external forces for change. Research reported by Lawrence and Lorsch[5] demonstrated over 30 years ago that the performance of organizations was related to the fit of their internal processes with the needs that arose from the level of uncertainty in their environment. The following list of environmental characteristics includes the criteria used by Lawrence and Lorsch in their research. They are expanded to reflect the continuing acceleration of change and increased uncertainty in today's world, only a few decades after the original research and findings.

- Rate of technological change (established vs. new or different/emerging technologies)
- Life cycle of new products/services — (number of new products required to compete; time to obsolescence in new applications)
- Customer product and service requirements (quality, improvements, costs, delivery)
- Rate of market growth (declining, growing with GNP, explosive; niche vs. broad markets)
- Size and diffusion of customer base (number, local/regional vs. national/global)
- Competition (number of competitors and ranking vs. competitors)
- Changes in supplier capabilities (including technological advances, potential outsourcing, technical support, etc.)
- Access to information from the environment (easy, inconsistent, difficult)
- Time required for definitive feedback on the results of decisions (immediate to extended)
- Environmental impact of business (minimal or demands much attention)

Understanding these environmental features provides data regarding the external forces for development of the capabilities of an ECO. As the degree of change in the current environment increases, so does the organization's need to become an ECO. Skills, structures, and processes for managing FOR change, continuous improvement, and continuous learning become more important. A stabilizing base that guides the organization through the increased turbulence, yet supports flexible behavior consistent with the external pressures, becomes a "must have" vs. a "nice to have." If, in addition to coping with a high level of pressure for change, the organization must also accommodate trends towards even more change, the magnitude of the challenge is compounded.

In high change environments, organizations are compelled to become more complex and flexible to deal with environmental demands. The proportion of the organization's total available energy dedicated to responding to external pressures must be increased unless new ways of organizing and operating the business support more proactive, leading-change kinds of behaviors. If not, more resources will be needed, overall, for operating the business. The result will be greater costs and missed opportunities and, therefore, fewer profits, on the one hand, or, on the other, attempts to increase prices in a competitive environment which is unlikely to tolerate such actions.

2. Stabilizing Base

As an organization exists and continues to operate in its environment, the ever-changing nature of that environment creates a continuing set of destabilizing forces and pressures for change. The organization is buffeted from all directions with forces of varying durations and intensities. Without the existence of a balancing and guiding set of counterforces the organization will soon be lost and will fail.

The stabilizing base of the ECO model consists of the features below. Together, these features create a supportive and nurturing, yet results-oriented "culture." It is predictable and caring and provides everyone with the capability and the freedom to act in ways that meet the organization's needs and their own self-interests.

These may be features of many organizations but are particularly important for organizations in high change, fast moving environments. Specifically, they must be in place and reflect the demands of the environment, e.g., "fit," to provide the balancing and stabilizing effects necessary for staying on course and surviving. The features are:

- Shared, positive values
- A compelling and living vision, explored to the point that all can understand it and its implications for their behavior
- Commitment to continuing improvement, learning, and change
- Clear and measurable goals and direction
- Operating practices that reflect belief and trust in people vs. a distrusting/blaming focus
- A stable base of people who know the organization and its values

- Flexible and adaptive systems, structures, and infrastructure to support managing FOR change
- Open access to data that allows all to act (proactively or reactively) easily and in the best interests of the organization
- Both a process and results orientation
- Balanced orientation to diverse demands

The features of the stabilizing base produce a culture that has staying power. It gives the organization the ability to survive and succeed in the midst of continual change. Such a culture is "built to last," in the sense described by Collins and Porras,[6] and sufficiently flexible to react or proact as required by forces for change from its environment.

3. Managing FOR Change

The extent to which an organization has designed its operating practices, business processes, structure, and infrastructure FOR change is a major determinant of the extent to which it has the capabilities of an ECO. As suggested earlier, our observations and experiences have identified many organizations designed more for permanence and stability than FOR change.

In the managing FOR change component of the ECO, a number of key features of the organization's practices are outlined. The presence or strength of these features defines the extent to which the organization is being managed FOR change. The list below briefly lists these features and one or two of the primary issues addressed by each. Each is discussed more fully in Chapter 4.

- Customer focus: Customers are a critical part of every organization's environment. What is in place that creates intense focus on customers and their needs, now and for the future? Is customer satisfaction diligently measured and pursued with a passion or not?
- Environmental sensing: Are mechanisms in place staying in touch with all key parts of the organization's environment? Are sensing activities supported financially and is proactive use of the data gathered expected and rewarded?
- Impetus for change: Is change dealt with proactively or does the organization simply wait for demands for change before acting? Is identification of opportunities for change and the initiation of action legitimate in all parts of the organization and at any level?

- Change planning and management: Do people throughout the organization employ tools to create readiness for change and for dealing with change dynamics? Are transition management processes understood and managed or do changes just happen?

- Systems approach to change and alignment: Does the organization understand that it is a system and also a part of a larger system? Is a systems model of the organization in use? Is alignment of the organization's design and its strategic direction an important consideration in change efforts?

- Change as a business strategy: Does the organization deal with change as a strategy for setting the competitive agenda and forcing others to be reactive while it continues to move forward? What portion of the available energy of the organization ends up being consumed responding to the lead of others?

- Adaptive leadership: Does the leadership of the organization adjust direction and strategy as conditions require? Are leadership processes and styles driven by the belief that everyone must be managed the same? As people and teams grow and mature, do leadership behaviors also change to utilize the growing skills and experience of the people?

- Change orientation of policies, procedures, and controls: Are procedures and controls designed to restrict people from implementing change or do they encourage and support independent action? Are the policies, procedures, and controls of the organization designed on the belief that self-control is much more powerful and change supportive than external control?

- Work design: Are jobs throughout the organization designed to allow people to manage their own work, individually and/or in teams? Are tools and information relevant to people's work provided to maximize their ability to contribute or are they withheld to protect the power of others?

- Use of change agents: Are Organization Development (OD) consultants or change management specialists and facilitators available to help the process of change throughout the organization? Are functions like these seen as frivolous overhead or as important investments for helping the organization and its management deal with ever-increasing demands for change?

Positive answers to these questions are characteristic of organizations working at the change-friendly or change-seeking end of the orientation to change continuum and behaving more as an ECO. Negative answers indicate the opposite, i.e., organizations that are change averse, resistant or managing and not functioning as high-level ECOs.

4. Continuous Improvement

It is hard to conceive of an organization without an organization-wide process of continuous improvement as an ECO. If continuous change and improvement is not part of what the organization values and makes part of each person's job, the organization would be in denial if contends that it is an ECO. Continuous improvement must be one of the five major components of any organization dealing effectively with continuous change.

Developing and managing a successful continuous improvement process takes time and hard work. Yet in the search for the proverbial "quick-fix" many organizations have begun and abandoned continuous improvement efforts in favor of new flavors of the month like "reengineering" with its promise of big, fast, breakthrough results. These organizations are not ECOs, or becoming ECOs, in the sense presented in this book.

As with the other components of the ECO model, there are a number of issues that are relevant to determining the extent to which the organization has effectively developed continuous improvement processes that support their need to be or become an ECO. These are briefly summarized below.

- Direction/Goals for Continuous Improvement: Has management established continuous improvement as a key goal of the organization? Have they communicated their own goals and expectations for improvement and targeted time frames for their achievement?
- Improvement Challenge: Is the challenge to the organization to be competitive or "good enough"? Or is the focus on continuing improvement as part of everyone's responsibility and on the use of tools like benchmarking to learn about and to exceed "what's possible"?
- Size of Improvements Expected: Are incremental improvements considered important or only large, breakthrough improvements deemed worth pursuing? Is improvement in any form and size valued, from all members of the organization?

- Common Language: Have a set of common definitions for continuous improvement been established to remove ambiguities and assure clarity of communications?

- Customer-Supplier Relationships: Do people understand that those who receive their work output are their customers and those who provide them work are suppliers? Are up-front agreements on requirements and feedback on performance accepted as critical pieces of the improvement process?

- Prevention Orientation: Does the organization recognize that preventing problems is the most profitable approach to improvement? Is preventing recurrence of problems viewed as a significantly better strategy for improvement than development of more elaborate tools for inspection?

- Systematic Problem Solving: Are common and systematic problem solving processes used by everyone? Is problem solving fact and data based and targeted at root causes?

- Process Improvement Methods: Is all work approached as a process that can always be improved? Do people throughout the organization map their work processes for shared understanding and as a basis for seeking improvement opportunities?

- Time/Structures for Continuous Improvement: Are people provided with structures like work teams, process teams, ongoing or temporary problem solving teams for doing the work of continuous improvement? Is time specifically allotted for continuous improvement work or must people somehow create their own time for such work?

- Strategies for Innovation/Creativity: Are obstacles to innovation and creativity eliminated to free up people for change and improvement? Are people provided tools and processes to tap their creativity? Is innovation in all aspects of work expected and valued?

If all of the actions implied in the issues identified above have been taken and are in operation, an organization has developed a viable continuous improvement process that will contribute to its ability to function as an ECO. If some or all of these issues have not been addressed, the overall system remains incomplete and requires additional development.

5. Continuous Learning

Organizations are human systems in which learning is occurring all the time. The overall issue, therefore, is whether learning is random or systematic and available to enhance the performance of the organization. The learning must help the organization cope with ever-changing conditions and prevent the costly process of having what someone has described as "…one year of experience ten times vs. ten years of experience."

Much has been written about learning organizations in recent years. More will be written. And, as learning about learning organizations continues, additional changes to produce ECO capability will evolve. For now, the following issues are those that are included in the continuous learning component of the ECO model.

- Investment in Continuous Learning: Are people recognized as the only renewable asset the organization has? Is money spent on their learning seen as an investment in the appreciation of those assets vs. as a discretionary expense? Are funds budgeted for continuous learning and must managers demonstrate that they have improved return on human assets with their investments?
- Life/Career-long Learning Support: Is life/career-long learning identified as important and available for all organizational members? Are the learning tools, materials, technologies, and so on in place to support this process? Are individuals given responsibility for their own development and supported in the process?
- Competency/Development Planning: Are jobs analyzed for the skills and competencies needed? Are individual competencies assessed? Are developmental plans for people based on current competencies and adding capabilities for potential future assignments?
- Structured Developmental Relationships: Do new or younger people have access to others that can help them learn? Are all parties to these relationships trained to get the most effective outcomes?
- Learning Critiques/Debriefings: Are systematic critiques of results conducted for learning purposes or does the learning that comes from the experience remain only in the individuals involved? Are formal debriefings required for tasks to be considered complete or does the organization simply move from one event to the next?
- Identifying Success and Failure Pattern: Are the results of similar activities analyzed to discern patterns of behavior associated with

success and failure? Is such learning used to guide the planning of future activities of a like nature?

- Archiving/Accessing Organizational Memory: Are processes in place for capturing and storing learning in an organizational memory rather than leaving the process open and informal? Is the organizational memory easily accessed for future reference?
- Identifying/Testing Assumptions: Is there a process available to help identify and modify faulty assumptions and improve results? Do people, in planning changes, make explicit and examine their assumptions and the behaviors they plan for a fit with the results they want?
- Learning How to Learn: Are models and tools taught to help people learn from their own experiences and that of the organization? Are these tools used and do they contribute to continuous learning for individuals and the organization?

If the processes and issues outlined for the continuous learning component of the ECO model are not in place, the organization is faced with the problem identified in the frequently quoted comment of Winston Churchill: "Those who do not learn from the past are condemned to repeat it!" Ongoing changes without continuous learning wastes resources and opportunities. Too much of the organization's limited energy is spent having to work without the benefit of prior learning. That energy is not available for helping develop the organization as an ECO and the danger of becoming more out of sync increases.

The components of the ECO model depicted in Figure 1.1 are linked to each other as part of the overall organizational system. This means that each must be designed to achieve its purpose and also fit with the others. Change in one part of the system will effect the other components of the system. Effort will be required to realign the components into an integrated whole. Understanding this concept is important in embarking on development of ECO capabilities. It is also critical to developing an integrated ECO strategy for the rapidly changing world of today and tomorrow.

VII. Implementing the ECO Model

The steps involved in planning and implementing increases in ECO capability are reasonably straightforward. Ideas discussed in this book provide a basis for development of such a strategy. The decision to grow the organization's capacity as an ECO is an important one. It places the organization on a continuing journey along a path not yet walked. It should not be made lightly or without sound business reasons.

The last chapter of the book is devoted to discussion of the process of implementing and building ECO capability meet or exceed the anticipated needs of the organization. We conclude this chapter with a brief outline of the process we believe offers the most valid base of information for the decision to implement and for sustaining the process through increasingly turbulent seas.

Following is an overview of the implementation process:

- Top executives become familiar with the ECO model and the range of issues it raises. Reading the book and sharing data from the "snap-shot diagnosis" starts this process. Discussion of the implications should be part of deciding to move to the next step, or not.

- Appoint a team of experienced people to conduct an in-depth diag-nosis of the organization's need and capacity as an ECO. Orient the team to their task and reasons for assessing ECO status. Convey that perceived long-term commitment to the organization, growth poten-tial, and the likely contribution of this assignment to their growth are all factors influencing their inclusion as a member of the diagnostic team.

- Train the diagnostic team. Assure that they understand the ECO model and its components. Determining needed ECO capability by focusing this effort on examination of the organization's environ-ment. Emphasize collection of facts and data describing the organi-zation's actual behaviors and the orientation to change they display in assessing status on the other ECO components. Also stress the critical importance of factual, open feedback to top management for creating a valid diagnosis and a sound basis for further choices.

- Meet with the diagnostic team offsite when their assessment is complete. Listen to the data and be prepared to spend time exploring the specific data and observations that resulted in their diagnostic conclusions.

- Continue the offsite meeting of the executive team to consider the results of the diagnosis. The executive team makes the decision to implement an ECO-building strategy or not as the next step. Part of that process includes creating a common vision of how the organization will function differently in the future when needed ECO capacity has been developed.

- If the decision is to move forward, select and prioritize the first set of change initiatives and define the process by which each will be planned and managed. Refer to materials in the managing FOR change chapter to guide the change planning and management activities.

- Establish an ongoing process within the executive team for managing the ECO-building process. Assign leadership roles, determine methods for review and approval of plans and progress, and establish a process using a tool like the management system model (see managing FOR change chapter) to align or realign operating practices with the new direction.

- Establish a process for communicating the results of the diagnosis and the decisions of the management team throughout the organization. Link the decisions to the features of the organization's stabilizing base. Assure that the communication process allows for discussion to reach understanding and that it is repeated regularly with updates on status of initiatives.

- Periodically repeat the steps outlined, including the diagnostic process, feedback of results, selection and management of new initiatives, and communicating progress and results to the organization.

An executive colleague of ours described the value of a process like the one outlined in terms of its impact on motivation to change. His comment was, "Motivation to change requires that you know three things: (1) where you are, (2) where you want or need to go, and (3) the first few steps you will take to close the gap between where you are and where you want to go." The process described develops the data needed for the decisions to implement and for building sustainable motivation to change in the executives involved. It gets the organization moving down the path to increased ECO capacity. The rest of the journey unfolds as the ECO-building process continues.

2 Environment

Understanding an organization's environment is critical to determining its need for being or becoming an Ever-Changing Organization (ECO). Of particular importance is the issue of the degree of change and uncertainty that exists in the environment. As uncertainty increases, the need for flexibility increases along with the need to build operating practices, policies and systems that encourage and support change. Working to become an ECO is not an option in highly uncertain business environments.

It is also important to be aware of the components of the environment that are likely to generate forces for change. Included are areas such as changing technology, customer expectations, competitors, suppliers, regulatory agencies, and so on. Organizations will have to address the forces that come from these areas whether or not they are aware of, or prepared for, the changes required.

The metaphor that comes to mind is that of the organization as a ship that travels the open sea. The sea and the atmosphere represent the ship's environment. The environment has changed and continues to change. Storms occur more frequently, many with greater force and turbulence than previously. The ship must be capable of coping with the changed environment. Ships that cannot cope flounder and fall behind or are taken out of service.

The ship may have been designed and in operation for many years. And the original design undoubtedly included the features necessary to function in the historically more stable environment. It may not include the features and advances in technology employed in current designs to allow navigation and survival in a more unstable and demanding environment. The design of the hull may be inherently less stable than current ship design. More advanced stabilizer designs have been developed for use in more turbulent seas. Global positioning devices provide more accurate understanding of the location of current ships and their proximity to potentially dangerous conditions. Improved sensors alert the captain and helmsmen to changes in depth or in bottom conditions that portend danger. Constant access to weather information and forecasts via satellite support selection of the most appropriate course for the ship. All of the adaptations in design and the application of new technology allow a ship to perform more effectively, in general, and in the ever-changing environment, in particular. Without these changes the ship's owners and operators could not compete and survive in the new environment. Similarly, organizations faced with increasingly unstable environments must anticipate or react to the increased environmental change and instability they face or become unable to compete and survive.

In this chapter we will be examining factors in the environment that increase uncertainty and some of the implications of those factors for the design or change of the internal operations and practices of the organization if it is to become an ECO.

I. Environmental Uncertainty and Change

Jack Welch, CEO of General Electric, has been quoted as saying, "When the rate of change inside an organization is less than the rate of change outside an organization, the end is near." The wisdom of this statement seems obvious. An organization that is not moving and adapting at, or faster than, the rate of change in its environment soon finds itself out of sync with that environment and its future is threatened.

Proactive behavior is impossible when the organization is out of touch with its environment. Being a leader in its chosen markets is compromised by the continual need to react to changes in the outside world for which the organization is not prepared. New products and technologies reach customers later than those of competitors. And those competitors keep moving forward while the organization plays catch-up or pursues the risky strategy of attempting to leapfrog competitors without the experience gained by them with previous generations of products or services.

A. Organization and Environment

Lawrence and Lorsch, in a significant piece of research in the mid-fifties, demonstrated a clear need to design organization and management practices aligned with the uncertainty of the business environment.[5] Uncertainty increases as increases occur in areas like the rate of technological change, number of new products required to remain competitive, globalization, difficulty of access to information, or feedback from the environment, and so on.

In environments with greater certainty, i.e., less uncertainty, the research found that simpler structures were associated with success. Traditional hierarchical means of communicating and coordinating among functions worked well in less complex structures and environments. In fact, the research indicated that designing in too much organizational complexity and flexibility could hinder performance of organizations in more certain environments.

In highly uncertain environments, on the other hand, Lawrence and Lorsch found that more successful organizations learned how to handle a double whammy associated with their uncertainty. First of all, they needed to create more complexity to cope with the greater uncertainty. They did this by developing more functional units that allowed each to handle a more specialized part of the increasingly complex environment. But the increased complexity and number of functions also created more difficulty in achieving coordinated efforts across the organization. Differences in goals, task focus, time orientations, and thinking processes of the various departments increased and became more "differentiated." And as the amount of differentiation increased, so did the difficulty of achieving "integrated" efforts and results on complex tasks.

To cope with this second whammy, more successful organizations in highly uncertain environments also created a variety of strategies for communication and coordination across departments. These included things like temporary project teams, ongoing coordinating teams, and entire departments or individuals whose primary role was to function as "integrators" to facilitate work across the larger number of more "differentiated" groups.

Without these adaptations, while also retaining the mechanisms needed for success in more certain environments, success was limited. Market shares were reduced, new products were limited, and bottom-line performance suffered.

B. Current and Future Environments and Uncertainty

In the decades since the original research, the level of uncertainty in the environment of all organizations has increased and will predictably continue to do so. The environments of many fewer businesses operating today would fit the criteria for "low uncertainty."

Additionally, a wide range of organizations that are surviving and successful today have adopted many of the practices found necessary for success in the higher uncertainty environments of the fifties. The existence of many more specialties in technical and engineering areas or in a variety of departments focused on the application of information technology seems natural today, but would have seemed unusual at the time of the original Lawrence and Lorsch research. The use of ongoing work teams, temporary teams, project managers, and so on are considered normal for coordinating complex work tasks and processes in medium- to larger-sized organizations. More and more managers and executives have found it necessary to add integrating processes like these, recognizing that the complexity of their world has made reliance on traditional hierarchical methods too cumbersome, inflexible, and obsolete.

II. Environmental Factors Influencing Needed ECO Capability

Executives need to understand the factors in the business environment that add to uncertainty and create needs for the capabilities of an Ever-Changing Organization. Equally important is to understand the trends of those factors as they relate to the organization's business. Use of the ECO diagnostic process found in the implementation section of this book (Chapter 7) provides insight about where an organization is at any point in time and assesses the trends in the environment. Consideration is given to the history of the environment and how it is likely to change in the future, recognizing that the environment is dynamic and will continue to change.

In this section the key environmental factors for determining the ECO needs of the organization will be described. Some of these have not changed from the time of the original research. Others have emerged in more recent times with the increased globalization of businesses and significantly increased demands and requirements from customers. And, of course, all of us have experienced the ongoing explosion of technology and its application to nearly all aspects of an organization's business. This is especially true in the areas of computer hardware and software and the incredible growth of the Internet and World Wide Web.

Each of the features of the business environment discussed below represents one of the areas examined in the ECO diagnostic of the environment. An overall pattern develops in the data that identifies the organization's level of need for ECO capability as well as where the environment is and will be going. This data assembled in the diagnosis helps executives make necessary choices for needed change and movement to the level of ECO capability required in their unique environment.

A. Rate of Technological Change

As the rate of technological change in an organization's environment increases, so must the rate at which the organization is capable of anticipating and adapting to new technology. Companies that once were in the business of selling individual copiers or printers now find themselves in the document services business with the growth of digital products and networking technology.[8] Wesley Cantrell, President of Lanier Worldwide, Inc., described the need to revamp many of his organization's practices, including the selling process, to cope with the advanced capabilities of the rapidly changing technology. Following are examples of rapid or accelerating change.

1. Semiconductor density
    Gordon Moore, cofounder and chairman emeritus of Intel, articulated what is today called "Moore's Law." It says that, in the world of semiconductors and integrated circuits, the number of components per chip doubles every 18 months. For this to happen there have to be major changes in the raw materials, i.e., in the silicon wafers or other semiconductor materials within which circuits are produced. New circuit fabrication, assembly, and testing processes must be created. New design and simulation methodologies become critical and the time to create and introduce products must be shortened. Applied Materials has grown to be a leading supplier of products to the semiconductor industry by learning how to move rapidly with innovative solutions to the fast changing needs of the industry. The complexity of current circuits is hundreds of times greater than it was 10 to 12 years ago. And Moore's Law says this rate of change will continue. For example, Dr. Asad Madni, CEO of BEI Systems and Sensors Company, described advanced development work in his organization with micromachining techniques. The ability to microminiaturize pumps, sensors, motors, actuators, and so on to sizes measurable in microns will allow them to be embedded in silicon wafers creating an even higher level of integrated systems and circuits.

Organizations in these and associated businesses are facing high levels of uncertainty that will continue to drive the need for ECO capability as time goes on. For them, performance measures like "time to market" are now critical success factors as opposed to interesting strategic concepts.

2. Information availability in transportation industry
The ability to know the whereabouts and delivery status of material consigned to a transportation company has rapidly become a strategic and competitive must. Ever more rapidly advancing information-processing technology has made it possible. And use of these technologies by leaders in the industry has changed customers' expectations dramatically. "Your shipment is on the road and should arrive by the middle of next week" is no longer acceptable. What's demanded now is "The shipment left Tulsa at 4:30 P.M. today and will arrive at our St. Louis terminal by 11:00 A.M. tomorrow. It will be delivered to your St. Charles factory no later than 3:30 P.M."

The president of a very successful regional trucking company understood the rapid changes occurring in both hardware and software for information processing as well as the advantages available from being early, if not first, with the application of the new capabilities. He devoted an unusual percentage of financial and people resources to projects for getting the capability. His company was among the leaders in this area. Yet he continually experienced frustration with the time required to fund projects and get the new technology successfully introduced. He could see the movement of competitors and was very much aware of suppliers' capabilities. The rapidly changing technological forces were clearly pushing him to develop greater ECO capacity in what was historically a relatively low-tech business.

3. Disk drive capabilities
Christensen, in "The Innovator's Dilemma,"[7] selected the disk drive industry as a primary subject of his research. This was largely due to the rate of technological change in the industry. So much change has happened in a brief span of time that it was possible to study several generations of technological advances in the relatively brief life of the industry (much like researchers who use short-lived organisms that multiply rapidly to study genetic factors and evolutionary trends).

In the disk drive industry a number of companies have led the industry technologically for brief periods. They have innovated and grown rapidly only to be supplanted by the next competitor who changes or takes the technology to a new level, succeeds wildly and then is also supplanted by the next innovator. Each new innovator and leader seems unable to sustain his lead or be prepared for the next generation of product. The result is a roller coaster ride from rags to riches and back again. And this phenomenon is observable in many industries where innovators are unable to maintain their position through continuing technological innovation and leadership.

Christensen's observations suggest that one important strategy for dealing with this dilemma would be to become more "differentiated" — create a new and independent unit to work on future generations of technology and products. This is akin to the creation of "skunkworks"[8] for getting projects done without the normal constraints of the ongoing organization. Provide that unit with all of the resources needed for development of new generations of technology and products to facilitate "integration" of efforts. Relieve them of the pressure of operating a successful and ongoing business and of the financial expectations for performance of an existing business. Free them from the limits of thinking associated with existing technology and give them freedom to explore what would be unthinkable and threatening in the current business.

In a business like the disk drive business, the rapid technological change may make such a strategy the only way to continue to innovate and lead.

Organizations faced with the rapid technological change occurring in industries like disk drives are definitely dealing with highly uncertain environments. As such they need to continue building their capacity as ECOs. The actions suggested by Christensen for innovators contribute to increasing ECO capabilities.

B. Product/Service Life Cycles

The life cycle of products or services is another major factor influencing environmental uncertainty and the need to become an ECO. For our purposes, life cycle refers to the period of time from the introduction of a product or service to the point at which it becomes obsolete for use in new applications by customers. As life cycles decrease uncertainty increases, and the need for creating increased ECO capacity goes up.

A number of forces in the environment can influence the overall life cycle of new products in a business. These might stem from customers and the demands for new products to meet their strategic needs. Competitor improvements in developmental processes, products, or technology is another. Availability of products and services from suppliers that accelerate the introduction of new products in the industry could be another influence. Changes in regulatory mechanisms, e.g., rules that define products or services offered by financial or insurance companies or actions by the FDA that reduce the approval times for new drugs, could suddenly mean that competing products are appearing more frequently and rendering existing products obsolete. Any or all of these forces would increase uncertainty as they contribute to shorter life cycles and increase the need for ECO capabilities.

Examples of rapid or reduced life cycles are:

1. Personal computers and integrated circuits

    Uncertainty reigns when the time period in which a product is viable for new customers is shorter than the development cycle of current design processes. At one point the life cycle of integrated circuits for new equipment designs had fallen below 18 months and the increasing complexity of the circuits mean development cycles in that time range or longer. At the same time the developer could expect to see the average selling price of new circuits decline by a factor of 3 to 4 or more when other suppliers matched or exceeded current performance or capabilities.

    The probability is high that you use a personal computer (PC). If so, you have seen the rapidity with which changes in product capability has affected that market. For example, the personal computer system used for writing this book was purchased less than six months prior to writing this paragraph. It was equipped with state-of-the-art capability at the time of purchase. In the past six months this equipment appears virtually obsolete for new sales. Systems with 50% (or more) capability are not only available, they are available at less than 50% of the cost.

    Major contributors to the rapid improvement in PC performance and pricing are the improvements in costs and performance of microprocessors, video and audio circuitry, memory devices, modems, CD-ROMs, and so on. The improvements are coming so rapidly that product life cycles are shrinking faster than ever. Many industry veterans would have scoffed at the idea of a complete PC system for less than $1000. Yet today these are commonplace and have incredible capabilities. And the drive of key semiconductor manufacturers is towards development of circuits with all of the functions of a PC integrated into one chip — the so-called "computer on a chip." It won't be long before this happens, probably before this book is printed.

The level of uncertainty in this environment is very high. As a result the need for ECO capacity is also very high. Some of the greatest certainty in these businesses is probably to be found in the predictability of continuing reduction in product life cycles, the requirement in the industry for continuous improvement in performance and quality, and ongoing reduction in "time to market" while reducing costs and pricing to customers. Without ECO capabilities the task becomes untenable.

2. Securities industry

A number of years ago Charles Schwab influenced a major change in the securities industry with the concept of a discount brokerage. Fewer other services were provided and the cost per transaction was significantly reduced. This eventually prompted the development of other discount brokerages and provided a viable alternative to many investors.

More recently, however, this industry has been turned upside down with the advent of online brokerages. Instant quotes and low-cost online buying and selling have taken off. Survival today requires fast response to new services and financial products and has clearly shortened the time frame within which new products are viable. As information processing capabilities grow, so do the applications of those capabilities in an ever-changing array of products and services while older products and services are replaced by newer innovations.

The historically staid and conservative brokerage industry must now allocate substantially more resources to creating new products and services to replace those that are being rendered obsolete. Moving from change-resistant to more change-friendly or change-seeking orientations is becoming a necessity for coping with the added uncertainty of shorter product and service life cycles. The pressure to become an ECO has grown and will continue to grow. Those who fail to make the necessary changes to increased ECO capability face the problem of obsolescence of their services and a severe challenge to their survival.

In contrast to the examples above are businesses where products and the processes that produce them are viable for many years. Some parts of the glass business come under this category. Corning Glass Works (now Corning, Inc.) created the "ribbon machine" for the production of the glass envelope for incandescent light bulbs in 1926. It produced an increase in productivity of hundreds of percents. Hand-blown envelopes could be produced at a rate of about 60 per hour. When the "ribbon machine" was fully operative it was producing at rates ranging from 600 to well over 1000 per minute. Over the years, these rates were increased even further and closed-loop process controls produced an even more consistent product. Yet the product itself has remained basically unchanged except for sizes and some modifications of shape.

This is not a situation in which the environment has created pressure for additional rapid change or acted to obsolete products. Rather it has become highly standardized for the glass manufacturer and producer of the completed bulb. Similar experiences apply to other glass manufacturing of such products as beer bottles and baby food jars, plate glass for windows and windshields, and scientific glassware. In these environments there is much more certainty and less external pressure for becoming an ECO than in many others.

C. Rate of Market Growth

Greater certainty is associated with markets that are stable or that grow primarily with the growth of the economy. In discussions with a production planning and control manager in a stable business environment a number of years ago, we were told that the ability to predict total annual shipments was a nonissue compared to other businesses in the corporation. The manager commented that he and his associates should be fired if their forecasts were off more than 5% since changes in volume were almost fully correlated with changes in the GNP. On the other hand, he described some of his colleagues in other divisions of the company as "lucky if they could forecast total volumes within plus or minus 20% of actual shipments." Environmental uncertainty was greater as a function of the more rapid and unpredictable market growth in some of the other divisions.

Rapid growth of the company or the company's markets adds substantially to the uncertainty of the environment. Dave Olsen, Sr. VP of Starbucks told us, for example, that many of their managers had come from successful positions in other businesses. Their experience allowed them to succeed in the early days of their involvement with Starbucks. However, the growth rate of the company was so far beyond what most had previously experienced that within a relatively brief time he described these managers as "hitting the wall." Previous experience was no longer useful at the accelerated rates of growth. The added uncertainty means that managers both learn rapidly and change to cope with the rapid growth or fail.

A division manager in a rapidly growing microelectronics company described how he had become a general manager at Texas Instruments early in his career as a result of unheard-of growth rates. "Guys like myself were promoted to fill positions we were not prepared for because there were no available candidates with the needed experience and skills." Under those conditions the organization was left with few options but to promote bright, young people who could tolerate the uncertainty and ambiguity of explosive growth and give them as much as they could take.

Another uncertainty added by rapid market growth has to do with decisions about the parts of the market to serve, i.e., whether to compete in all segments of the broader market or focus on more limited, niche markets. Other decisions might involve whether to do the entire range of tasks required to be in a market or to buy various services from specialists to keep the task and costs of entry manageable. The extremely large investments required for manufacturing semiconductors led to the creation of a number of companies, e.g., Chips and Technology, Cirrus Logic, and S3, who rely almost completely on contract manufacturers for the production and testing of their products while they concentrate on design and marketing of the products. Companies like Solectron, ANAM, and others have become large and successful contract manufacturers by servicing the growing market for others who outsource some of their traditional functions.

With rapid market growth also comes a number of testy financial issues that add uncertainty. Make vs. buy decisions involve a number of key strategic questions as well as issues related to cash flow, availability of financing, and so on. When and how to add capacity or people or facilities become more complex issues with rapid expansion of markets. Will the growth continue and for how long? What share of market can we expect to have or gain?

The tendency towards unbridled optimism is a difficult one to overcome when things are going well. Reality checks are difficult. In many situations of rapid growth the person who questions ambitious forecasts or cautions against letting expectations surpass what is likely may be seen as a non-team player. The euphoria of growth may cause some or all of the managers or executives of the organization to withhold concerns. The result can be decisions or predictions that no one really believes, but also avoids confronting (this is the type of decision-making process Jerry Harvey calls the "Abilene Paradox."[9]) The uncertainty created by rapid market growth only adds to the likelihood of such things happening. Acknowledging that the growth trends will not continue indefinitely, on the one hand, is accompanied by the excitement of the opportunity to continue to grow, and the excitement often wins the argument.

D. Changing Customer Requirements and Expectations

In the period of rapid industrial growth that followed World War II, organizations were able to sell virtually everything they could make. If costs increased, prices were raised. If quality was poor, customers ordered more inventory and returned the faulty product. If delivery was unreliable or partial orders were shipped, customers would simply order additional inventory to cover shortages associated with off-schedule deliveries. Customers had learned to expect little from their suppliers. Although they were never happy with this situation, there were generally no alternatives available.

Then a number of things began to happen to change this environment for most businesses. International competitors invaded markets previously owned almost exclusively by American businesses. The Japanese, for example, were forced to rebuild most of their industry from the ground up. They realized that the option to compete with Americans on the basis of productivity was not viable. The direction they selected was to rebuild their businesses with a focus on quality and meeting customer requirements.

Suddenly levels of defects that had been presumed to be "natural" were shown to be excessive and unnecessary. Customers began to realize that it costs less, not more, to produce quality products and services. The expectations of customers and consumers were irrevocably raised and continue to grow today. And these expectations apply to services and customer support as well as to products.

Failure to meet customers' higher expectations means loss of business to competitors who do. And meeting higher expectations is not a one-time thing. This is not just a blip about which one can say, "This too shall pass." It has become a permanent part of virtually all business environments. Some examples are:

1. Customer quality requirements for automobiles

    No more making lists of defects for the first few weeks and then returning the car to the dealer for a day or two to get the first bunch of problems fixed. Not acceptable, especially at higher prices. "Make it right the first time!" is what today's consumer expects. And the new car is also expected to be reliable and not contain what customers previously thought of as "planned obsolescence" where components broke down shortly after the end of a warranty period. A number of car makers today are building engines that need no primary service for 100,000 miles.

    An airplane conversation with Jim McHugh, President of McHugh Lincoln-Mercury, confirmed the changing customer expectations as well as Ford's response. Jim was President of the Lincoln-Mercury Dealer's Association of America at the time. He recalled earlier times when the dealer would not immediately make new cars available for sale. All new cars were put into the shop for testing and fixing first. Today, he said, they are cleaned of dirt accumulated in transit and place in the showroom. Increasing environmental pressure from customers is driving such performance and will continue to do so.

2. Demise of acceptable quality levels (AQLs)

    In some industries it was common for manufacturers to negotiate an AQL with their customers. The concept was that it was difficult and expensive to test for and find all defects. It was said to be too expensive to design and build manufacturing processes that would always meet customers' requirements. Therefore, let's agree that you, the customer, will test our incoming product and only return it if the defect level exceeds an agreed upon level of defects. This concept has faded in use.

    One indicator of the shift away from an AQL mentality was observed when a purchasing manager from a major customer was addressing one of his suppliers at a quality improvement celebration. He told the group that he understood that his company had agreed to an AQL and that they would honor it. At the same time he asked them for a favor. Since it cost him so much time and money to find the defects being received, he asked that they help out by putting the defective parts all in one bag to keep them separate from the good ones. Customer expectations today no longer need to accept the AQL notion, and this ongoing force for improvement from the environment creates added pressure for the capabilities of an ECO.

3. Requirements to demonstrate improved processes and results
   Many customers today will avoid suppliers who have not achieved
   ISO-9000 certification. In a related area, two of the early winners of
   the Malcolm Baldrige National Quality Award, Motorola and IBM,
   notified suppliers a number of years ago that they were expected to
   pursue the award as a condition of doing business. Ford, always
   among the more demanding suppliers, has greatly expanded its performance expectation from suppliers. Knowing that quality improvements also result in lower costs and reduction of cycle times, they
   now require suppliers to negotiate improvements in a growing range
   of performance measures. Included are the areas of reduced pricing,
   improved lead times, and "just-in-time" delivery in addition to quality levels previously thought to be impossible. They expect to benefit
   from the gains of suppliers that result from their improvement efforts.

E. Competitive Situation

A number of factors in the competitive situation an organization faces contributes to the level of uncertainty of the environment and the needed ECO
capacity. In general, the number, size, market share, and product leadership
position of competitors influence uncertainty. Larger numbers of competitors all scramble to grow and increase market share. An examination of the
3- to 5-year plans of the many competitors in a crowded market usually
shows a total market in future years well in excess of any predictions and
combined growth rates that far outpace the industries' expectations. Greater
uncertainty is the result.

Larger competitors have more resources with which to compete. Smaller
competitors face more uncertainty and may find it necessary to focus on
narrower, niche markets. Competitors with the greatest market share often
have the most influence with customers as to pricing and product direction.
The additional learning experience of producing more product helps with
productivity and process improvement and often creates a cost advantage.
The additional uncertainty for those with little share of market might come
from preemptive pricing by larger competitors or from limits on their ability
to provide additional services. Product leadership can be a significant advantage. It provides leverage to lead further as followers rush to catch up, only
to find the leader moving further ahead again. Intel and Microsoft offer great
examples of this leverage in recent history.

Another issue in the environment that impacts uncertainty based on competitive positioning has to do with vulnerability of attack from others. When the potential exits from existing competitors or suppliers for integration into your markets, uncertainty increases. A major semiconductor CEO we know found it necessary to modify key portions of his product strategy as a result of the threat of further integration by an industry leader that would render products obsolete before they were developed.

In other businesses, the threat of attack by competitors using different materials or new design or development processes or technology can significantly increase environmental uncertainty. In the medical supply field, for example, the use of paper-based, disposable products has displaced reusable cloth products as plastic disposables have generally replaced reusable glass products.

Other examples of the impact of competitive positioning on environmental uncertainty are:

1. Product leadership

   Intel has become dominant in the world of microprocessors to such an extent that others question its business practices as being anticompetitive and monopolistic. Yet Intel has pursued product leadership as a major strategy from the inception of the company. When Intel introduced the industry's first MOS RAM, the 1103, the additional capability provided to customers commanded a premium price. Competitors quickly followed to offer an alternate source. And, as soon as such sources became available, Intel took two additional competitive steps: (1) it significantly lowered the price and (2) it introduced a newer and faster version of the product that continued to command the higher prices. The competitors were still learning to make the product and they struggled to make money at the lower prices while Intel reaped great margins both from their lowered costs on the older version of the product and from the higher pricing of the newest versions.

   This strategy continued through each level of complexity of the product until their experience and time advantages had shrunk significantly with the challenges from the Japanese. At this point, Intel left the market it had created and moved into other markets, notably the microprocessor. And the Intel strategy had remained much the same. It is based in large part on the concept advocated by Andy

Grove, retired Intel CEO, that to become and remain a leader one must be paranoid, i.e., always fearful of competitors who are out to get you. The only argument we have with Grove's concept is that he's not talking about paranoia. It's only being paranoid when they're not really out to get you and, in Intel's case, they really are!

The product leadership strategy practiced by Intel has provided it a major competitive advantage while maintaining a sustained high level of uncertainty for competitors like AMD or National Semiconductor and others.

2. Growth of superstores

In a number of businesses there has been a major shift from small, local, family-owned businesses to super- or megastores. These stores offer a greater range of products and lower pricing based on their volume buying power. They are often able to drive the smaller guy out of business. Consider, for example, the likes of Costco or Sam's Club in the wholesale warehouse business, Blockbuster and Hollywood Video in the home video rental business, Wal-Mart and K-Mart and the dominance of markets once served by organizations like Woolworth's or Ben Franklin.

Home Depot, Home Base and others have captured large portions of the market in the do-it-yourself world, often driving the small town hardware stores out of the market. Small bookstores have become almost extinct with the growth of organizations like Borders or Barnes and Noble and others. And similar changes have happened in many other consumer products businesses such as pharmacies, audio/video equipment, and even garden supplies.

The effect of this change to megastores is to create uncertainty that smaller competitors cannot cope with. They continue to get business for smaller purchases, and customers appreciate their more personal service. Yet they are unable to compete for larger purchases where they historically have made the greatest profits. They are forced to accept a more limited, niche position in their markets or, more likely, to quit or sell out in some form of merger or acquisition.

3. Online commerce

We have just discussed the demise of the small business as a result of the creation of megastores. Yet today, many of these businesses are faced with growing uncertainty from newer business forms not even possible until recently. Amazon.com has become a major force in the field of book selling by offering access to millions of titles via the Internet. Barnes and Noble and others have had to scurry to cope with this new uncertainty by creating their own virtual bookstores. And Amazon.com is continuing to move forward. They have created an online offering for music in almost any form, i.e., tapes, CDs, and the emerging new technologies such as DVD. How many other businesses will have to face the additional uncertainty associated with this new form of commerce? Most likely, nearly all consumer businesses will see this type of competition to some degree and have to be prepared to deal with it. This was clearly illustrated by the recent advent of a full-blown fashion show by Victoria's Secret broadcast on the Internet.

Although developed originally based on advances in telecommunications technology, the enormous growth of catalog shopping will undoubtedly continue and will integrate even more virtual shopping. And this will also impact on the enormous success in recent years of television shopping and TV networks devoted just to that business.

All of the examples and issues discussed above influence uncertainty in an organization's environment stemming from the competitive situations it faces. And, as seems obvious, all of these forces and trends show no signs of waning. Instead they are likely to increase in strength and create continually increasing uncertainty for competitors in these businesses.

F. Globalization of Businesses and Markets

Businesses that operate in local or geographically limited arenas generally are functioning in an environment of less uncertainty. They are able to see and touch base with customers on a face-to-face basis. The buying habits of their customers are well understood and rooted in a single culture. The customers and the supplier are likely to share a set of reasonably common values.

As the territory of a business expands, many things change. Direct customer contact is limited. Customer expectations are more varied and requirements for products and services also tend to be more variable. When extended to international and then full globalization of a business, even greater uncertainty is added. Selling in different cultures requires understanding and adapting to the ways of doing business in the foreign environment. Successful operation of manufacturing plants or distribution centers in other countries means needing to understand the culture and legal systems of those countries as well as what behaviors are acceptable or unacceptable. Simply transplanting native operating systems and management practices to foreign environments is a formula for disaster.

Eric Herr, President of Autodesk, shared his sense of the difficulty presented. Autodesk is a major supplier of PC design software and multimedia tools. They provide more than a dozen basic products servicing five markets with business in 150 countries and 19 languages. They have built an organization that uses third-party software developers and value-added resellers to service the unique needs of end customers around the world. He stated very clearly the company's realization that they "are just not smart enough to dictate from the top down what happens around the world with that range of products and applications."

Many attempts at globalization of a business have been based on the size and attractiveness of current or projected markets. Little attention has been paid to the significantly increased complexity associated with doing business in foreign lands. The result has been preventable failure. Recognizing the additional complexity and uncertainty and creating additional ECO capability could have prepared the organization for success in both the short and long term.

Let's look at just a few examples:

1. Managing with expatriates

   The insertion of expatriates into top management positions of new or acquired business in other countries is a common practice of many business organizations. Often these managers are sent to their new assignment with a minimum of training and preparation, i.e., intense training in the language of the country. Knowing the culture and values of the people and what they expect is given little emphasis. Rather, the manager is oriented to the expatriate policies and financial benefits and approaches the new position eagerly — often with a rather high level of arrogance about the effective way to manage, obviously based on what works at home.

   After a considerable amount of consulting work in Thailand and several other Asian nations, we have seen firsthand some of the effects of unprepared expatriate managers. Managerial actions that would never happen in the local culture are common and resented. The issue is never confronted, however, because to do so would be inappropriate in the culture. Intense but subtle forms of resistance often result. Unfortunately, the problems that surface do little but confirm the expatriate manager's assumptions about the difficulty of managing in the environment and the keen insight of management's decision to use expatriates in the first place.

In one situation we observed, a talented and very successful Korean executive was suddenly taken from his position in Korea and placed in the comparable position in his organization's subsidiary in the Philippines. The changes were announced and implemented with virtually no time allowed to prepare for the transition or to learn about the culture and working values of the Philippine people. This executive was forced to rely on a management style that had served him well in the Korean culture but was an unmitigated failure in Manila.

A colleague of ours, Kevin Wheeler, spent several years in the Peace Corps in Thailand. He learned the Thai language, became immersed in the culture, married a Thai national, and became a Buddhist. And with all of this background, he still acknowledges the care it requires of him to function effectively in the country. Imagine how he shudders when he observes the behavior of many foreigners ("farang" as they are referred to by the Thai) who work and manage in the country with virtually no preparation. Yet Thai nationals are managing few foreign companies in Thailand. Foreign companies that have sent poorly prepared expatriates to do those managing jobs have added to an already high level of uncertainty that they and their representatives are not prepared for. And the result in many cases has been, or will be, disappointing performance vs. expectations.

2. Language issues

England and the U.S. have been described as allies separated by a common language. Certainly both countries speak the English language but often in different ways. When conducting business among people from the two countries it is easy to assume that the use of English means that communication has occurred far more often than is true. British English and American English differences add a degree of uncertainty to business transactions that is often subtle and unknown until something doesn't happen as expected. "But you said..." is followed by "But I thought you meant..." and so on. Another example of uncertainty created by untested assumptions.

Working for an American company acquired by the Dutch multinational, NV Philips, demonstrated the subtlety of these problems. English was always used as the language of the business. In fact, the Dutch were so fluent that some American managers were reluctant to ask questions to clarify potential miscommunications. Not wanting to embarrass a visitor from the parent company meant that questions sometimes did not get asked. Likewise, the Dutch were sometimes reluctant to ask the meaning of terms that would indicate limited fluency in English. As the president of the American company often said, "The question that has not been asked cannot be answered." Yet many were left unasked and resulted in problems that might have been avoided.

The effort required to understand the "common" spoken language (assuming it is English) and the accents of others can be very trying. Being sure of what is meant requires time and patience. In working with a management team composed of foreign and Thai nationals, one of the foreign managers expressed frustration about getting agreement on tasks without getting results. After some discussion one of the Thai managers commented, "But you failed to get the second 'yes' you needed. When you asked if the task was understood and heard 'yes', the answer indicated understanding of what the task was. However, you needed to ask further if there was agreement to complete the task. Without the second yes, there was no commitment to do what had been discussed." Taking the time to clarify agreements and to test for both understanding and commitment was necessary in that situation.

Organizations in global businesses need to recognize that uncertainty is increased by the complexity of communication in such an environment. Additional time may be needed to assure complete communication even though spending time on such a process runs counter to the need to reach conclusions and move on.

These are just small examples of a simple but important type of uncertainty associated with the globalization of businesses. Relying on the communication practices of organizations from different parts of the world because the language in use is assumed to be "common" is foolish. It reflects a failure to recognize the need, and cope with the changes required, to become more of an ECO in a more global business.

G. Application Base of Products or Services

In environments with a widely varied set of customers and applications, environmental uncertainty increases. Implications for flexibility in design for ease of application vs. customization for specific applications vs. creation of a range of products or services must be considered in product strategies. Customer needs for technical support are likely to be greater as is the need for creating a greater range of selling and distribution options, i.e., via distributors or manufacturers' representatives or online or direct selling.

Understanding the specific demands of various market segments may lead to the need for specialists oriented both to the product and to the market segment. Along with the addition of specialists come additional costs, not only for the people but also for their travel and the ongoing training required to keep them current on the products and their applications. In the electronics distribution business, for example, the development of more application engineering roles (or technical sales engineers) reflects the added product complexity and growth in the range of applications. And the investment required in training and maintaining their knowledge of the avalanche of new products being developed is extensive.

Additional effort may be required to understand the variety of applications being used — and the probability of inappropriate applications may tie up resources trying to help the customer understand the problems that are created. This problem is not uncommon in the application of computer software to situations beyond those for which the product was designed. Customer or technical support people find themselves involved in trying to understand and isolate an assumed "bug" in the software only to find that the problem is in the customer's application, not the software. With a broad range of potential applications it becomes virtually impossible for the designer to anticipate them all. Autodesk's use of third-party software developers in its wide ranging markets acknowledges the inability of the original designer to understand the application of the product in all situations. Breadth of application in the environment creates additional uncertainty and the need for additional ECO capacity.

H. Access to Information

In more certain environments it is much easier to gather market intelligence or to assess the likely response to a decision or strategic direction. Typically, there are fewer and bigger customers with whom long-standing relationships exist. These customer are an important and easily accessible source of information regarding competitors, and feedback from just a few will provide a sound basis for assessing the impact of, or response to, decisions.

As the size and geographic dispersion of the customer base increases, uncertainty increases. As the number of competitors and the variety of options available to customers from different materials or technologies increases, uncertainty increases even further. In more uncertain environments, much more effort is required to gather market intelligence regarding competitive direction or the overall needs of the customer base. Feedback is more difficult to obtain and more time-consuming to evaluate. For example, data on the acceptance or rejection of price increases may take months. Customers in uncertain environments may simply shift business to competitors leaving the impact unknown for an extended time. In more certain environments, on the other hand, the feedback needed to assess the results of a pricing change may be available via a handful of telephone calls.

The cycle from introduction of a new product through its evaluation and acceptance by a customer and on to its purchase and use requires additional time in rapidly changing markets, creating an extended period of uncertainty. Deciding how much manufacturing capacity to create or how much inventory to produce is more difficult. Culling information from the environment about requirements for the next generation of products is also more difficult and time-consuming.

To cope with lack of information or delayed feedback organizations must invest more resources or be left behind. The greater use of internal specialists or external consultants for market research or of trade associations for compilation of data and forecasts increases. Added responsibilities for collecting data from the customer and competitive world to the sales role may be required to get rapid and up-to-date information for strategic decisions and product development direction.

As additional mechanisms are created to collect data and feedback, the organization must also add resources to process and interpret the data. This often involves data-processing capabilities as well as departments or review committees assigned to consolidate data and prepare reports. Without such capabilities the organization accumulates data but very little intelligence, and their ability to cope with the additional uncertainty is diminished.

I. Environmental Impact of Business

Uncertainty has been added to the external environment of many businesses by the growing concerns for our overall environment, both physical and social. Advocacy groups such as those associated with Ralph Nader, Greenpeace, or the Sierra Club are visible and powerful forces for change in the behavior of many organizations — groups that in earlier times would never have needed to address the issues they now raise. Groups concerned with such issues as depletion of natural resources, e.g., old-growth redwoods or whales, or of extinction of rare species of plants or animals, and so on, have spawned the growth of governmental agencies like the Environmental Protection Agency. The policies of such agencies add time and costs as well as uncertainty to the efforts of many organizations.

Environmental forces have greatly increased for the reduction or prevention of pollution. Worries about issues like depletion of the ozone layer or the threat of global warming bring added pressures to some organizations to change materials or improve waste processing or make changes in their products to achieve the same ends. In the chemical industry, the industry association has developed a set of environmental standards subscribed to by all of its members. Complying with these consumes time as well as human and financial resources.

Safety and health concerns have increased, and pressures and uncertainties are added for organizations by agencies like the Occupational Safety and Health Administration (OSHA) and its regulations.

Organizations that move manufacturing capabilities offshore to reap the benefits of lower skilled but less expensive labor are finding that they must also consider the social implications of the working conditions in the facilities that produce their products. Michael Jordan and Nike, for example, and others have had to pay attention to the working conditions and issues like abusive child labor practices in their factories in foreign countries. Again, advocacy groups produce very embarrassing and negative publicity even though the practices may be within the norms of the culture in which the producing takes place. Strong messages from consumers indicate that they expect organizations to behave in a socially responsible manner no matter where the products are made. Uncertainty is added because of the need to assess and consider an additional set of factors in making decisions about where and how to produce.

Much of the additional uncertainty related to the environmental impact of an organization stems from greatly increased communications capability. Many see the media as primarily concerned with "bad" news. This plays directly into the hands of those who have a specific issue they wish to highlight and have addressed. Acceptance of this environmental reality and the additional uncertainty it creates has become a more important factor to be dealt with in considering an organization's need for capabilities as an ECO.

III. Acceleration and Compression of Time in High Uncertainty Environments

Increasing environmental uncertainty leads to the acceleration of all aspects of a business and increasing emphasis on doing things in less and less time. Shortly after moving from Corning Glass Works to the much more uncertain environment of the semiconductor industry, one of us consulted with two departments about a process for improving their working relationship. When told two and a half days were "normally" required for the process, the managers asked, "What can we do in one day?" Agreement was reached to try a one-day process. The consultant then began looking for a time to meet sometime in the next four to five weeks, a normal lead-time in his previous experience. The manager's reaction was "What's the matter with Tuesday?" And that is when the meeting was scheduled. Leaving the meeting the consultant thought to himself, "Wow, welcome to the fast lane!" He was beginning to understand at a very personal level what being in such a high uncertainty environment meant and how it affected his work as well.

Chuck Harwood, Signetics' president, encountered a situation some time later in which he had lunch with a colleague who was president of a business in a much more stable environment. After sharing experiences during the lunch, the colleague commented that both he and Chuck were faced with the same types of issues for making their businesses successful. However, he observed, he had the luxury of dealing with those issues in a four- to five-year time frame while Chuck was forced by his environment to deal with them in a year. Here was another, external observation of the acceleration and time compression that comes with operating in a very high uncertainty environment. Chuck amusingly described the personal impact of such an environment in his response to a question about how he was able to sleep while having to deal with all of the rapid change and uncertainty. His response was, "I sleep like a baby. I wake up every two hours and cry!"

In a broader sense, the general increase in uncertainty in today's environment has resulted in the emergence of time to do things as a major focus in many organizations. "Time to market" has become a key measure of performance in new product development efforts. Major work on process improvements with a focus on reducing cycle times is another indicator of the effect of added uncertainty and what organizations need to address as they adapt their practices to a generally more uncertain environment.

IV. Implications of Uncertainty for ECO Needs

As environmental uncertainty increases, the need to develop the capabilities of an Ever-Changing Organization also increases! A primary implication of this statement is that it is important for executives to examine the level of uncertainty in their business environment. They need to understand not only the current pressures for change but also the extent to which these pressures have changed and will continue to change (or not) in the future. It is difficult to see the level of capability needed as an ECO without a clear picture of the environment and its trends. Specific materials and guides for their use in carrying out an environmental assessment are presented in the implementation section of this book.

Many executives express awareness of an increase in the number of changes they must implement and manage. At the same time they express concerns and frustration with the slowness and difficulty of making change happen. Wesley Cantrell, CEO of Lanier Worldwide, was asked whether his expectations had been satisfied for a number of change projects he had initiated. He said, "... I always say that a CEO is never to be satisfied with anything — he's not supposed to be. I am pleased with the progress we've made, but not satisfied." He, like many others, realizes that more capacity for change is needed in addition to improvements in the manner in which changes are implemented.

Yet not many have taken the time to do an overall analysis of the forces for change in their environment and how these have grown. Without documentation and facts, these executives are left with the uneasy, gut feeling they should move their organizations forward towards becoming an ECO. Holding still is not the answer, but setting the direction to develop increased ECO capabilities is a major step with ongoing implications for the executives themselves and for their organizations. The lack of data only adds to the difficulty of the decision to commit to such a direction.

A CEO friend of ours, in discussing his decision to embark on an organization-wide continuous improvement process a number of years ago, acknowledged his awareness of the need to initiate the process but also to be sure he was selecting the right direction. He knew that he couldn't be wrong, because in moving ahead he was setting a direction with long-term implications for the company. Examination of data from the business' environment and an analysis of his own company's performance convinced him it was not only the right thing to do but that it was also his obligation as CEO to create the capacity for continuous improvement. Subsequent examination of available approaches helped him find a process that fit his organization's need and culture.

This book describes a process similar to the one used by the CEO above. It begins by helping to identify the need for ECO capability through an assessment of the environment (historically, currently, and in the likely future). Where the environment is uncertain and/or is likely to become more uncertain, there is a strong probability of a need for greater ECO capability. Internal changes to align current and future practices with the need to become more "change friendly" or "change seeking" will be critical.

Assessing the level of uncertainty in the environment is an important first step towards becoming an ECO. The other steps in the process involve assessing where the organization is on the other major components of the ECO model and then the ongoing prioritization and implementation of change initiatives to move to the needed level of ECO capacity. The remainder of this book addresses the composition of the other components of the ECO model as well as the processes for assessment and implementation of changes for increasing ECO capability.

3 | Stabilizing Base

The accelerating and ever-changing nature of today's environment creates an unending set of destabilizing forces and wide range of pressures for change. The organization is buffeted from all directions with forces for change. Increasing the capacity for change is a big part of what this book is about. At the same time, however, there is a need to create an additional set of forces that provides an organization and its people with a degree of stability as they work to negotiate the turbulence of the environment. Note that we did not say "stable" or "fixed" or "inflexible". Too much stability creates paralysis. Nor do we say to open up the organization to all of the forces coming at it. This destabilizes the organization and its people and produces uncontrolled drift. Rather, the emphasis is on modulating the forces acting on the organization. A stabilizing base allows the organization to cope with the pressures without being overwhelmed, while maintaining a sense of direction.

This set of balancing forces is called the organization's stabilizing base in the model of the Ever-Changing Organization. This terminology conveys that the base must be designed to support the organization's need to flex and adjust to the forces it experiences, but not break. The people of the organization need something(s) they can hold on to. They need things they can count on as they cope with the unsettling effects of the change around them. As the organization is pushed or pulled in different directions, the features of the stabilizing base are reliable points of stability. In an Ever-Changing Organization, the components of the stabilizing base provide comfort and support, on the one hand, and guidance and the freedom to act on the other.

The metaphor of the organization as a ship in an increasingly turbulent and changeable environment includes the need for stabilization to allow the ship to operate and navigate. Without stabilizing devices, the ship is tossed

around and from side to side. The crew is unable to work. They are forced
to hang on and seek safety. But the use of ballast and devices such as a winged
keel and flume tanks modulate the pitching and rolling of the ship, providing
enough stability so that the crew is able to act. They can maintain the ship
in the proper position to reduce the threat of being overturned. They can
plot the best course toward their destination. They can use their experience
and training, not only for assigned tasks but also for dealing with unusual
conditions that require quick and decisive action. The features of the stabilizing base perform similar functions for organizations in uncertain environments and help them become more of an Ever-Changing Organization.

I. Stabilization vs. Rigidity

Creating a stabilizing base in the face of increasing forces for change is a
challenge. The components of the stabilizing base need to be designed to
achieve a balance between the need for stability and the trap of creating
rigidity that inhibits change. Kevin Wheeler, former senior vice president of
Charles Schwab and now president of Global Learning Resources, describes
this dilemma quite clearly. He emphasizes that an organization cannot effectively move forward without a group of people who act and think alike based
on a common set of values. On the other hand, the base cannot be so strong
and rigid that it impedes change.

The question Kevin poses is "How stable is stable?" If the stabilizing base
itself does not value flexibility and change, the operating practices and behavior of members of the organization will become inflexible and act as obstacles
to becoming an ECO. On the other hand, when the components of the
stabilizing base are unclear and ambiguous they can have the opposite effect.
Instead of producing too much stability and inflexibility, unreliable components of the base or the failure of the organization to assure their alignment
creates confusion and mixed messages. The effect of this condition is not too
much stability and rigidity but the opposite. As the world changes more
rapidly, organizations with a poorly designed stabilizing base are a party to
their own downfall.

What is needed to provide a stabilizing base while preserving the flexibility needed to cope with the growing demands for change the organization
faces? Can this be achieved without sending members of the organization
confusing signals? We obviously believe this is possible and that addressing
the issues presented in this chapter is key to doing so.

II. People Need Stabilizing Forces

A professional colleague of ours, Jeanne Cherbeneau, Ph.D., reviewed and commented on an early draft of this book. Jeanne has been dealing with change, learning, and improvement for over 25 years. Her initial impression was that the book was much like other writings on change and its pervasiveness. She then read about the stabilizing base of the ECO model and came to a different conclusion. Her observation was that the ECO model offers something different and that the idea of a stabilizing base should receive even more emphasis as a component of the ECO model. Her experience has convinced her that "there is a desperate need for stabilization within the context of managing ever-changing situations and demands. People need things that are familiar and reliable and that provide them with a sense of being in control." Without a well established stabilizing base these needs cannot be met in increasingly uncertain and changing work situations.

The components of the stabilizing base discussed in the following sections of this chapter are the ones identified at this point in evolution of the model. Some of these features are not unique to organizations working to build their capacity as an ECO. They are characteristic of many effective and successful organizations, what Collins and Porras call visionary organizations.[6] Other features are particularly important for building the stabilizing base of organizations in high-change, rapidly moving environments. As you read the rest of this chapter, consider whether or not your own organization has developed a stabilizing base appropriate for its needs, both now and into the foreseeable future. Does what you have created actually help to stabilize the organization in the midst of the turbulence it encounters? Or, does your stabilizing base add rigidity on the one hand, or contribute to already increasing levels of instability on the other? Neither of these conditions will support efforts to increase the organization's capacity for change nor the process of becoming more of an Ever-Changing Organization.

III. Shared Values

Commonality of values is an important part of communicating what is important and must guide people's actions. Mr. Robert Miller, former CEO and President of Charles of the Ritz, described his perception of the importance of shared values and the implications of values for change.

To effect change in any organization, there must be good communication so that employees can understand not only what must change and how, but why. To facilitate change it is important that this communication not start only when change is required. We established a set of shared values, a statement to everyone of what the company stood for. No policy or procedure manuals could possibly foresee the different circumstances the company might face, so it was important that employees understood the basic principles that would guide our actions and proceed accordingly.

Shared values shape the boundaries within which behavior is viewed as appropriate and acceptable as well as that which is out of bounds and unacceptable. Anyone who is unable to accept and act in ways that are consistent with the core values of the organization will experience discomfort and a lack of fit. Where the values are particularly compelling they will often influence an individual's decision to stay or leave the organization.

A. Starbucks

David Olsen, senior VP of Starbucks, defines the overriding value that drives their company as "growth." The shared values of the company are strong and greatly influence people's behavior, always with a dominant focus on continuing growth. One of Starbucks' shared values is individuality, i.e., the idea that each person, individually and as part of a team, can create what they need to create to make the business succeed and grow. Starbucks' values exert a powerful influence in selecting and orienting employees to the Starbucks culture. Mr. Olsen commented that the impact is so great that, in a short while, people either adjust to the values or they don't survive. The shared values help the people who survive and become part of Starbucks cope with rates of growth and change that most have never experienced before.

B. Ann Taylor

Pat Spainhour, Chairman and CEO of Ann Taylor, a major designer and retailer of woman's fashions, inherited what he called "a demoralized organization in which nobody felt valued" when he took over in 1996. Among his early actions was an assessment of the organization which revealed broad-scale dislike and distrust among employees, poor communication, and other symptoms of uninvolved and disenfranchised people. From this data, Pat and his human resources VP led a process of developing and dispersing a set of positive and shared values. "Caring about people" was defined as the basic and driving value of the organization. Focus on the shared values now permeates everything he and other executives talk about with the people of the organization. Mr. Spainhour continually works to convey his deep personal conviction that caring about people builds positive relationships and that the strength of those relationships allows people to work through difficult circumstances. His belief that "positive relationships are the key drivers of everything" is at the core of the values that contribute to building a stabilizing base for Ann Taylor. They have helped support other significant internal change that has returned the company to positive financial performance and growth.

C. Making Shared Values Come Alive

Writing and distributing statements about an organization's shared values has increased markedly in the later years of the 20th century. Executives who read about the importance of shared values often take their management team to an offsite retreat. There, with the help of a consultant, they wrestle with what the basic values of the organization really are or need to be to carry the organization to long-term success and survival. Upon their return a report is made to the people of the organization about the new or reconfirmed values and, typically, a nicely packaged, written statement of the values is provided to everyone. The expectation is conveyed that these values must guide everyone's actions and become the foundation for the organization's future.

At the same time, it is not uncommon that little or nothing is done to create an understanding of what the values mean. There are no discussions, other than the informal talks in the hallways or at the water cooler where people speculate about what the values mean or if they really mean anything. People are left to their own devices to decide whether or how to change their behavior to comply with the stated expectations. If people are told, for example, that "individual initiative" is a key value of the organization, they wonder how they are expected to behave differently. They may have concerns about taking actions that they believe are acts of individual initiative when similar actions in the past have been subject to reprimand or have required review and approval by the next two levels of management. Will such action be supported? Or are the newly stated values little more than proper sounding words? Without understanding what it means to act in line with the new values and how that action will be supported, people are likely to resist or assume that the values are not meaningful and make few attempts to change.

1. Explore Values, Their Meaning, and Expectations for Behavior

The process of making values come alive requires several steps in our experience. The first step involves providing a legitimate vehicle for exploration of what the values mean among peers and managers: allow people to describe situations they might encounter where the values could influence their decisions about how to act; encourage discussion of what they think would be appropriate ways to act as well as actions they think would be inappropriate; let them ask questions about their manager's expectations and how his or her response to their actions would be different in light of the stated values. And these should not be one-time discussions. Ongoing discussions of experience with the meaning and application of the values build understanding and commitment. And, as understanding increases with experience, more and more individual decisions will be made that are consistent with the values.

2. Align Operating Systems and Practices with Expectations

The second step involves the use of "systems thinking" to identify components of the organizational system that support or inhibit behavior consistent with the values. What features of the organization's measurement and control systems, the appraisal and reward systems, goal-setting processes, skill-building and learning mechanisms, and so on send messages to people about the appropriateness of certain behaviors, e.g., taking individual initiative in the example above? Reinforcing things that support the newly expected behaviors and eliminating or changing conditions that block those behaviors is important. Confusing and mixed signals are eliminated and the management actions involved communicate their commitment to making the values legitimate influences in the day-to-day life of the organization. Preferably these issues are addressed even before the values are introduced.

We recently were told about an organization involved in supplying products to the health care industry where this step was not included. The company had been working through a process to support a turn-around of lagging performance. In addition to developing new business partnerships and a number of acquisitions, the process involved reassessing the organization's mission and shared values to support improved performance. A middle manager we talked with was convinced the organization was doing a great job and that growth in the price of the company's stock was an indication.

However, he was confused by the recent introduction of a "shared value" focused on continuous learning and improvement. After an offsite executive meeting, top management returned to their respective locations to introduce the new value and to stress making it a reality as a very important, current challenge. His reaction was, "Wow, this is great. I can't wait."

Two weeks later he and all other managers were notified to begin the budgeting process for the next year. They were given specific direction to keep the budget flat and, where possible, to reduce operating costs. The manager's comments reflected the failure of the organization to consider needed change in operating practices to support the espoused value. He said, "I don't know what I am supposed to do with that. Those are mixed messages." He wondered how the confusion in the management ranks might have occurred, saying, "Maybe the financial people who are in charge of the budget weren't at the management meetings or the executive briefings. Maybe they don't understand that building a continuously learning and improving organization has just been defined as a critical shared value for our future and a current priority. And that an investment will be required to make this value real." He speculated, "I think what I am seeing is that we have two visions at the top. And I have a good idea that the financial vision will win out over continuous learning and improvement. " Management statements about the shared values of an organization, when not aligned with its operating practices, only produce confusion among its people and inhibit their pursuit of behaviors that would make the value come alive.

3. Legitimize Upholding the Values

Making shared values come alive requires conditions that make it legitimate for everyone in the organization to uphold the values. This includes allowing a person to refuse to act, and to do so without threat of retaliation, if directed or pressured to behave in a manner that is not consistent with the organization's shared values. Likewise, confronting actions that are inconsistent with the values must be legitimate. Support for these behaviors provide some of the most compelling evidence of the importance of the values to the organization and its people. When everyone is expected to behave in ways that are consistent with the values, and can do so without fear, the frequency of that behavior increases and becomes ingrained in the people of the organization and its culture.

We have lived in the San Francisco Bay area for many years. Conversations and participation in many meetings with employees of Hewlett-Packard have provided us with a view of how this highly respected company establishes and sustains its key values. Stories about how the values are defended and supported by the founders abound. Training that involves exploration of the values and "The HP way" actively helps the assimilation of new employees, at all levels. And people speak with pride about their freedom to behave consistently with the values and to tell others "That's not the HP way" when they experience deviant behaviors. The shared values of HP are not just statements. They are living guides to people throughout the organization and provide them with stability and comfort in their reliability and with the freedom to act in ways that are consistent with the values. They are a critical part of the organization's stabilizing base.

The development of shared values at Ann Taylor has already been discussed. The new values were not just established and communicated to people. Substantial effort was also made to deploy and make those values a living part of the organization's culture. The values were introduced one at a time in a setting that provided the opportunity to discuss and understand what each really means, i.e., how you live and show the value in your personal behavior. The company's actions were based on awareness that the newly created values would not come alive immediately. Ann Taylor employees were not expected to change overnight. Therefore, the values were introduced as "aspirational values," values the organization believed in and wanted to make real. The CEO, Mr. Spainhour, felt strongly that the battle in establishing positive values would be won when people really aspired to live those values. And the battle could not even begin if people did not know or could not recognize, in his actions or the actions of others, that the values existed as guides to the actions of Ann Taylor people. As people have learned the meaning of Ann Taylor's values and have aspired to act in accordance with them, the shared values have become part of the organization's stabilizing base. They lend stabilization and support as the organization works through the ongoing change it encounters in an industry characterized by frequent change.

IV. Living Vision

Shared values convey what is important to the organization and guide people's day-to-day actions. A living and compelling vision describes a desirable future for the organization. It identifies what the organization will strive to become and guides people's actions as they make choices to support movement to the future. Clearly, a living vision is not about today. It is about where we want to go and what we aspire to become. For this reason, it is important that the top manager of the organization owns and leads development of the vision. To become a living vision, the people must know that the leader believes in it and intends the organization to go there.

A. *What's In It for Me?*

While shared values provide stabilization by being consistent and reliable guides to what is important, an organization's vision contributes to its stabilizing base in a different way. It is an attractive beacon in the distance. It is a desirable place where the organization wants to go. And it needs to be attractive to the members of the organization. It will not be a guiding beacon if just top management or the owners or shareholders of the organization own the vision. Too much is unknown about the steps to the future to have the vision guiding a small percentage of the organization. It needs to provide energy and excitement for all.

Everyone must know what the vision is and how it translates to two areas that directly effect them. First, people need to be able to see "what's in it for me" (WIIFM) to work towards the vision. Do I really find the vision attractive and in tune with my personal vision of the future and of a place where I would be proud to work? Will I feel better about the organization and myself if the vision is realized? How can I contribute to achieving the vision in ways that will be satisfying to me and meet my personal needs and expectations? Unless people can relate their own self-interests to the vision and its achievement the motivation to change or contribute will be lacking, or maybe negative.

Second, support must be provided to help members of the organization at all levels see how the vision relates to their work and how they can help move towards it. As already described in the discussion of shared values, the steps needed to provide this help are often missing. Somehow it is assumed that the overall desirability of the vision will be clear to everyone and that no additional effort is needed to make it clear. It is also assumed that people will easily make the connection between the vision and how it relates to them and their work. The failure to articulate and test these questionable assumptions results in the omission of activities where exploration of the vision and its implications take place. Plaques are created and posted and/or other forms of one-way communication used to deploy the vision. People see or hear the vision and are cast adrift on a rough and shifting sea. They must fend for themselves, trying to make sense of the vision and what to do about it. The end result is the conversion of the vision into another part of the organization's uncertainty as opposed to having it act as a guiding beacon pulling everyone forward and as a stabilizing force as choices are made.

B. Creating a Living Vision

In a rapidly changing world a static vision loses meaning or attractiveness. Instead of functioning as a beacon pulling and guiding the organization towards it, the static vision may become the flashing yellow light warning the organization and its people away. For example, new possibilities may be created which render an existing vision obsolete or at least point to new directions. These possibilities might be the result of internal or external discoveries, e.g., from the organization's own R&D efforts or that of customers, suppliers, or other research efforts. They might open up as a result of the capabilities gained via an acquisition or merger. Whatever the reason, under changing conditions it doesn't make sense to be tied to a vision that is "cast in bronze" and mounted on the walls of the organization.

We characterize visions that have lasting value as "living" visions because they, too, continue to evolve and change. People today frequently read or hear about the acceleration of change. Most accept the reality that more change will result in more effects on them, even though they recognize that the effects may not all be beneficial. Our observations suggest that change is more disconcerting and frightening to people when the organizations they are associated with behave as if change is not the new reality. Many have seen the effects of failure to adapt to change and of stubbornly holding to a direction or vision. And invariably the result of denial of the reality of change is negative, either for the organization or its people and customers or all of them.

Many organizations have developed processes for regular communication with their people. These processes may be used to share results or improvements in products or services or business goals and so on. Properly designed, these processes can also be used to make the organization's vision a living vision. As suggested above, it is important to assure that people understand the vision and its attractiveness to the organization. And the process must also allow people to make the WIIFM connection. Discussion and exploration are at the heart of processes that achieve these purposes. As conditions change, the use of established processes of exploration maintains awareness of the vision and stimulates discussion of the advisability of maintaining or changing the vision. The discussion process can also be designed to encourage consideration of ideas for near-term action to facilitate movement towards the current version of the living vision. In particular, as organizations develop their plans, discussion of what needs to happen in the next planning period, e.g., quarter, year, three years, etc., allows groups and individuals to select goals that will continue to drive the organization on a path towards its vision.

C. Documentum Corporation

Jeffrey Miller, CEO and President of Documentum, presented his vision to all employees of his organization in 1996. He called the presentation the "Millenium Mission." His intentions in creating the vision were to provide the organization with a sense of (a) where they were going, (b) what it would look like when they got to the future, and (c) his expectations about the changes they were likely to encounter on the journey. Mr. Miller's approach to setting out the vision was not to search for the 100% right direction. He stressed that his objective was to begin with something that was 80% right. He said, "If you are 80% right on something, and if you apply your energy to it with 100% focus and vigor, you will be phenomenally successful." Mr. Miller mentioned that the effect of this strategy is sometimes kidded about in the company when people report, "We may not always be right, but we are never confused." He believes that a leader should, "…get it pretty much right and drive the whole organization down that path. And of course correct along the way, taking into consideration those factors that are either going to require you to change or that you are going to seek out for change."

Documentum has developed these strategies and processes to make their vision come alive and to guide people's actions to be aligned with the vision along the way. Annual and quarterly goal-setting processes focus on high priority results, i.e., the five or six most important things to make happen in the next time period, starting from the top and working on down through departments and to the individual level. The high-priority results are aligned with the vision. Mr. Miller says, "What I tell people, in all seriousness, is every day one of the things you ought to do is to look at the company's corporate objectives and your quarterly objectives. If what you are doing does not apply to those objectives, you either stop doing it or you do something else or go ask your boss or manager why you are working on something that apparently has no connection to the corporate objectives."

An important source of confirmation of the pervasiveness of the vision and goals of the company comes from interviews Mr. Miller has had with candidates for jobs at Documentum. He is proud of uniformly receiving feedback from job interviewees who tell him, "I have talked with ten people in your company and they all have said the same thing. People in the organization all talk about the same goals, they all have exactly the same vision, and they all understand what is important here. I'm really impressed with that." The processes developed at Documentum have not only produced a "living vision." They have translated that vision into working objectives and day-to-day actions and clearly provide an important part of the organization's stabilizing base. And the vision and style has made Documentum become one of the fastest-growing software companies in Silicon Valley at the end of the millenium.

D. Maintaining Positive Tension

A living vision is always being moved forward and into the future. It is not like a goal or objective to be completed. Rather, the living vision represents a positive mental image of where the organization is going. Approaching too closely to a vision reduces the positive tension between what is and what is desired. The effect of getting too close is the reduction of the motivation and drive to pursue the vision. The nature of the living vision is that it does continue to move out and continues to exert a pull based on the tension of now vs. the future. A living vision continually provides the beacon that beckons the organization onward into an ever-changing but desirable future.

V. Commitment to Change, Learning, and Improvement

Creating increased capacity for change, learning, and improvement is important in increasingly uncertain environments. Most organizations in uncertain environments will discover that they need to become more of an Ever-Changing Organization if they undertake a careful assessment of their ECO capabilities. The people of the organization know that ongoing change is a reality because they experience it. In organizations with limiting orientations to change, i.e., change averse or change resistant, people often exhibit a personal orientation similar to that of their organization. For this reason there is also a need for people to become more change friendly or change seeking in their personal orientation. But, unless they know that the organization is firmly committed to change, learning, and improvement it is difficult for people to commit themselves to that direction. If an organization is not actively investing energy to increase its capacity as an ECO, its people are unlikely to become "Ever-Changing Persons" (ECPs).

A. Walking the Talk

In eighteen-plus years of experience with organizations specifically focused on increasing the capacity for quality and continuous improvement, we have seen that people readily recognize the truth in the statement, "People watch your feet, not your lips!" President George Bush demonstrated that he understood the importance of making a statement about what he was committed to when he used the now famous expression, "Watch my lips, no new taxes!" in a speech to the American people. What he somehow missed was the even greater importance of matching such a statement with his actions if he was to be credible. People clearly watched his feet when he later signed a bill into law that was inconsistent with what they heard from his lips and the discrepancy damaged his credibility.

B. Learning to Walk the Talk

Norman Gottschalk is President and CEO of Marmon/Keystone, Inc., a major distributor of steel pipe and tubing. Norm was first exposed to an organization-wide quality and continuous improvement process in a public seminar in 1988. It was suggested that he phone a random sample of his managers and ask the question, "How's it going?" to find out what they felt he was really committed to. The first issues addressed in response to that question would indicate what "it" meant to them. They would be the areas the managers had learned were of greatest importance to him.

Upon returning to his office, Norm called the manager of his California facility. The first several responses to the "How's it going?" question suggested that his greatest commitment was to issues of dollars shipped, operating costs, incoming orders, and so on. He then asked, "How's your quality today?" After a stunned silence, the manager indicated that he thought it was pretty good but wondered why Norm had asked. Norm replied that he had decided that quality and continuous improvement had become critically important issues for the future of the company.

A few weeks later Norm was talking with the same manager. After a few minutes the manager interrupted, saying, "Why haven't you asked me about my quality today. I'm ready to tell you about our shipment errors and late deliveries. I now get a report on these quality issues every morning." Norm chuckled when he reported these exchanges to us. Not only did he learn that his behavior at that time indicated that other things were more important to him than quality, he learned that by simply asking about the subject he had increased perceptions of its importance to him. And he had created the expectation that his actions would be consistent with his verbal statements.

From this experience, Norm has made many changes in his personal behavior that communicate a significant commitment to quality and continuous improvement. For example, he will not allow a planned visit to any of his facilities to be scheduled at a time when he, or members of his staff, cannot sit in on a regular improvement meeting with an employee improvement team. On plant tours he regularly asks people, "What is the dumbest thing we ask you to do that wastes your time and the company's resources?" All of the answers he gets to that question are taken as potential areas for analysis and action by one of the employee improvement teams. The result of these changes and many others instigated by Norm and his management team has been a sustained period of growth and improvement in market share. Further, sustained savings from the company's improvement efforts have contributed to financial performance that outpaces others in the industry. Mr. Gottschalk really understands what it means to tell someone you are committed to a new direction. He has learned how to make statements about his commitment credible by changing his personal behaviors so that he "walks the talk." People do not receive mixed signals because there is a consistent match of words and actions. This kind of reliability adds to the stabilizing base and eliminates confusion about what is expected and important from the top of the organization.

C. ECO's Commitment to Change, Learning, and Improvement

Managing FOR change, continuous improvement, and continuous learning are three of the key components of the ECO model. Becoming committed to increasing the organization's capability in these three areas is critical for organizations that acknowledge the need to become more of an ECO. This does not mean leaders making statements about commitment but not implementing changes that demonstrate the commitment. It does not mean creating slogans and publicity about being committed that are not backed up with action. It does mean that a commitment to these areas needs to be articulated and made public. But to be believable and to generate sustainable support for this direction, it means much more. Executives who elect to move their organization in the direction of ongoing change, learning, and improvement must also demonstrate their own willingness to learn, to change their own behavior, and to improve the organization's processes for making change happen.

Assume, for example, an organization with a history of change initiatives that have begun with statements about management's commitment, only to fade into oblivion or be replaced by another initiative after a brief period of high focus and intensity. Think of situations where you have experienced this pattern. Ask yourself, as an employee being led in this direction by his management, what it would take to make statements of commitment believable this time.

We have encountered many people in a wide range of organizations undergoing change over the past 20 years. Nearly all of the organizations had experienced limited success or failure with one or more previous change initiatives. The questions raised about management commitment in our conversations were strikingly consistent. Following is a sample of what we have heard:

- Why this new initiative? Are there sound business reasons for doing this or has the boss read another new book? It sounds like another version of God, motherhood, and apple pie to me.
- Management says they are committed to this initiative. They've said that before and then not really supported the process. Why believe them when they say this time's different?
- What is management's role in the process? Is it more than just talking about it?
- Is this just a direction from the top or has middle management bought into it, too? If my boss doesn't buy it, forget it. Nothing I can do will help and if I try I may create a problem for myself.
- Have we learned anything from our previous initiatives that will help this effort succeed where others have failed?
- Will we be trained on the new skills we need to do this or are we just supposed to pick them up by osmosis?

- I've gotten behind other change initiatives and really started to work on implementing them only to see them dropped. Why should I believe this one is real and will last?
- Is this another thing I'm supposed to somehow find time to do by squeezing it into my already overcrowded schedule or will time be made available?
- If this works, is my position and that of my peers and associates threatened? Is this just another attempt to get us to help and then use the gains we've created to justify why some of us are no longer needed?
- Is management going to participate in this process or are they just setting a direction that we are supposed to implement while they continue with business as usual?
- If this initiative succeeds and I contribute to the success, what's in it for me (and for the rest of us)?

These, and many other issues, are very real concerns to people in organizations taking on a change effort. Unless they are dealt with in advance or people can be shown a plan and process for addressing the issues, management commitment will be questioned and support for the new direction severely eroded. Personal commitment of members of the organization will be difficult to develop.

It is a simple fact that most people in organizations already feel overburdened. Time is a precious commodity. It is becoming more scarce as the rate of change impacting organizations increases. People have no choice but to set priorities to assure that the most important things get done. Highest priority is given to things they perceive to be most important to their management. This is why a clear and unambiguous commitment to change, learning, and improvement is important. And it must be demonstrated in observable behaviors as well as in oral and/or written statements. Under these conditions the commitment becomes a stabilizing force to be depended upon. Ambiguous and mixed messages about commitment to these areas create additional uncertainty. The thrust for change, learning, and improvement becomes a distraction and another destabilizing force.

D. Profiles of ECO Components

The diagnostic process outlined in the implementation section of this book provides a way to profile the organization's status on each of the major ECO components. If a well-planned assessment results in profiles that are primarily in the middle of the various scales or below, the reality is that the organization's commitment to change, learning, and improvement is limited, at best. The observable behaviors of management and the operating practices of the organization convey tentativeness in the commitment. Or, the average will be mid-range because there is wide variation across the various scales. This situation sends mixed signals to the members of the organization, i.e., some actions portray high levels of commitment while others are low. Management has not made up its mind or has not considered the confusion created when their practices are not aligned. Only with consistently high profiles in the areas of managing FOR change, continuous learning, and continuous improvement is the organization's behavior demonstrating real commitment to these areas. When this happens, the consistency involved increases the organization's stabilizing base and supports development of greater capacity as an ECO.

VI. Clear Goals and Direction

Clear articulation of an organization's goals and clear direction for achieving the goals is important for creation of a stabilizing base. Lacking these, the people of the organization must make assumptions about what management wants to accomplish and make guesses for themselves about how to contribute to getting there. It is unlikely that the goals of individuals and groups that depend on each other will be aligned. More likely, in fact, there will be goals and direction that are in conflict. Resolution of the conflicts will require additional time and consume more of the organization's limited supply of energy, making it unavailable for use in the best interests of the organization.

A. S.M.A.R.T. Goals

One of the most useful acronyms we had found in consultation with organizations and individuals is used to remind people of five critical attributes of meaningful goals. Goals or objectives that meet all five of these criteria have positive motivational impact. If any of these criteria are not met the opposite is true. The acronym is SMART. Meaningful goals are:

Specific
Measurable
Agreed upon
Realistic
Timed

"Specific" goals have meaning because they are focused on a particular outcome, e.g., sales volume, new product introduction, cost reduction, and so on. Generalized statements of a goal are not meaningful in that they do not focus on the area within which a result is to be achieved, e.g., "Do things right the first time" or "Make continuous improvements." Such statements do not identify what things are to be done right or what is to be continuously improved and do not meet the criteria of being specific.

"Measurable" goals identify the indicator that will be used for determining whether or not the goal has been met. Measurable goals may be quantitative, i.e., numbers, percentages, ratios, etc., or digital, i.e., yes/no or above/below or increased/decreased, etc. Unless specific and measurable, achievement or not is a matter of judgment. Evaluations of performance leave great room for disagreement. Asking how the organization or person performed vs. the goal could be answered with an equally nonspecific and unmeasurable response such as "not bad" or "reasonably well." In fact, the person with the goal and the person assessing performance to the goal are likely to be testing the performance against different and subjective criteria. Neither really knows how well the goals have been met and will make judgments consistent with their own needs. The tension produced and the negative residual effects are eliminated when goals meet the criterion of being measurable as well as the other SMART criteria.

"Agreed upon" goals are meaningful because those working to achieve the goal and those to whom they are committed have discussed the goal, its meaning, and its relevance. The parties involved know specifically what is to be accomplished, how performance will be measured, and why it is an important result. There is mutual buy-in and commitment to the goal. And the buy-in and commitment is greater than the feelings of ownership for dictated or imposed goals.

"Realistic" goals are important because the level of realism impacts the motivation to achieve the goal. The phrase "tough but achievable" is often applied to the idea of realistic goal setting. Realistic goals that produce the greatest amount of energy for accomplishment are not so easy that they can be accomplished with little or no additional effort. Neither are they so difficult that the people involved feel there is virtually no chance of meeting them or they can only be made with luck. In the latter case a "why bother" response is likely and the motivation to perform is low.

"Timed" goals put a necessary boundary on accomplishment instead of leaving it open-ended. Setting an objective and giving it an indefinite time frame such as "as soon as possible" or "when feasible" makes the goal less meaningful and also makes determination of achievement subjective. Timing gives a goal a high level of specificity, i.e., "…by 2/15/00" or "on or before the close of business on 11/20/00."

We have observed a number of management groups that failed to articulate specific improvement goals that met the SMART criteria. In one situation the president of the company simply gave his top managers and division managers the direction to read a then-popular management book and to get started on the process as it applied to their business. Several months later he was upset when little had happened. When asked about progress, answers from the executives involved ranged from "We have a specific plan, five goals for the next year, and have begun training our people in the process" to "We've been talking about the process and are planning to get started soon." The lesson regarding the importance of providing SMART goals was clear. When the CEO later became a consultant to top management teams, he insisted that they attempt to write SMART goals as part of preparation for implementation of the process. He personally offered critique of their attempts and shared his own problems when he failed to provide SMART goals.

Another consultation we were part of involved spending a few days with the top management team of a division of a high technology plastics company. The focus was on review and critique of the first year of a continuous improvement effort. The team had struggled with the issue of providing specific goals that met the SMART criteria. They had concluded that setting general goals would be preferable. They did not want to impose or dictate specific targets to their subordinate managers, preferring that the next level select the specific targets while they provided general direction and guidance.

Reviewing the results achieved vs. the generalized goals set a year previously proved to be very instructive. Asked about their performance to the goals, team members comments included "we've definitely made progress," "better than I expected," "not bad for the first year," and so on. Asked to discuss the facts and data that were used to reach their conclusions, the group recognized that they had no idea what their actual performance was and that their comments were little more that guesses and "windage" based on what they hoped had happened. They also realized that they had created a problem for their people with the generalized goals they had set. Some assumed that the goals had been set for other departments and did not apply to them. Others took the signal from the top to mean that they, too, should pass the general goals to the lower levels and let them figure out more specific areas to attack. The outcome was a year with a fair amount of effort invested but with little demonstrable gain. This was accompanied by a high level of questioning about management's commitment to the process. After all, "when anything is really important to them they have no problem setting extremely specific goals and direction." With what we called Avis goals, i.e., "try harder," the organization read the message as tentative and lacking in commitment. The goals established by this management team for future years were tested against the SMART criteria. The result was increased acceptance and greatly improved performance.

At the beginning of this section on the stabilizing base, we described the features of the base as providing comfort and support to people, on the one hand, and guidance and the freedom to act on the other. SMART goals, as seen in the two examples above, operate in ways that qualify them as features of the stabilizing base of an ECO.

B. Goal Alignment

Increases in the size and complexity of organizations has led to the development of processes for building internal alignment of goals both vertically and horizontally. As the rate of change increases, the added need for flexibility and decisive action adds to the need for goal alignment.

Without goal alignment processes the probability of conflicting objectives increases. The additional time and energy spent resolving this conflict detracts from the organization's ability to meet its objectives. More uncertainty is produced and the diversion of energy needed to cope with it has a destabilizing effect on the organization. Misalignments of goals that are not identified make some form of fire-fighting response the only option. Work that has been done in good faith but in ignorance of the impending misfit with the work of others must be reworked or scrapped. Costs are increased, delays are experienced, and errors occur. And all of these effects must be absorbed by the organization without adding in any way to the value received by its customers. These effects are destabilizing and totally unacceptable as rates of change continue to increase.

Some other approaches to goal alignment have grown to be overly complex and bureaucratic. The time to achieve alignment is excessive and requires so much effort that people become frustrated and tend to give the process lip service. Multiple cycles of direction setting, goal setting, sharing, and approval (vertically and across functions) are aimed at alignment at such a detailed level that little time is left to do the work. Further, the complexity involved leads some organizations to attempt to align goals for extended periods of time, e.g., a year, even though everyone would agree that locking onto a set of goals for that amount of time is unreasonable in their environment. Priorities will change, projects will be cancelled or new ones added, people will leave or be moved, external changes will render corporate goals obsolete, and so on. Yet, the process marches along with goals aligned towards targets that no longer exist or are irrelevant.

We have heard expressions of frustration and confusion in organizations with complex processes for goal setting and alignment — for example, product designers whose goal document remains the same for a year despite the cancellation of key projects and reassignment to others. Goal documents are not changed to reflect the new assignments. Yet the originally negotiated document continues to function as the primary reference for performance appraisal and review. In fact it has no meaning to the individual or the person charged with conducting the appraisal, leaving the appraisal process to subjective evaluations or to the good will of the appraiser. And this creates even more problems when it comes to setting goals and creating objectives for the following year. People see little value in the process, invest almost no effort, and produce another set of documents with little or no meaning. The next appraisal is even more subjective and meaningless. Yet organizations continue to invest significant amounts of energy in this flawed process. Documents are created, reviewed, and discussed vertically and horizontally, and finally set for the following year (or quarter). The decision to use such a process is characteristic of decision-making processes that Professor Jerry Harvey of George Washington University calls the "Abilene paradox."[9] No one agrees with the process, but none will challenge it for fear of being seen as disloyal or against motherhood and apple pie, i.e., goal alignment in this case. Therefore, the organization moves forward with a process no one believes in and invests significant amounts of energy in attempts to make it useful. This approach to goal alignment is not just destabilizing. It is paralyzing and part of a base that inhibits change. It is most likely being used by organizations that are change averse or change resistant, making it difficult to move to greater levels of ECO capability.

Goal alignment processes in organizations with greater capacity for change are clearly more flexible. As the world changes, goals are realigned to reflect the changes. But the process of change is designed to be easy and ongoing. It is not an annual event occurring over a period of several months. Instead, it is part of the ongoing dialogue within the organization. Regular vertical exchanges and reviews of direction and priorities support goal alignment at the various levels of the organization. Likewise, ongoing exchanges and reviews among internal customers and suppliers who make up the chain of steps in the organization's business processes allows anticipation of change, testing, and easy realignment in a proactive mode. Goal documents are fluid, being adjusted as needed to reflect what is needed now and not what was imagined a few or several months ago that is no longer relevant. Goal alignment processes with these characteristics contribute to the organization's stabilizing base. Uncertainty is reduced because people know that their current goals are relevant and their work output will mesh with the work of others. As such, the goal alignment process provides comfort and guidance on the one hand and the freedom and flexibility to focus efforts on what is important and relevant to achievement of the organization's objectives. These are characteristics of the stabilizing base required for operating in a more rapidly changing world.

VII. Belief and Trust in People

Organizations that believe in and trust people behave in very different ways from those that distrust people. The consequences of those beliefs are similarly different. There has been much discussion of the idea of the "self-fulfilling prophecy."[10] If I believe you are capable and, as a result, treat you in a way that conveys my expectations, my beliefs will be self-fulfilling, i.e., you are much more likely to succeed. Likewise, if I do not believe in you and your capability, I will treat you as if you are not capable and you are likely to fail. In the musical *My Fair Lady*, Professor Higgins' belief in Liza Doolittle and her potential caused him to treat her in a way that produced dramatic changes in her, a self-fulfilling prophecy. Originally a lower-class flower girl with a heavy Cockney accent, Liza was transformed into a "fair lady" whose speech and manner fooled even those in the English upper crust.

In the same manner, the behavior of people in organizations is a Consequence of the Assumptions that guide the Behavior of managers and executives who deal with them (note the ABC model described in the introductory section as the model that applies to the self-fulfilling prophecy). People treated as capable and trustworthy will behave that way. Or, conversely, people dealt with as incapable and untrustworthy will eventually behave that way.

A. Start with Positive Beliefs and Trust — or Prove It First?

We have observed behaviors in many organizations that convey the message to people that they are trusted but have to prove it. The words say "trust" but the reality is that what you do or intend to do must be reviewed and approved before you can act. Only after you demonstrate that you have good judgment or are concerned with the organization's success will you be given more freedom. And, in those situations there are generally no criteria for having demonstrated trustworthiness. Then the self-fulfilling prophecy takes over. Additional freedom is withheld and, eventually, a response to management's behavior is observed that can be taken as less than completely trustworthy. The original belief that people cannot really be trusted is confirmed. The policy of withholding trust continues, paralyzing the organization's ability to function in conditions of rapid change.

1. New Employee Practices

When you examine the practices of many organizations in the early stages of an individual's employment, it is easy to find differences in their beliefs in people. Some recruit people aggressively, subject them to many interviews, offer them a position with the organization, and work hard to impress them with the good choice they would be making to join the organization. However, once the offer is accepted and the person reports to work, a different message is given. They are told that they are not yet full-blown employees. The first 90 days are to be a probationary period. During that period both the person and the organization will be able to decide whether or not there is a good fit of the person and the job and the organization. If everything is a "go" at the end of this period the person's status changes from probationary to full employment. And, not uncommonly, the person does not accrue normal benefits during the period of probation.

What messages do these policies and restrictions send to the person? Several seem obvious, including:

■ We're not sure it was a good decision to hire you and we're covering our tails in a way that makes it easy to get out of this situation if we need to;

■ You're sort of joining this organization but will remain a second class citizen until you prove yourself;

- All of the good things we said about you to get you to accept the offer we didn't really believe;
- The financial value of the offer we made is actually less than for other people in the same job because you must prove yourself worthy of getting our normal benefits before we invest in you;
- Our legal and/or HR people prevailed in this situation and have pushed this policy into effect to protect us from you in case we decide to terminate you early on; and so on.

The excitement of joining a new organization and starting a new position is pretty well drained for most people under these conditions. The organization demonstrates that it doesn't believe in or trust the individual. The individual, in turn, begins employment with concerns about the organization. Why establish policies that suggest it doesn't trust or believe in me before our relationship has begun? Now I wonder if I've made the right decision. What else might they do to me if that's the way they feel we need to start?

At the other extreme are organizations that begin from a position of full belief in the person and their ability to succeed. People joining the organization are entrusted with full employment status. They are not treated differently from other members of the organization except as policies require various degrees of longevity for particular benefits, e.g., vacation accruals or the beginning of insurance coverage or the prorating of increases or bonuses. The organization greets the person with open arms and with the expectation of success. A formally scheduled period of review may be included, e.g., after the first 60 or 90 days. However, its purpose is to assure that unanswered questions or issues are addressed and discussions of needed changes or adjustments by the individual or the organization take place. This discussion is not for letting the person know whether or not they have "passed" and will be retained as a full-blown employee or terminated. The first type of organization begins with tentative beliefs in the person and looks for things that suggest failure. The second begins with positive expectations. They look for indications of success and to make sure everything is right for the ongoing employer-employee relationship. The self-fulfilling prophecy works in both cases.

2. Trusting People to Change Behavior

Another example related to starting from positive beliefs and trust comes from our consulting experience with the sales organization of Signetic's Corporation, now Philips Semiconductor. The president and new sales vice president of the company, after intense deliberations of the theme for the VP's first national sales conference, settled on "The Professionals" as the theme. The prior behavior of the sales organization could best be described as not highly professional. The planning for the meeting focused on establishing understanding and acceptance of the definition of "professional" behavior. Belief in the ability of the sales force to function professionally would be demonstrated by treating the group as professionals in the design and conduct of the meeting. For example, participants were provided blazers instead of the more traditional T-shirts and windbreakers. A full afternoon workshop was scheduled on the subject of what "professional" means. In addition the VP outlined his minimum expectations for professional behavior at the beginning of the conference, including his expectations for participation and learning during the conference.

However, at one of the last planning meetings a lively discussion occurred about how to get people up on time and how to prevent them from renting unauthorized vehicles for trips to the city nearby for late night activities. Several types of externally administered controls were considered. Finally, however, someone suggested that such actions were inconsistent with the idea of treating the group like professionals. The team recognized that they were reverting to prior approaches and assumptions about their people. The discussion shifted to consideration of how to achieve the same result while treating participants as professionals.

The vice president's opening remarks included sharing his personal expectations of appropriate behavior during the conference. He told the group that he was not going to "police" their behavior. What they chose to do would be their choice. At the same time he told them that he expected that they would behave as professionals, would attend all scheduled sessions, and would be alert and able to profit from the learning experiences provided. Soon afterwards, a district sales manager approached a member of the planning team. He commented that the VP's remarks and spelling out of expectations was the best thing that had ever happened for him and the sales force. He said, "I'm now free to go to bed early and sober and to be ready for a full day of meetings and workshops tomorrow. In the past I would have felt compelled to prove that I could drink and play cards until morning and still make it to the meetings. Now I can behave professionally, as I see it, and not feel guilty or that I will be viewed as outside the group." In fact, the changes in the behavior of the sales team at that meeting, while not free of all previous shenanigans, were dramatic and marked the beginning of a very successful transition. It was widely accepted that trusting the group to operate up to new expectations had been instrumental in getting the transition off on the right foot.

B. Belief and Trust and the Stabilizing Base

When people know from the behavior and policies of their management that they are trusted, they are freed up to act without fear that their actions will be misinterpreted. Good intentions will be assumed and, even if the results were not as intended, the situation and outcomes will be reviewed for learning as opposed to seeking to blame and punish. This contributes greatly to creating a stabilizing base in situations where rapid change often leaves little time for reviews and approvals and requires innovative, fast actions.

Eric Herr, President of Autodesk, and CEO Carol Bartz, have changed the company's decision-making process for release of new products based on trust in people to make the right decision. The development and market groups are told, regarding the decision, "…it isn't about revenue; you ship the product when it is ready." The top executives recognized that, while these are very important decisions, the development group is in the best position to make the decision. The trust was not misplaced. Eric's comment was, "They made a wonderful decision."

High levels of belief and trust in people also leads to treatment of all members of the organization as sharing an interest in the success of the company. It is assumed that no employee would take deliberate action to harm the organization. After all, each person's personal success is somehow tied to the success of the organization. So the organization begins from a belief in trustworthiness as a valid assumption for virtually all employees. Policies and operating practices that apply to everyone are designed on this assumption and not to cover the small percentage of people where the assumption may not be valid. Only if there is specific data and observable action indicating a deliberate violation of the organization's trust will limits be imposed or employment terminated for an individual. Even then, the organization gives the person the benefit of the doubt. People live up to the expectation of trust and the organization's belief in them.

People who experience not being believed in or trusted also learn not to trust those who lack faith in them. They feel unable to influence their management and, in turn, are less willing to be influenced by management. Where trust is low, policies and management actions are driven by the belief that the total influence in a relationship is fixed, i.e., a zero-sum game. The inappropriate assumption at work says, "If I allow my people to increase their influence on me, I will have less influence on them." Where there are high levels of trust and positive beliefs about people, the assumption is "To the extent that I allow my people to influence me, I will also increase my influence with them." In other words, total influence is a function of the mutual willingness and ability of people to be influenced by others. Behaviors built on these assumptions open up organizations and give managers and their people the freedom to act. They help build a stabilizing base that will support an organization in an ever-changing environment.

VIII. Stability of Employee Base

The stability of the employee base of an organization can be a plus or a minus for organizations experiencing increased change. Very high levels of employee instability are destabilizing. Very high levels of stability, on the other hand, can be paralyzing. The other features of the stabilizing base determine whether or not destabilizing or paralyzing effects happen. When the organization has a set of shared and positive values, a compelling and "living" vision, a commitment to change and improvement, clear direction and goals, and so on, the level of stability of the employee base is less of a factor. People learn to operate in ways that are stabilizing in the face of turbulent conditions when they know what is important, where the organization is going, and that change and improvement are part of what is expected. They learn not to fear change and feel free to act in ways that serve the best interests of the organization.

A. Excessive Stability

Too much stability in the employee group can make change more difficult and have a paralyzing effect. There is a lack of new people with different perspectives. Exposure to a rich diversity of approaches from a variety of other experiences is missing. This leads to a sense that the way the organization operates is the only right way and increases resistance to change and improvement efforts.

Tony Ridder, CEO of Knight-Ridder, described to us the need to change ways of thinking in the tradition-laden newspaper business. He noted that, in effect, the business is highly inbred and has a stable base of "newspaper people." People tend to join the business early in their careers and stay with it even though they may eventually work for several different newspaper organizations. The result is that the thinking about how to operate tends to be similar in most newsrooms, for example, and sustains old ideas from journalism schools about the role of an editor in giving people what he or she decides they need.

This high level of stability increases the difficulty of moving into delivering news in the way many of today's customers want to get their news, such as via the Internet. Some younger and well-educated people have never developed the habit of reading a daily newspaper. At the same time their parents often feel that an important part of their day is missing if they do not read their daily newspaper. Bringing new people from different backgrounds into the newspaper business is part of what Mr. Ridder sees as necessary to help change the thinking patterns in the industry and respond to changing customer needs. Part of his response to this need has been the move of Knight-Ridder headquarters to Silicon Valley and the hiring of people from outside the industry, including people with technology backgrounds. He has also created what is called "The Media Group," a group of approximately 45 people under a senior VP, chartered to investigate how Knight-Ridder can be competitive using new technology. Without the infusion of "new blood," the broad stability of the employee base would have a paralyzing effect on efforts to change. It would be very difficult to develop the stabilizing base needed to cope with rapid technological changes impacting the business.

Employees entering organizations with a highly stable and entrenched employee base frequently encounter behaviors that display an unwillingness to change. Comments like, "We've always done it that way" or "We've tried that before," quickly teach the newcomer that new ideas are unwelcome. The embedded employee base pounds the new kid on the block into submission even in the face of greater needs for change. This happens in organizations that have a stabilizing base designed for conditions of high certainty and low levels of change. It is characteristic of organizations that have a change-averse or change-resistant orientation.

B. Too Much Instability

The lack of stability in the employee base can have a destabilizing effect on the organization. Rapid turnover or very rapid growth often leaves a small base of employees with understanding of the features of the stabilizing base, even if the basics have been put in place. In one microelectronics company we heard many comments about the lack of a unique and common culture and the negative effects of this on achieving coordinated efforts. Comments like "The design group head is a TI guy, the marketing guy is from Fairchild, the manufacturing head is an old National Semiconductor person, and they all want to run things like the companies they came from. We don't have a single culture that we've developed. It makes it really hard to get things such as the design and introduction of new products done in a timely manner." In this case, not only was there a lack of a stable base of employees, the top management had not gotten its act together to provide the other components of the stabilizing base. The overall effect was very destabilizing.

Another example of the destabilizing effects of a limited employee base was observed in the start-up of a new manufacturing facility in a new location. A few people were relocated from the organization's headquarters location. Nearly all others were recruited locally or from competitor's facilities in other locations. People joining the organization came into a situation with a new management team, a new manufacturing process, a different work design concept, a new and not yet debugged facility, and with very little experience in the business. Without a stabilizing employee base and the need to merge diverse cultural experiences into a new organization, the situation was destabilized to the extent that the time from start-up to full operation took substantially longer than originally anticipated.

In another situation in a "white goods" company, we observed destabilizing effects in a downsizing effort that included incentives for voluntary early retirement. It turned out that a large percentage of the organization's "corporate memory" was lost when many of the development engineers for a particular type of appliance accepted the retirement incentives and left the organization. The history in this organization was that the older engineers passed along their knowledge over time to the newer engineers. Nowhere was this valuable core of knowledge captured and available for use once the old-timers were gone. Even though the organization had many of the other pieces of the stabilizing base in place, the loss of key members of the engineering employee base in that part of the organization proved to be destabilizing and costly. Delays and repetition of problems previously solved cost time and money. And, ultimately, a number of the retired engineers were rehired as consultants to the newer people at rates well beyond the salaries previously paid.

C. Employee Stability that Strengthens the Stabilizing Base

All of the components of the stabilizing base are important if the organization is to capitalize on its employee base to add stability in the face of change. The employee base must be (a) aware of and personally aligned with the components of the stabilizing base and (b) given responsibilities and roles that allow them to act in ways that build the stabilizing base. Taking the steps outlined in the various sections of this chapter will develop employees that are attuned and personally aligned with the organization and its values, vision, direction and goals, commitment to change, and so on. Additional steps are needed to include appropriate responsibilities and roles for building the stabilizing base.

Assignment of people to roles such as mentors and coaches, and providing training to develop their skills for carrying out those role assignments, is one step. Some portion of the responsibility may be focused on transferring specific skills to new people while other portions involve help in assimilating the person to the organization, department, or specific job. While the formal role of coach or mentor may only last for a limited time, the relationships developed continue and serve the organization's needs informally for many years.

Making it the responsibility for all to operate consistently with the organization's values, as in the Hewlett-Packard approach to "the HP way," is another step. Included with this step is the requirement to make it everyone's responsibility to confront inconsistencies, to guide new people, and to reject directives that are out of line. At the same time, it needs to be appropriate for anyone to consult with others, peers included, about the appropriateness of something they intend to do. This action uses the stabilizing effects of the employee base. Feeling free to act increases when a support system of others is available for consultation as needed. As a colleague once commented, "I will play a better game of tennis on the top of a tall building if there is a fence around the court. I know where the boundaries are and don't have to take my concentration from the game worrying about falling over the edge."

We were involved with an organization experiencing annual employee turnover rates of 100% among first-line manufacturing employees. There was great concern that this situation was too unstable to allow the organization to cope with high rates of change in its products, equipment, and manufacturing processes. Yet performance in the affected areas remained strong. Analysis of the turnover data revealed that approximately 50% of the employees were stable and had been with the organization for a number of years. The other 50% of the people turned over twice a year. Obviously, this situation was not acceptable and a process was initiated to improve the turnover rate among new people. Yet an important finding was that the high stability among half of the people created a stabilizing base for the entire area. These people knew the organization and its values. They were excited about their jobs and, among other things, found satisfaction in their mentor-like role of helping new people learn their positions and become productive. In addition, the supervisors of the areas involved were often young and inexperienced college graduates. The actions of the more stable group of employees helped their peers and provided support and continuity for the ongoing flow of new supervisors.

D. Managerial Transition Meetings

A colleague of ours, Jerry Pike, retired from the U.S. Army as a lieutenant colonel. His last assignment was as head of the Concepts Directorate of the Organizational Effectiveness Unit at Fort Ord, California. A continuing issue in the military is how to deal with the movement of officers from one assignment to another approximately every two years. The time required to transition into a new position as well as a few months of winding down and preparing to move on leaves a limited time when the officer is fully productive. Mr. Pike was involved in developing processes to facilitate and shorten the transition into new assignments.

The process involved a set of meetings among the incoming officer, the outgoing officer, and the direct subordinates of the position. The discussions covered issues such as what people were working on, current goals, what had been accomplished or was unfinished, the expectations and preferences of the incoming officer, concerns and hopes of the subordinates, and so on. Putting this process at the beginning of the new officer's tenure in the position saved a significant portion of the time normally wasted in getting up to speed. The period of testing the new boss to learn his style and preferences was reduced. The period of probing by the new person to understand the history and norms of the unit was shortened. Issues normally covered in a safe, unplanned, take-them-as-they-come, manner were dealt with up front and directly and in a supportive environment. Transitions supported by this process are less destabilizing and the process employed strengthened the unit's stabilizing base.

An adaptation of this process was used in a consulting assignment with a newly hired CFO. The process was called "Interview and Press Conference: Everything You Always Want To Know About Your New Boss But Don't Usually Ask." A set of interview questions was prepared in advance by the consultant and discussed with the new CFO. Included were questions related to what he expected from people working for him, what kind of things pleased him vs. what really upset him, how he liked to work with his subordinate team, what his technical hot-buttons were, and so on. In the meeting with the executive and his staff the consultant played the role of interviewer (he was called Walter Cronkite). After 20 minutes of questioning by the consultant the CFO's subordinates were invited to act as members of the press and ask any questions they wanted to. Since the new CFO had demonstrated his willingness to discuss tough questions, the interview session was lively and very informative. Later in the meeting, each person also reported on their work and needs and the CFO asked questions designed to bring his understanding of the department and the people up to speed as quickly as possible.

Two months after this session the CFO contacted the consultant to report that he felt the process had reduced his time for getting up to speed by more than 50%. Opening up the flow of information allowed the new executive and his people to deal with important issues early in the relationship. The more stable group of subordinates helped add stability to the organization during a period of substantial change.

To summarize the idea of stability of employee base as a component of the organization's stabilizing base, the employee base can be an important contributor when used appropriately. Planning is required to prepare people for roles that are stabilizing vs. paralyzing. Too much stability can be paralyzing. Too little stability is destabilizing. Making sure employees are attuned to all parts of the stabilizing base and that each component of the base is in place allows the organization's people base to contribute stabilizing effects.

IX. Flexibility of Systems, Structures, and Infrastructure

Among the most paralyzing features of organizations in uncertain environments are inflexible systems and structures and a rigid infrastructure. As the rate of change increases time becomes an ever more precious commodity. Consuming additional time to work through rigid systems, seek approvals through a complex hierarchy, or deal with bureaucratic hassles is a formula for disaster. There simply is no available time to waste without losing ground in today's rapid-change environment.

A. Inflexibility and the Cost of Energy to Change

Kurt Lewin developed a widely recognized change model.[11] The model describes three phases of change and calls them unfreezing, change (or learning), and refreezing. Energy has to be applied to bring about change. In this model, energy must first be applied for unfreezing to take place. Often this energy comes from a discrepancy between where things are and where we want them to be. The greater the discrepancy, the greater the energy release and the greater the motivation to change. Without unfreezing, change will not occur. Changing also requires energy for moving from where we've been to where we're going. And, finally, refreezing requires energy for the change from a fluid state back to a fixed state.

Beverly Scott, a colleague and former director of organization development for McKesson, discussed her concerns about inflexible structures and infrastructures and the energy required to cope with more and more change. She said:

> We can't freeze, unfreeze. We don't have time to unfreeze. We need to learn to live with ambiguity…to constantly communicate about the organization's values, vision, direction, and overarching goals. Understanding these gives people some sense of being able to cope with the amount of change within the slush of ambiguity.

Building the elements of the stabilizing base provides comfort in the face of ambiguity and makes change easier. Organizations faced with growing pressures for change have to create flexibility (and with it some additional ambiguity) so people can act and not be paralyzed (frozen).

Organizations have a finite amount of energy available for conducting their work. In rapidly changing situations they often consume more energy than is available. People work overtime to get things done because there is not enough time to get them done in the normal course of working. This increases the amount of debilitating stress in the organization and consumes even more energy in nonproductive ways. The continuing consumption of excessive amounts of energy leads to a deficit that must be repaid. Often the repayment is in the form of inefficiency and reduced productivity, a condition sometimes described as "flailing." There is the appearance of high energy and lots of effort but with little progress and limited results. It is similar to what happens when the heart goes into a state of fibrillation. All of the muscles are working but are operating independently. No blood is being pumped and, unless defibrillation occurs very soon, death follows shortly.

Organizations that are change averse or change resistant generally have designed more inflexible systems, structures, and infrastructures. And the costs to the organization as pressures for change increase are incredible. Lost time, wasted human resources, high levels of non-value-added effort in the name of control or of protecting the power of managers and administrative/support groups, and so on, add up to huge costs that do nothing for the organization's customers and can never be recovered.

B. Flexibility Is Stabilizing

Designing or redesigning for greater flexibility is not just an activity undertaken for purposes of treating people better or making it easier for them to get things done. In fact it is, or will become, a matter of survival in the ever more rapidly changing world. The payoff to the organization is in the creation of a broader stabilizing base. Making change and getting things done easier means they will consume less energy. The energy savings then become available for further change, learning, and improvement. And the cycle continues, paying off continually.

A good example can be taken from the world of quality and continuous improvement where there has been a great shift from creating ever more elaborate inspection capabilities to eliminating defects and improving processes with a focus on prevention. When the root causes of defects and errors are eliminated and prevented from recurring, costly inspection becomes unnecessary except to confirm that processes are operating in control. Time, money, and energy are saved and become available for further improvement and improved financial performance.

As with other components of the stabilizing base, increasing flexibility allows more freedom to act. It does not, as many people worry that it will, result in the loss of control. Instead, people are able to make and implement decisions more readily and act responsibly in doing so. The people whose time had been consumed in non-value-added efforts to control others are freed up to pursue more productive efforts or become unnecessary in a very positive way. That is, they are no longer operating as impediments to getting the work of the organization done by the people assigned to do it.

The need for greater flexibility does not mean the elimination of systems, structures, and infrastructures. Too much flexibility and ambiguity leaves people unable to act. The CEO of a client organization that had grown very rapidly acknowledged the importance of this statement as it affected the performance of his organization. From the beginning of the company until the time of our discussion, the company had grown from almost nothing to around one billion dollars in sales in a ten-year period. The CEO was virtually obsessed with avoiding the paralyzing effects of rigid systems and bureaucracy and keeping the organization fluid. Working on the leading edge of technology coupled with an incredible growth rate drove him to want to prevent the creeping paralysis he had observed in other organizations.

Yet the company experienced a very difficult period of reduced sales, an insufficient flow of new products to the market, and growing challenges from competitors. He commented that, "We finally realized that you can't grow a company from nothing to a billion dollars in sales without providing the needed systems and infrastructure." The absence of these components of the stabilizing base had been destabilizing and costly. He realized that the answer rested in creating flexible, but nonparalyzing, systems, structures, and infrastructures. These had to be designed to guide and support people for timely action but not hinder them.

The company found that the development of flexible, but common processes for product development was important. These processes had to be flexible enough to accommodate the unique development needs of different product types but provide commonality to assure that a systematic overall process was in use. At the same time, the processes needed to be facile enough to dramatically shorten the organization's "time to market." Extensive effort was invested in the design and development of such processes. The result was a stabilizing base better suited to the needs of an organization in a very high uncertainty environment.

C. Features Adding Flexibility

Adding flexibility happens in a variety of ways. Some of the options follow:

- Create the ability to act by giving everyone wide access to data and information that are relevant to their activities. Informed people are able to act.
- Place the authority to act at the lowest possible level. Those with direct contact with an issue are in the best position to take action. It is commonly known that the best sources of ideas for change and improvement are those who do the work.

- Minimize restrictions on people's actions from requirements for multiple approvals. Where approvals are necessary, i.e., where experience is lacking or information is not available, put limits only where they are relevant, not on all areas where an individual might take independent action.

- Require that changes to operating systems or the infrastructure include a simple process for subsequent change.

- Create systems that include all necessary steps but allow adjustments for the unique needs of the groups that use it. Don't let the design of systems assume that "one size fits all."

- Make temporary structures available for specific tasks such as project teams or task forces. Dissolve the structure when it has served its purpose. Assign people based on the need for their contribution and not on irrelevant factors such as organizational level, time of employment, or position power.

- Create ongoing structures to manage and coordinate tasks or processes horizontally, e.g., cross-functional process teams. Minimize requirements for such teams to check with higher levels before acting.

- Trust and empower people to use their best judgment when action is required. Provide for subsequent review of actions for learning purposes but not for blame or punishment.

- Set criteria for policies, procedures, or controls that assure flexibility and minimize bureaucracy. Equal or better outcomes are achieved when such criteria are used.

- Require all systems, structures, and components of the infrastructure to maximize people's ability to manage their own work. Work from the assumption that self-control is more powerful than attempts to control people's behavior externally, especially in conditions of high change.

Systems, structures, and infrastructure designed around these ideas produce a "stabilizing base" in the face of increasing change. There is the freedom associated with more flexibility and the comfort and support of established boundaries. And, while building the stabilizing base, they avoid the destabilizing effects of insufficient support and guidance while preventing the paralyzing effects of excessive bureaucracy. These are critical issues to address when greater capacity for change is required and the decision is made to move towards a higher level of capability as an Ever-Changing Organization.

X. Access to Data and Information

Increased openness and sharing of information with everyone becomes more important as the rate of change increases. Without full access to information the organization moves too slowly. Uninformed people have no choice but to wait for instructions because they have no basis for deciding and taking action on their own. Informed people are able to make decisions and take action when needed.

A. *Control of Access and Effects on Stabilization*

"People get information in this organization on a 'need-to-know' basis." That quote could only come from an organization with legal restrictions on dissemination of information, i.e., suppliers to the defense establishment, or with a paralyzing stabilizing base. Anyone setting such a ground rule undoubtedly recognizes that "knowledge is power" and that knowledge comes from being informed. Controlling access to information is one way to protect the power of those with the data.

Any organization that only shares data on the basis of the "need to know" is doing so based on a change-averse or change-resistant orientation. This orientation will be obvious in many other aspects of its operation beyond how it controls or shares information. Management may deliberately keep information in the hands of a few as a strategy to limit exposure to the potential for change. It is also obvious that they do not trust people to use information in ways that are in the best interests of the organization. No matter what the rationale for the need-to-know approach, someone in these situations has taken on the role of deciding for others what information or data they need to do their job. The net result is a set of people who are unable to act in situations where they could act with relevant information. Managers could not perform their jobs without information and data. Other people are similarly hampered in managing their own work and in coping with needs for change. Overall, "need to know" as a basis for information availability is a paralyzing prescription for dealing with accelerating change.

Organizations faced with increasing change help themselves create an effective stabilizing base when they open up access to data to all that might use it. People may or may not actually access the data, but they know what is available and how to get it when needed. They are not restricted from access when *they* decide it would be relevant and useful. Others do not presume to be in the best position to decide for them. People are trusted to make decisions about the information needed and to use data appropriately.

People are more willing to act and to take risks when they have full access to information. Uncertainty is reduced and people can be more confident of their choices. Lack of information is destabilizing. People rightfully feel that they are taking greater risks when they need to act but lack the data to guide their actions. They are forced to guess or make assumptions in lieu of data. Timely decision making is avoided or delayed, usually at an unknown cost to the organization. Withholding of information sends the message that people are not deemed capable of dealing with it or are not trusted. Failure to act based on lack of data is a valid explanation for a person's lack of action. Restricted access to data does not support the need for flexibility and quick action associated with accelerating change.

B. Information and the Response to Change

One manager we talked with told us his organization was in the process of reinventing itself. Acquisitions and top-level changes were occurring and the organization's mission had been redefined. He observed that management had substantial amounts of data that would help people understand the new environment and the company's direction. But the information was not being shared. He said, "Lack of open communication is very unsettling. We are like an old clunker of a ship out in the ocean. Many of the people here have tenure of 25 to 30 years. They know the "old" company. Can you imagine what is happening to them? They don't understand what is happening to the company. It is reinventing itself but it can't do it by osmosis." He continued, "Little news bulletins and telephone conversations are just not going to do it. We need to share information openly and allow people to act or change easily. We need to give individuals access to information from our new environment." From this manager's description of what was happening, the failure to share or deliberate withholding of information was having a destabilizing effect on the organization's recognized need to reinvent itself.

Another person told us, "We have employees who now have access to huge amounts of information that used to be what managers and executives had. But we haven't developed an organization that enables them to make decisions. The organization doesn't know what to do with the information. We haven't taught people how to sort through the information they have in order to use it in a wise fashion. People closest to change should be making changes, but hierarchy does not allow it." Here is a situation in which opening up access to information has destabilized the organization. People are overwhelmed with what is available to them. They lack the skills and guidance to use it well. So while too much information can be destabilizing, lack of skills and a rigid structure can be paralyzing. The stabilizing base in this case is working against the organization in both ways as it undertakes major change.

C. Dramatic Effects from More Open Access

A consulting assignment in the early stage of our careers provided another illustration of the power of information for influencing and supporting change. A small group of employees in a glass manufacturing plant were assigned to jobs inspecting and repairing imperfections in the surface of blueprint cylinders. One was part of the quality control department and the others were in production. Imperfections in the surfaces of the cylinders were identified by the inspector, repaired by the production operators, and reinspected. The production employees had established a fixed rate of 44 per shift and produced at that level each day. In addition to a fixed output level, the quality of the work required nearly 15% rework.

Several changes were introduced in the work area. The inspector was moved into the production department, although the job did not change. The group became a team and was treated as if they were running the blueprint cylinder business for the plant. They were provided information on inventory and order backlog. Correspondence from customers, sales people, and marketing people were provided to them and the production data was made completely available including rates and rework levels. The department manager met with the group regularly and a link to the quality department was maintained by having a quality technician available to the team on an as-needed basis.

Changes in performance and attitude towards the business were almost immediate. Feedback from customer letters, especially, was eagerly sought and discussed. The team reviewed production data daily. Discussion of new orders was a topic at all meetings of the team and the backlog and inventory reports were reviewed weekly. The fixed production rate began to vary and within two weeks had increased by over 10%. Even more striking was the improvement in quality. Rework rates dropped from nearly 15% to less than 1% within the first week and active discussions took place about what was missed whenever a piece requiring rework was identified. Armed with information and data, a group of people that had been perceived as restrictive in their output and in conflict between departments took on responsibility for a small business as if it were their own. Prior lack of data and involvement had created a paralyzing base for employees' actions. Open communication and the trust it conveyed built a stronger stabilizing base for the business, even in what was a relatively certain business environment.

The managers of the plant where the blueprint cylinders were made learned from another experience to further open up communication with their people. Specifically they made changes to include information about the applications for their products available to everyone who worked on a product. A long-term employee had visited her brother-in-law in a nearby hospital shortly after open-heart surgery. She noticed a part that she and others in the plant produced connected to a suction machine used to keep the chest free of fluids and the lungs inflated. Upon return to the plant she told everyone what she had learned and that she had never realized why the specifications on the part were so demanding. Understanding the life-and-death nature of the product's application led to an immediate improvement in the quality of that product, although there was a temporary decline in output rate as people learned to produce improved quality at prior production levels. Plant management soon requested that more customer data and application information be provided to them for sharing with employees. They realized that the ongoing task of doing work without understanding what was being produced or how it was used makes the job "just a job" without purpose and meaning. Changing that situation increases the stabilizing base. As product designs are modified or quality specifications tightened, understanding of why the change is necessary is more readily achieved and resistance to the changes substantially reduced.

D. Technological Change and Availability of Information

Ongoing advances in information processing and computer technology have greatly increased an organization's ability to make information available to anyone. Computers make real-time access to information possible and, if not real-time, make getting information to people in a timely manner much easier. The development of software and interconnect capabilities facilitates communication via local areas networks (LANs), Intranets, and e-mail linkages, and the Internet gives people access to information virtually anywhere in the world.

Among the concerns to be addressed with the growing potential for access to information are such things as:

- How to help people decide what available information is most useful and how much information is enough;
- How to have the information presented to make it useful data and not just an unintelligible and overwhelming mass of information;
- How to teach people to use the equipment and the information it makes available in ways that are most useful and efficient; and
- Resolving security issues for information that needs to be protected, e.g., personal data or financial statements or legal documents, or where limited distribution is required for proprietary purposes.

As with other areas of the stabilizing base, an important consideration is providing access to available information in line with the felt needs of the individual person doing a job. The comfort of having necessary data to guide decisions and actions augments the organization's stabilizing base. Too much information can produce paralysis and the inability to act. Too little information, on the other hand, can be destabilizing by increasing the uncertainty of any situation. Providing open access and maximizing the individual's skill for selecting the information they access provides the greatest chance for a solid stabilizing base. Balance is needed and is best achieved by open access to informed users.

XI. Emphasis on Results and Process

A. Only Focusing on Results Doesn't Work

How many of us have been told at some point in our careers that what is really important is getting results *no matter how they are achieved*? Levinson[12] described the situation of a manager sent into an operation in deep trouble with just that instruction. A year later, the organization is in the black and "turned around" in the eyes of the manager told to "just get the results." But this manager is unceremoniously terminated despite the change in results. He is admonished for destroying the fiber of the organization and creating a situation that will require a very difficult rebuilding of the trust and the culture of the organization.

The message, of course, is that the requirement to "just get the results" was incomplete. Nothing was said or discussed about limitations on the process to be used. Nor was the idea of "results" defined to include outcomes that maintained and protected the culture and good will of the organization. Even though the financial numbers were achieved, the other "results" indicated destruction of the human system and ended up being more important in the manager's performance evaluation. Even a brief discussion to explore the instructions given to the manger could have clarified the range of outcomes and processes that would be acceptable in seeking to produce the turnaround.

The ABC model described in Chapter 1 helped a frustrated information systems executive deal with problems he was having much like the plant manager in the previous example. The executive described what he had hoped to achieve (desired consequences) very simply, saying, "The only thing I want is the most cost-effective decision for the company when we purchase computing equipment." He was responsible for review and approval of decisions for purchases of individual desktop computers or engineering workstations. His customers were other managers submitting purchase requisitions for equipment. Each situation requiring approval was ending up in a win-lose confrontation between the IS executive and his "customer." He would reject requisitions that did not meet his criteria and return them with a note dictating the selection of equipment meeting his singular decision criteria for cost effectiveness.

Once the executive was able to include a broader range of desired consequences in his thinking, e.g., satisfying the customer's requirements and reaching a decision that improved or maintained working relationships, he was able to identify and modify the assumptions driving his win-lose behavior. The modified assumptions allowed him to adapt the process for reaching decisions into a win-win, problem-solving approach that would meet both parties' requirements. In this situation failure to consider the full range of effects of his behavior in defining desired outcomes and stubbornly clinging to a no-win decision process had put the executive on a path towards failure in his job. The ABC model helped bring focus to the broader systems effects of his actions and to support change from a unilateral to a mutual decision-making process.

Much greater awareness that all results are achieved via a process that transforms inputs to outputs (results) has developed in business circles in the latter part of the 20th century. There is much greater understanding that unacceptable results cannot be improved directly except via rework and added costs. Continued improvement occurs only when changes are made to the process and/or to the inputs to the process. The use of business process mapping as part of ongoing improvement processes and the use of statistical methods for improving process control are two areas where the increased awareness of the need for both results and process focus can be seen.

Systems' thinking has also increased awareness that the results of decisions and actions occur throughout a process or system whether or not the effects of the action in other areas are considered. Failure to consider effects in other parts of a system is a result of oversimplifying situations beyond a useful level. Including consideration of the effects of decisions or changes in all key components of a system must be or become an important part of strategies for prevention of failures and improving the organization's ability to avoid the extensive costs of inspections and rework.

B. Both Results and Process, Not Either-Or

Consideration of the results to be achieved is important to success. Considering the process used as a key factor in achieving the results is equally important. This is not an either-or issue, it is a "both-and" issue. Organizations facing rapid change need to escape what Collins and Porras[6] call the "tyranny of the OR." Saying that only results count and process issues are unimportant restricts consideration of processes that could produce better results. It may also be paralyzing if the results targeted lead to processes that ignore the effects of the intended action in other parts of the system. Even more problems are likely to be created that further inhibit achievement of the desired results.

Organizations working to move towards higher levels of ECO capability adopt a balanced orientation to results and the processes used to achieve them. Both areas must be addressed where change occurs more rapidly to keep the organization on a steady course. Paying attention to both issues adds to the organization's stabilizing base.

XII. Balance

The last component of the stabilizing base addresses the need to provide balance. The concept of a stabilizing base, by itself, suggests the need to operate in a manner that creates forces to counterbalance the ever-increasing forces and pressures for change. Not, as stressed in the introduction to the section, for the purpose of repelling or neutralizing the forces, but to modulate their effects so that the organization can maintain its course and continue to operate amid the turbulence. The counterbalancing forces of the stabilizing base are intended to keep the organization from extreme conditions where it becomes rigid and unable to move or flex, at one extreme, or finds itself adrift and unable to navigate its course at the other.

Some of the challenging areas where balance adds stabilizing forces are identified and discussed briefly below.

A. Time Orientation

Pressures for near-term performance must be balanced with the need to sustain activities for the achievement of longer-term goals. Organizations that sacrifice product/service or human resource development efforts to bolster short-term earnings confuse their people with the variation in emphasis and the overbalance of focus towards immediate needs. People are able to deal with reduced budgets or spending constraints when the need is clear, but feel lost when projects with future payoffs are cancelled or departments doing the longer-term work are eliminated. Instability increases when management is perceived as unable or unwilling to seek solutions to short-term problems that sustain movement towards the organization's vision. At the other extreme, an organization that stubbornly drives primarily for future gains in the face of indicators of short-term failure paralyzes the organization and subverts energy for performance improvements and problem solving.

B. Work and Personal Time

Some organizations take great pride in the number of hours worked by people exempt from the overtime provisions of the wage and hour laws. Norms in these organizations put pressure on people to get to work before their boss and to leave after he or she does. Whether or not the individual is able to operate efficiently is not a consideration. The amount of time spent on the job is taken to indicate one's level of commitment to the organization. Even though there is powerful evidence that too much time at work lowers effectiveness and efficiency, these organizations drive everyone to work long hours with the implication that anyone working less must not have enough to do.

Documentum president Jeffrey Miller takes a different approach based on the advice of one of his mentors while at Intel. The counsel of the mentor was to find a pace of working that was right for him and that could be sustained in order to prevent burnout and frustration. Even though there were sure to be times when it was necessary to exceed that pace for brief periods, selecting the right pace and then intensely focusing only on top priority issues would pay off handsomely in performance and growth. Mr. Miller provides the same counsel to his people at Documentum. Providing balance between work time and personal time in fast-paced businesses ultimately produces sustainable high levels of performance and a stabilizing effect for employees.

C. Stakeholder's Needs

Organizational stakeholders include owners and shareholders, customers, employees, local communities, suppliers, and so on. The needs and demands of these groups often are in conflict. Organizations build a more powerful stabilizing base when they work to balance the needs of all stakeholders. Maximizing attention to the needs of one or a few stakeholders is destabilizing in the long run. For example, failure to address employee needs may lead to instability in the employee base or to actions that force consideration of their needs through vehicles such as unions, regulatory groups such as OSHA or the Department of Labor, or legislative bodies. Failure to meet customers needs leads to loss of revenue and market share, reduced access to information on future needs or trends, and so on. All stakeholders are part of the overall system within which an organization functions. Their needs and the organization's needs are interrelated and impact each other. Balance among the needs is critical, especially as change rates accelerate.

If the needs of any stakeholder groups are not addressed they will feel disempowered and will react. Their reaction will be designed to demonstrate that they really do have power and will often be counterproductive for the organization. What they do will reflect a variation on an old expression, "Power corrupts, powerlessness corrupts absolutely." The effect of their actions will add to the level of uncertainty the organization faces and reduce the ability of the stabilizing base to support the organization through increasing amounts of change.

D. Freedom and Control

A number of other areas exist where there is a need for balance, many of which are variations on the need for balance between freedom and control. One of our mentors, for example, often talked about the need for balance between trust and distrust. He spoke of trusting people to act in the best interests of the organization without tempting them to violate that trust unnecessarily. While providing greater spending authority conveys trust, leaving the organization's cash box open to all would be foolish.

Balancing delegation and participation while avoiding the extremes of abdication and anarchy vs. dictation and autocracy is important. While balancing freedom and control is also important, shifting the balance towards freedom and self-control becomes more important and less dysfunctional as the rate of change grows. The stabilizing base is extended vs. constricted by such a shift in balance.

Balanced practices in each of the areas mentioned lend balance to the organization and build the stabilizing base necessary in turbulent times. Imbalance in either direction contributes to an erosion of the stabilizing base, moving the organization into areas of greater uncertainty and instability or towards rigidity and inflexibility that limit its ability to function in the face of change.

XIII. Summary of Stabilizing Base

With the overall trend of organizational environments towards greater change and uncertainty, all organizations can benefit from examination of the components of their stabilizing base and the implementation of changes to strengthen it. As the base becomes more supportive of change the organization will find it easier to move towards more change-friendly or change-seeking levels of managing FOR change, continuous improvement, and continuous learning. The capacity for change, learning, and improvement will grow to meet the demands of the environment and will support continually becoming more of an Ever-Changing Organization.

The following three chapters will spell out more of our thinking and research on the other components of the ECO model and the major subcomponents of each. The information presented will allow readers to explore their organizations' ECO status today and will help identify missing or weak elements for the level of ECO capability needed.

4 Managing FOR Change

The world around us continues to move more rapidly! The forces FOR change are increasing! Yet many organizations continue to function with operating practices and systems that are, or were, designed for a more stable and certain business environment. The messages to members of the organization are clear. They indicate that change is unwelcome and the province of a select few. Ideas for change are difficult to get approved, requiring multiple reviews and signatures, even though leaders proclaim that everyone needs to look for opportunities for improvement and feel free to initiate change.

In this chapter, we examine important aspects of an organization's behavior which reflect the extent to which it is being managed FOR change vs. actions which indicate more restrictive orientations to change, i.e., averse or resistant. The issue of managing FOR change is particularly critical for assessing the fit of the organization's practices with the demands for change capability that arise in its environment. It is impossible for executives to talk their way into managing FOR change. Unless the operating practices and behaviors of the organization support the need for change, the levels of individual resistance and the difficulty of making change happen will be high.

I. Customer Focus

As customer focus increases, the extent to which the organization is managing FOR change increases. Organizations high in customer focus put significant effort into understanding the current needs of customers as well as their business strategies and product direction. Important information about competitors and their strategies is often a by-product. This effort allows proactive, timely, and focused development of products and services that

107

meet customers needs. Organizations with this focus are influenced by their customers and, in turn, gain influence with the customer.

A. Customer–Supplier Partnerships

The result of high levels of customer focus is greater interdependency between customer and supplier. The relationship becomes a partnership. Each party recognizes the value of the relationship and learns to trust the other to deal with them collaboratively and to their mutual benefit. Being certain that customers' needs are satisfied is a primary concern. Adversarial, win–lose actions are replaced by problem-solving, win–win behaviors. The relationship is viewed as long term, and both parties realize that such a relationship cannot be sustained unless both benefit. Discussions and agreements about how to work together as business partners clarify what it means to engage in a customer–supplier partnership and how to make the partnership succeed.

Wesley Cantrell, CEO of Lanier Worldwide, Inc., has led a change effort to build partnering relationships with customers. One customer used the phrase "an intimate relationship," a description of the relationship they have been striving for with larger accounts. Mr. Cantrell describes the desired link with customers as, "…a relationship of trust and confidence where they would stick with us if little or bad things happen …and the same way with us to them."

Jeffrey Miller, CEO of Documentum, describes a similar transition from selling a particular product to a consultative partnership focused on an overall business solution. Mr. Miller says this is a change that, "…sometimes requires different people. It requires people to think differently. It requires a change in the relationship with the customer from individual transactions to building relationships, and requires a team approach." He describes that approach as one that they have been developing for more than five years and that he believes is succeeding because, "it is consistent with our culture and values."

Much more emphasis is placed on short-term business relationships with low levels of customer focus. The customer is viewed more as a necessary evil to be overcome. There is more concern with getting the order than with meeting the customer's needs.

High levels of customer focus are built on the belief that the customer is the reason for the existence of the supplier. This contrasts dramatically where there are low levels of customer focus. In those situations the supplier's behavior conveys the feeling that they are the customers. If you supply them with money they will exchange it for the product or service they have decided you want and choose to supply.

Our personal experience with a number of banks has indicated such a belief. We have been treated as if the bank was giving us the privilege of depositing our money in their institution or of taking a loan and should feel happy that we were being allowed to do so. Instead of feeling like a valued customer we ended up with the sense that the bank was our customer and we were fortunate to have been included among those who were privileged to do business with them.

In contrast to this feeling, we have found a new focus as customers of Safeway, the large supermarket chain, under the leadership of Steve Burd, CEO. When wandering the aisles looking for something, store employees we encounter, no matter where they were headed or what they were stacking on the shelves, stop to ask if they can help. And when we explain what we are looking for there is no hesitation. Instead of being directed to aisle 8, we are taken to the location of the product we seek and shown the options we have. The impression created by this behavior is that meeting our needs is as important as, or more important than, whatever else the person was doing. Even if it means driving extra distance, we now find ourselves heading to a Safeway to shop. We know we are valued customers and are the focus of the work of the employees of the company.

B. Feedback and Customer Satisfaction

Organizations with high customer focus become almost obsessed with collecting feedback and data on customer perceptions and satisfaction. And their concern is not seen in some form of annual, third-party customer survey. Rather the data they seek is collected on an ongoing basis and by the people in the organization who must act on it. Without this data they could not manage FOR change because they would be unaware of conditions needing change. Armed with the data they can implement changes rapidly and prevent further problems. Or, they can see trends developing that can be remedied before a more difficult situation evolves.

Solectron Corporation, a contract manufacturer serving the electronics industry and twice winner of the Baldrige Award, is an outstanding example of a high-end customer focus organization.[13] Weekly feedback from customers is agreed upon contractually. Contact with all customers occurs a minimum of once a day and up to ten or more times per day in critical periods of a contract. Reports of defects and errors are reviewed regularly, discussed with responsible parties, and assignments made for corrective actions. Servicing many of the blue chip companies in the electronics business, e.g., HP, IBM, and so on, Solectron's high level of customer focus has supported a high level of sustained growth and long-term partnerships with its customers.

C. Customer Linkages at Many Levels

At high levels of customer focus people at many levels of the organization are involved with the customer. This ranges from the executive level, sales and marketing, customer service, engineering and manufacturing levels, quality and reliability people, financial people, and also includes exchanges among people at the operating level. Understanding the customer's direction and business strategy is important to the supplier. Knowing the nature of the customer's application and the difficulties encountered helps the supplier anticipate or respond to issues that benefit both the supplier and the customer. Design and process engineers who understand the way in which customers install and use their products can often improve the design of a supplier's products for manufacturability. And operators familiar with the tasks and problems of their counterparts may be able to make changes or improvements that benefit the customer's people. We observed an example of such a change in the Butler, Pennsylvania warehouse of Marmon/Keystone Corporation, a distributor of steel pipe and tubing. While visiting a customer, members of a warehouse improvement team were asked by their counterparts if it was necessary to place the metal binding strap on bundles of tubing as far from the end as was their normal practice. The placement of the strap created a difficult reach for the customer's people as well as a potential safety hazard. The visiting team agreed to move the straps to a position that was easier to reach and safer, with full support from their management.

Customer links at the various levels of an organization are not random or casual. Rather they are planned and deliberate. Money to support the costs of the exchanges is budgeted. People and time are allocated to the task. In the financial services industry, for example, certain partners are designated as "client service" partners for key clients. Their role is to maintain personal and social, as well as business, relationships with key executives of the client organization. Their activities are supported with their time as well as with financial resources.

Sales personnel in an organization we have consulted with are assigned the responsibility to have lunch with a number of existing and potential customers regularly. Money is budgeted and the number of lunches is tracked to assure that the investment is being made. This organization believes that at least a part of being customer focused includes building relationships that exist beyond the customer's offices or facilities. Greater trust and openness comes with improved communication and relationships. The organization gains awareness of additional business opportunities. Additionally, potential problems can be identified and resolved before becoming major issues.

Organizations with low levels of customer focus are much less likely to build relationships with customers except at necessary interfaces. The time and costs involved are seen as expenses and not as an investment in a long-term relationship. A type of paranoia often exists that displays concern about the loss of proprietary information, whether technical or financial, or recruitment of people by customers. The supplier tends to view the customer more as a threat than as an ally. Restricted access to information and contacts that could strengthen the relationship with the customer is the result. Less information and trust reduces the capacity to anticipate and manage FOR change.

D. Ease of Customer Access to Supplier Organization

With high customer focus also comes a willingness to make it easy for customers to access people and information and have questions answered. Specific individuals or departments are identified to provide a direct link. In one organization we have worked with, Viking Freight System, people throughout the organization, including the officers of the company, answer their own phones. Among the primary reasons given for this is that "the caller might be a customer." Ease of customer access is facilitated in some organizations by direct phone lines to sources of frequently needed information. Key customers may also be provided direct access to information in the supplier's databases and computers, i.e., inventory levels or order backlog or shipment status.

Customer-focused executives frequently consult those who are in regular contact with customers to obtain feedback and observations about what is happening or needed. Despite a very busy schedule, the president of one electronics company makes it a practice to meet with members of the field sales force on any occasion he can. They provide him with up-to-date information and allow him to conduct reality checks about what is going on with specific customers and in the broader marketplace. Jeffrey Miller, Documentum's CEO, also spends as much time as possible with his field forces. He says, "I am always amazed and astounded ...by how much incredible knowledge is out there in the sales force." Access to that knowledge supports the ability of these executives to manage FOR change.

An organization's ability to manage FOR change is enhanced by in-depth and sustained high levels of customer focus. Without the intelligence and understanding that comes from the processes employed, proactive changes are "iffy" and successful outcomes improbable. With high customer focus, on the other hand, comes more valid and useful data for setting direction to meet customer needs. In addition, relationships are built that are enduring and more capable of surviving the inevitable ups and downs of any ongoing business relationship.

II. Environmental Sensing

In the discussion of the environment as a key component of the ECO model, it was emphasized that the need for ECO capability increased as uncertainty in the environment increased. If more things are changing and they are changing more rapidly, more effort is required to assess what is happening in the environment that will require change, either proactively or reactively.

Organizations which are high in the area of environmental sensing develop and support a wide variety of ways for sensing their environment. These organizations are likely to be high in customer focus and they will have created ways to sense other aspects of their environment as well.

A. Technology Sensing

Vehicles will exist for staying tuned with the relevant technologies of the organization. These will include memberships in trade organizations and technical associations where future technologies are discussed or research is reported. University researchers or specialized consultants may be retained to help stay abreast of technical developments and forecasts.

Attendance at professional meetings or industry conventions is widely supported, even in more difficult times. Technical people are encouraged to publish as a vehicle for establishing external technical contacts that provide access to technical developments. The participation may occur even in organizations lower in environmental sensing. In higher level organizations, however, there will be more structure built into the process to assure best results from the sensing activities. For example, attendance at a full range of meetings will be planned and allocated in advance. Within a particular meeting, plans will be made to assure that all key sessions are covered. And, when the meetings are over, reports or review processes will be used to share the learning from the meetings among participants and others who will benefit from what was learned.

B. Competitive Sensing

Extensive efforts are made in the area of competitive sensing. Customers are used as a source of competitive information. Suppliers who provide parts or materials (or whatever) to competitors are another source of input. Information derived from the meetings and conventions discussed above also add competitive intelligence. Market research firms and internal marketing departments produce studies and reports of the structure and direction of the marketplace and the position of the organization in the market. Sampling and testing of competitive products is conducted to assess manufacturing capabilities or give insight into features of competitive design processes. Input from sales people is sought to determine competitors' priorities and pricing strategies. Newly hired people from competitive organizations are debriefed for information they can legitimately disclose about the competitor's activities or direction.

All of this information is collected, some formally and some informally, and utilized to manage FOR change in the competitive marketplace. Product strategies or pricing plans or targeting of particular segments of the market may be confirmed or modified as a result of the competitive intelligence obtained from the variety of sensing activities.

C. Other External Sensing

Virtually all functions have external sources of influence whose actions produce the need for change. Organizations high on environmental sensing formalize and legitimize the sensing activities of these functions. Each department is chartered to stay in touch with relevant happenings in the external world. What is happening or is likely to happen that will create a need for change? What trends are developing that we should be preparing for even though their influence may not be felt for a number of years?

One feature of organizations high on environmental sensing is the assignment of permanent cross-functional teams to assure ongoing improvement of key business processes, e.g., order fulfillment, inventory management, product and process development. These same teams are charged with looking beyond their own organization and processes to determine best practices in current use. Benchmarking of the practices of recognized leaders in the use of a particular function is one way to manage FOR change. Instead of simply seeking moderate or incremental improvement, the purpose of benchmarking is to make the organization aware of "what's possible" instead of asking, "how are we doing vs. our competitors." Knowing what can be achieved, whether in the same business or another industry, creates openness to major process changes.

Functional and cross-functional process teams are also charged with ongoing awareness of the emergence of products, services, or technologies that may change the nature of their work processes in the future. Taking steps to prepare for or lead the change to the new processes is part of managing FOR change. External sensing supports proactive actions rather than having the organization itself "managed" by unanticipated changes beyond their control.

Some organizations create special roles or departments to sense the activity of regulatory agencies or legislative bodies and to exert influence in the best interests of the organization. Or, they may fund sensing and lobbying efforts of trade associations and professional societies. Making such an assignment an add-on part of a busy person's job, especially in high uncertainty environments, relegates an important task to just one of many tasks clamoring for priority at any time. Under these conditions, longer-range tasks are almost always overwhelmed by shorter term pressures, i.e., the "squeaky wheel gets the oil" syndrome. Adding specialized functions is one way to address an uncertain environment and puts the organization in a better position to identify needs and manage FOR change.

Other forms of external sensing include the collection and review of trip reports, lost business reports, post-mortem reviews of external visits, and collections of materials from clipping services that scour newspapers, magazines, and other print media for information on competitors and suppliers.

D. Internal Sensing

Organizations working to increase their capacity as an Ever-Changing Organization (ECO) also sense the internal environment as it is managed FOR change. People's experience with attempts to innovate or propose change is an important indicator of the extent to which movement has been achieved along the "orientation to change" scale, e.g., from averse or resistant to managing, friendly, or seeking.

Particularly important is the extent to which management behavior is consistent with pronouncements about the importance of change. We have reminded many management groups that "people watch your feet not your lips" when it comes to believing and committing to management direction. Failure to behave in a manner that is consistent with spoken or written statements of intention results in withholding of effort and the increase of resistance. Likewise, support that varies under different conditions or is applied differently to some groups or levels increases resistance. Unless inconsistencies are explained so that the rationale is understood and makes sense to the people affected, people believe what they observe and not what they are told.

In implementations of major organizational change efforts it is not uncommon to observe people wince and roll their eyes in looks of disgust when informed about the new management direction for change. A young marketing manager in a major white-goods company once asked if he couldn't just skip the new change initiative and wait for the next one. In this organization, as in many others, people were extremely skeptical of another "program of the month" that would begin with a round of hype and training. Their reaction was to wait to put energy into any new process until they observed changes in management's behavior that indicated that the change was "real" this time.

Employee surveys of people's experiences with change efforts is one way to handle internal sensing. In our experience, however, administering a questionnaire that results in a set of numbers and statistics from a set of attitude scales yields rather sterile data. At a minimum we recommend that any such questionnaire also ask for descriptions of actual experiences and behaviors that influenced people's choices of a particular scale point. Analysis of the data is more involved but produces a richer understanding of what is happening. The information derived from the analysis provides much more guidance to management. Changes needed to move the organization forward on the march to higher levels of ECO capability are clearer. Choices are based on examples and stories and not just a set of statistics.

"Sensing meetings" conducted by managers and leaders of the organization are a fruitful form of internal sensing. Groups may be composed of people from a specific unit or from several functional areas. The number and composition of groups is designed to provide input from a reasonable cross-section of the members of the organizations. Leaders of the discussions may be the managers of the groups involved. The leaders might also be from areas other than those represented by the participants. This approach is used where there is concern about comfort and openness. Either way, the group discussion is structured around the issue of change and the conditions that exist in the organization that support or inhibit change. Participants discuss their observations and experiences with change, providing as many specific examples as possible. The results of the sensing meetings are discussed among the leaders and recommendations for changes prepared. The richness of the outcome of sensing meetings is worth the additional effort required.

Organizations lower in concern with environmental sensing will be inclined to use anonymous and impersonal ways of internal sensing, if any. They may use things like suggestion boxes, forms for written input to management or the human resource department, or other one-way communication processes. It is unlikely that they would use a more systematic approach to sensing the internal environment for change.

Overall, organizations with a high level of investment in environmental sensing recognize the importance of formal processes for broadening their perspective on the world. If anything, they are obsessed with a fear of being unprepared or unable to lead and being forced to change. Their overall orientation to their environment is to be in touch with it and to use the information and insights that result to function in proactive and anticipatory ways. They manage their organizations FOR change instead of having to divert resources and implement changes in reaction to forces in their environment.

III. Impetus for Change

The key questions in the area of impetus for change have to do with what triggers change activity in the organization and where in the organization changes originate. The impetus for change in situations where managing FOR change is strong comes from any and all parts of the organization. Management is not the only or primary force for the initiation of change. Nor do change initiatives come primarily from specialized groups such as industrial engineering or only from certain levels.

A. *Change as Everyone's Responsibility*

Change-averse or change-resistant organizations highly restrict the responsibility for initiating change. Organizations that are managed FOR change, on the other hand, broaden the range of responsibility for change. With high impetus for change, identifying and initiating change is explicitly defined as part of each person's responsibility. Waiting to be asked is inappropriate. Each person is assumed to be aware of needs for change and the issues that impact the performance of their work. Living with the job on a day-to-day basis produces insights that are unavailable to anyone else. This fact is recognized by the organization.

Yet the initiation of ideas for change is not left to chance. Time is made available for examining one's work performance and exploring ways to improve. This might be done by individuals but is more likely to be done in groups. Members of work teams meet regularly, and one of the continuing agenda items is consideration of ways to improve their work processes and performance. Opportunities for discussion with people in the same or similar job on different shifts or working in different facilities helps to highlight issues, share best practices, and stimulate ideas for change. Participation in benchmarking studies or, at a minimum, being informed of benchmarking results, is another source of ideas about what's possible and ways to change to make the new possibilities happen.

People in organizations high in managing FOR change also are provided measurements and data about the performance of their unit. They are given the opportunity to visit with people in other areas, i.e., their internal customers or suppliers, to understand how their performance impacts, or is impacted by others. Exchange visits are arranged with people in similar jobs in other companies to broaden awareness of the work processes or equipment employed and how they might relate to potential changes in their own work. The result of data provided to people and the outcome of these visits is an increased capacity of those involved to manage their own work FOR change. They do not have to rely on others for ideas and are able to translate their observations and discussions directly into making change and improvements in their own areas.

B. *Problems or Opportunities?*

The behavior of organizations with limited impetus for change conveys to everyone the idea "If it ain't broke, don't fix it!" Change is not viewed as an opportunity to improve but rather as an unfortunate need to respond to a problem, i.e., "Something's broken, we have to fix it!"

Organizations with high impetus for change are looking for ways to improve no matter what the reason. If problems exist, the focus is on resolving them. But the emphasis is not on simply stopping the problem. Instead, focus is on understanding the cause of the problem and corrective action that keeps it from happening again. Knowing the root cause of a problem leads to solutions aimed at preventing recurrence as opposed to changes that fix the immediate problem but not the underlying cause. (More discussion of this subject is presented in the continuous improvement chapter).

People throughout organizations with high impetus for change understand the importance of seeking opportunities for change in addition to solving problems. Management's behavior clearly communicates its support of people's efforts to improve, with particular attention to being proactive. Prevention of problems frees up time previously consumed in reactive problem resolution. People learn tools for mapping work processes and use those maps to explore opportunities for change and improvement.

C. Incremental or Breakthrough Change?

We have been surprised by the number of arguments that arise regarding the importance of incremental changes vs. breakthrough change. Some argue that the principle of "kaizen" common in Japanese improvement efforts is slow and even has the potential to stifle creativity when everyone is looking for ways to make a 1% improvement in several hundred areas. Others argue that looking for breakthrough opportunities and only supporting major change efforts cuts off gains possible from a significant percentage of the resources available to the organization.

The issue is not an either–or but a both–and issue. Organizations with high impetus for change address both incremental and breakthrough change. The CEO of one high-tech company commented that it was important for everyone to be involved in ongoing changes to improve his or her own work processes. He made no distinction between small, incremental changes or changes that came from a whole new look at how things were done. At the same time, experience had convinced him that some key business processes needed to be redesigned on occasion, starting from scratch. In these areas it was likely that external support was needed, whether via benchmarking to add awareness of new possibilities or via use of consultants with independent perspectives and broader awareness of the options. In his organization the objective was to identify opportunities for change and improvement without consideration of the magnitude of the impact.

D. Change Stemming from the Absence of Change

Where impetus for change is high, questions are raised when specified periods of time have passed without any change. This behavior is based on the assumption that improvement is always possible. The failure to identify and initiate changes within a period of a few to several months triggers questions about the improvement process, not the assumption that the work process needs no improvement. Obstacles to change are identified and, as necessary, removed to get the improvement process moving again.

Many organizations recognize that established policies or rules often do not change, despite other changes that render them impractical or obsolete. Those with a high impetus for change go beyond being aware of this condition to acting on it. Periodic reviews and updates of policy manuals and operating procedures are required to assure that existing ones are updated and changed when they are no longer relevant. The concept of "sunset clauses" is attractive to these organizations. Instead of providing for continuation of policies or rules, they are required to include a time for termination. Unless the policy or rule is reconfirmed to be of value — by the issuer as well as by those affected — it must be rewritten to make it relevant and useful or it dies. With high impetus for change, organizations are unwilling to tolerate continuation of irrelevant and obsolete practices. Instead of allowing them to continue, the absence of change causes the "sun to set" and they are eliminated.

IV. Change Planning and Management

A must for an organization working to increase its capacity as an ECO is to create effective processes for the planning and management of any change effort. The organization cannot be said to be managing FOR change without such processes. Change-averse or -resistant organizations generally have not established methods for dealing with change. It is dealt with primarily by brute force. Changes are announced and implemented and people are expected to comply with whatever is handed to them. They are not given the opportunity to participate in either the decision to change or in planning the implementation of change that impacts their work.

A consequence of the way changes are imposed by these organizations is strong resistance from the affected people and frustration among the executives and others who impose the change. They find it difficult to understand why people would be irrational and not accept their direction. They do not see people's reactions as similar to their own reactions when change is imposed on them. Not understanding the dynamics of imposed change, the leaders of the changes see no reason for different ways of communicating or involving people and, therefore, end up viewing change as undesirable and as a battle.

A. Predictable Responses to Imposed Change

A number of people have written about the effects of imposed change.[18,19] They describe a predictable series of emotional responses in people. These reactions are normal and are neither antiorganizational responses to be suppressed nor indications of a natural resistance to change.

The typical initial response to imposed change is some form of denial that the change will happen. Evidence of the certainty of the change is needed to move people beyond the period of denial. With continuation of the change effort, however, a phase of resistance appears. Responses range from ignoring the change to explaining why it won't work or will only make things worse to actually sabotaging efforts to implement the change. People eventually move beyond resistance if, or when, they have had the opportunity to work through the issues influencing their resistance. They then move into a phase where they examine the positive sides of the change, exploring how it will benefit them and how they will use it. Once this has been accomplished, there is movement into the last phase. At that point belief in the change and a personal commitment to make it work develops.

Organizations where change planning and management is lacking either do not understand that these phases of response to change occur or believe that they can use their power and influence to force people into being committed to a change. Changes are often introduced with lots of hype and hoopla. People are told what will happen and when and that the change is important for the success of the organization. They are asked to signify their acceptance and buy-in to the change in some way such as signing a pledge or becoming part of a team to make the change happen.

Management and change leaders (often the same people) leave these sessions with a sense that the change has been sold and people are committed to make it happen. They have done nothing to help their people deal with their feelings of resistance or their need to understand "what's in it for me" (WIIFM). And they will not understand the resistance that appears later and the accompanying delays in implementing the change.

Executives and change leaders in these organizations have created conditions that produce the illusion of commitment via symbolic acts that people feel compelled to take. They still need to work through feelings of resistance, to become comfortable that the outcomes of the change are not threatening, and to explore how the change affects them before they reach a real state of commitment.

Several years ago we experienced a client organization that was implementing a major change process but with very little change-planning. The president had decided to pursue an organization-wide quality improvement effort and was strongly committed to it. He arranged an executive workshop in which the management team was acquainted with the process and a model for planning and managing its implementation. At the end of the workshop the team appeared committed and anxious to move the process forward.

The management team was cautioned against introducing the process prematurely with statements about the importance of the effort and the personal commitment of the executive team. Conducting an assessment of the current situation, both internally and with customers, was recommended to provide data to support the decision to go ahead. It was also recommended that the management team develop specific plans for the implementation before laying out their intentions to the company. The team chose to disregard these recommendations and scheduled meetings with all employees within a few days.

Management was disappointed with the response of the employees. Post-meeting comments indicated a lack of buy-in to the process and why it was being done. Continuing to ignore the initial recommendations, a second round of meetings was held. Management felt that their message had not been heard. Repeating it was necessary for the message to get through. But the reactions to the second meeting were no different.

At this point the recommendations were accepted, an assessment taken, and more specific plans put in place that could be communicated to employees. Armed with specific data from customers, facts regarding their own performance, and additional information on competitors' improvement activities, management then held a third set of meetings. There were follow-up discussions in each department regarding how the process would apply.

Reactions were very different and positive. When asked why they felt differently, management was told that the earlier meetings seemed aimed at getting them charged up, once again, for a new program. They knew that management didn't make important decisions without facts. Yet they saw no specific facts that convinced them that it was important or that management was serious this time. When the third meetings provided answers to their questions and gave them a sense of what it meant for them, they were much more willing to give the process a try.

The initial meetings were those of an organization with no systematic approach to change-planning and management. They did not understand the dynamics of change. No effort was made to help people with their personal responses to the change. The process to prepare for and conduct the third set of meetings employed a much more useful approach to planning for and implementing a major change, with confirming results.

B. Change-Planning and Management Factors

Organizations strong in change-planning and management are aware that people must go through the various phases of responding to the change. They legitimize their reactions and support people through the phases of change. They realize that people cannot simply jump from hearing about a change to fully accepting and committing to it. Some time will be required, and management provides for that in their planning. Following are some ideas for improving the effectiveness of change-planning and management.

1. Use Understanding of the Phases of Change

Some of the factors that make change planning and management effective were described in the minicase above: Provide people with data and facts that have been used by management to choose to change; don't try to introduce change with a lot of hype, especially in lieu of facts — the message won't be believable.

Explain the organization's awareness that there will be reactions to the change, including feelings of resistance and concerns about how it affects each person. Acknowledge that these reactions are normal and appropriate and that time will be provided to discuss people's concerns. Then provide them with an opportunity to explore the implications of the change for themselves. Make this exploration two-way and with their supervisors and managers (this should be taken to apply to middle- and upper-level executives as well as to those at the lowest levels of the organization). Should I be concerned that the changes will negatively impact me personally? Will I have to learn new skills or ways of working or will the change fit into how we operate now? How can we know that getting excited about the change and putting our effort into making it succeed will be worth it vs. having this be another new thing that starts and then dies? And so on. Legitimizing and dealing with these issues helps people move more rapidly through the phases of denial and resistance and on to examination of the change for its benefits and uses. The investment of time in planning and supporting such processes is well worth the effort and is characteristic of organizations high on change planning and management.

2. Minimize Imposed Change and Maximize Participation

Research has demonstrated that participation in decisions to change and/or in planning for the implementation of change has strikingly positive influence on the outcomes of the change. Some of the original research on participation[16] over 60 years ago sought to reduce regular drops in productivity that occurred with each change to new styles in a pajama factory. The drops occurred even though the basic work tasks did not change. The finding of the research confirmed that participation by those doing the work in planning for the changeover virtually eliminated the periods of reduced productivity. Management continued to make the decisions about what styles to produce and when the changes would occur. But the participation of the employees created understanding and buy-in to the change and how it would occur.

Where change-planning and management are important components of change efforts, research like that in the pajama factory leads the organization to seek greater levels of participation by those impacted by a change and the minimizing of imposed change. Wanda Lee, senior VP of PacifiCare, a major HMO, shared experiences that have convinced her organization that changes that effect the doctors in their system will not work unless the doctors participate in the process. Doctors are now part of change processes and, in addition, are trained in change management to improve their ability to participate.

As the capability to function as an ECO increases, so does people's confidence that they will be provided with the opportunity to participate in change decisions, as appropriate, and in planning how to make the change work. In working to increase participation, however, organizations also need to learn to manage expectations about participation. Many managers working to increase participation have told us over the years of their frustration with participative management. Most often their concerns have centered on people's expectations running amok.

When people were told that the organization was moving to implement participative management, discussion and clarification of what that direction meant was missing. Did increased participation mean involvement in all decisions or in how decisions were to be implemented, or both? What criteria would be used to decide when and who would be involved if everyone would not be involved in decisions? Without such discussion, people became excited about the change and expected to be involved in any and all decisions that affected them. Supervisors or managers were challenged and confronted when they informed their people of decisions they had made without participation. To the supervisors it seemed as if the idea of participation had been displaced with expectations that participation equaled abdication.

What is needed in situations of greater participation is for management to provide the boundaries within which the participation will occur. The manager may clearly reserve certain decisions for him/herself. Even with those decisions, however, it may be that there would be participation in plans for how to implement the decisions. With the boundaries clarified, managers can work with their people to build a set of criteria and ground rules for involvement and how they will work. An important example would be the need to establish who gets involved and how decisions are made when time is not available for the entire group to work on the issue. Or, which decisions will involve the group and which will engage subgroups or individuals? Establishing common and shared expectations makes it much easier to manage the participative process.

Our experience tells us that one of the most problematic issues in becoming more participative occurs when the leader of a group implies a greater level of participation than is suggested by his or her subsequent behavior. People quickly pick up signals that indicate the leader has already reached a decision. When a leader's actions communicate that he is not really receptive to participation by others, people quickly learn to sit back and simply wait to hear what the manager has decided. Leaders are much better off letting people know where they stand in making a decision than pretending in any way that the decision is open when it is not.

3. Capitalize On the Energy Released by Change

Energy is released when change occurs. That energy can end up being used in ways that support the change or make implementation more difficult. Where change-planning and management are weak the energy is often exhibited as obstruction and resistance. Consider, for example, the amount of time and energy spent in hallway discussions or behind closed doors when changes are announced or imminent. The expenditure of energy is very high, non-productive, and primarily speculative.

On the other hand, actively involving people in developing plans for implementing a change and making it work positively focuses the energy to the advantage of the people and the organization. Concerns and sources of resistance are addressed in the process and buy-in is developed for the change more easily. Those involved feel ownership of the implementation plan and personally committed to its success.

4. Assess and Develop Readiness for Change

Highly capable organizations in the areas of change planning and management invest the effort needed to assess readiness for change. They create plans to improve readiness and to reduce or eliminate conditions that will contribute to failure. They recognize that the effort involved is minimal compared to that which will be required to recover from a poorly planned and managed change process.

Many questions are asked and the answers used to optimize the probability of success. Is there a leader for the change whose skills are appropriate for the task and whose leadership will be accepted? Are those whose support it critical to success on board or are they likely to be obstacles? If so, what is needed to gain their support or, at a minimum, to prevent them from behaving in ways that could cause the change to fail? What resources and support are needed (time, people, and financial) and have they been allocated? How will the success of the effort be measured? Is there a communication plan in place for the introduction of the change and for keeping people informed of progress? Can the reasons for the change be articulated and supported with logic and fact? Will the people of the organization understand why the change is occurring and what's in it for them? Has an analysis been done of potentially serious problems and plans developed to prevent their occurrence or to minimize their effect? And so on.

Some organizations never ask these questions or ignore the data if they become available. They are so action oriented that processes for developing readiness seem wasteful. Yet they often end up spending even more time after the change is introduced dealing with resistance and other actions required to "sell" the change. Such groups are clearly lacking in change-planning and management and fall at the change-averse or, minimally, change-resistant point of our change orientation scale.

V. Systems Model for Change and Alignment

At higher levels of ECO capability, organizations manage FOR change using "systems thinking." The importance of this approach is based on the reality that organizations are living systems. They are composed of a number of key components that are highly interrelated. Change is one component of the system that impacts the others. Failure to consider this fact leads to changes that produce tension among the system components. Inconsistencies exist that send mixed messages to the people of the organization. For example, are we to believe statements that the new effort is a top priority of management when performance in that area is in no way reflected in the reward system of the organization? Or, how can I be expected to spend at least one hour per week on improvement activities when the structure of my job requires me to be at my workstation eight hours per day? When mixed messages like these exist, people are forced to resolve the issue on their own or to ignore the change and continue to act as they always have.

A key benefit of a systems model is that it forces the organization to look at the change in the context of what already exists as well as to examine the broad range of potential issues of compatibility and consistency. The likelihood of a successful change is greatly enhanced when adjustments are made to the interrelated parts of the system to assure alignment with the change.

The "Seven-S Model"[17] and Weisbord's "Six Box Model"[18] are two widely used systems models. The award criteria for the Malcolm Baldrige Award, although originally developed with a primary emphasis on quality, have continued to evolve from their original form into a broader organizational model. Examination of these award criteria involves consideration of an extensive range of interrelated issues in the areas of change, learning, and improvement discussed in this book.

MANAGING ELEMENTS

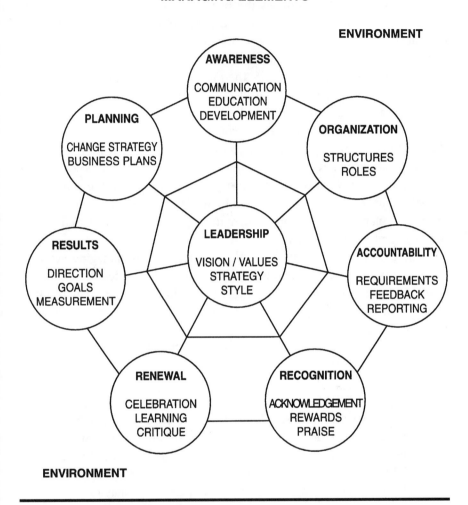

Figure 4.1 The Management System Model. Eight elements of the management process that must be aligned or realigned to support successful change.

A. The Management System Model

A systems model we have found particularly useful is the Management System Model (Figure 4.1). This model was strongly influenced by the work of Weisbord, referenced above. Pieters[19] developed this model for the change process used in organization-wide quality and continuous improvement efforts by clients of The Quality Improvement Company he cofounded.

Prior to implementation of the overall quality improvement process, executives are oriented to the model and its implications. Assessments are conducted of the organization's external environment, with emphasis on its customers and competitors, and of its internal operating practices. The assessment provides data to clarify the present state of the organization and to arm the management team with factual data to confirm their decision to move ahead. The data also provide data for communicating the "why" to the people of the organization in a way which reduces perceptions of pursuit of the latest fad and the beginning of a process likely to fail. Creation of a vision statement about where the organization intends to go also precedes implementation. In addition, support is provided for organizing the work of the management team along with written manuals and tools. The support tools guide the planning of the implementation process and are based on the Management System Model.

The eight components of the model are referred to as managing elements. Each is examined for the actions needed to support a successful implementation and to assure consistency among the various elements. The resulting plan is shared with the people of the organization with regular updates on progress and results.

A brief look at the issues addressed by each of the managing elements follows:

- **Leadership**: What is needed to allow all members of the management team to accept and be willing to work to see this change fully implemented? How do we assess our current situation, both internally and externally? How do we state our vision for the future in a way that will guide us down this path and elicit support from our people? What changes are necessary in our personal behavior, other than verbal support, to convey to others that we are fully committed to the effort?

- **Awareness**: How will we communicate with people about our decision to implement this change and why? What ongoing or new communication processes are needed to keep people informed of progress and results? How do we orient our people, providing them the opportunity to explore the new direction in a way that facilitates their buy-in to the change? What training is needed to provide knowledge and skills for effectively operating in the ways expected as a result of the change?

- **Results:** What specific results do we want to achieve as a result of this change and when? How will we measure and report the results of the change? How do the overall results we are pursuing get translated into goals and objectives for all those affected by the change?
- **Organization:** What are our roles, within the management team and in the implementation process in our own areas? What roles are people impacted by the change expected to play? How do we use our existing structure in implementing the change? What additional roles or structures are needed to support the change effort?
- **Planning:** How shall we develop the overall plan for the implementation of the change? How do we maintain and update the plan as we move forward? What plans are to be developed by those at other levels and what will be our involvement in the review and approval of such plans?
- **Accountability:** How shall we measure and ask people to account for their progress in the implementation? What process will be used, and at what frequency, for people throughout the organization to report progress of their plans and results achieved?
- **Recognition:** How will contributions and results be recognized? How will performance in the area of the change be integrated into the organization's existing reward and recognition systems?
- **Renewal:** What must be done to sustain the change and the new processes involved? How do we learn from experience so the processes can be improved and not fall into disuse? How shall we celebrate progress and results in a manner that will invigorate the effort and renew our energy for the change?

When teams planning change deal with questions associated with each of these elements, they have used systems thinking to guide their work. It is not unusual for teams to ask which of the managing elements is most important and which could be eliminated. It then becomes necessary to remind them of the interrelated nature of a system and that change in one of the elements impacts all of the others. Without the effort to address and align all of the elements the effectiveness of the change will be impaired.

We have utilized the Management System Model with over 200 management teams. The organizations involved varied from quite small (under 100) to very large (20,000+) and are involved in businesses ranging from travel agencies to chemicals to high tech to health care to glass manufacturing and so on. Our experience with the model has convinced us that it addresses the primary areas of concern when planning and managing a change. In addition, client executives have frequently shared the perception that this model has broad application to any significant change effort.

B. Selection of a Systems Model for Change

Organizations high on managing for change select a systems model to guide their change efforts. In general, which model is chosen is less important than selecting one the organization finds useful and will apply consistently. Change leaders and planners are educated about the model and the importance of a systems orientation, including awareness of the larger systems within which they exist. Management expects plans for change to address the full scope of change required to bring the affected system into realignment.

C. Use of Systems Models for Prevention

Systems thinking can be used to minimize or prevent problems with change at any level of an organization. A simple tool helps guide the thinking of work teams planning to implement changes in their work process. It helps them consider the other people or groups that are part of the overall business process they are involved with. This tool is a solution–effect diagram (see Figure 4.2). It is a variation of the tool commonly used to isolate root causes in problem solving processes, the cause–effect diagram. In this case, however, the solution (change) to be implemented is examined for its likely effects (both positive and negative) on others in the system. Those planning the change use the tool to consider issues like (a) who will be impacted by the change, (b) how should we involve and communicate with them about our plans, (c) are we likely to produce effects that create more problems in other parts of our system than we solve, and so on. From the analysis, modifications of change plans and improvements in communication often result. Organizations high on managing FOR change will include tools like the solution–effect diagram in training people to plan and execute change effectively. And they will be expected to use the tool prior to implementing changes that affect others.

Systems thinking and consideration of the system effects of a change are not included in introducing change in organizations with little or no capacity to manage FOR change. Even the effects on the immediate internal customers

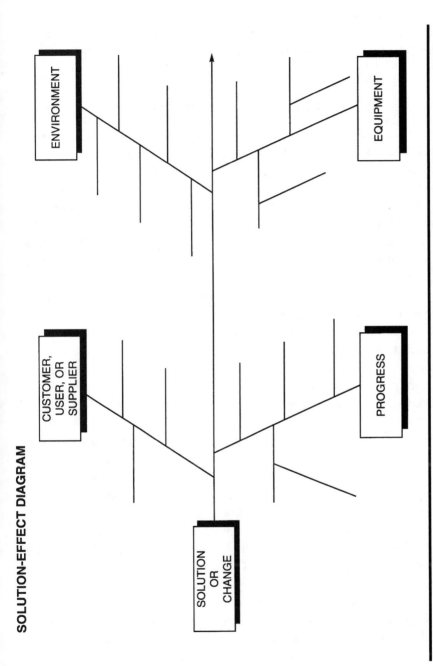

SOLUTION-EFFECT DIAGRAM

Figure 4.2 Solution–effect diagram. Identifies potential impacts of change and allows planning that prevents creation of new problems in change implementations.

or suppliers of the group making the change may not be taken into account. These organizations often experience additional time and costs in implementing change or need to reverse decisions to change because they fail to understand the systems nature of work processes and organizations.

VI. Change as a Business Strategy

The issue in this area deals with the extent to which an organization has an explicit strategy to lead and create change in its businesses. At one extreme would be organizations that manage themselves to preserve and protect the business as it is. Avoiding change is a more apt description of their strategy — to "milk" the existing businesses and only change when customers or competitive conditions leave them no option, or strategize to protect what they have and be prepared to fight off those who challenge the established business.

A number of years ago, Corning, Inc. ventured into the field of plate glass for automobile windshields, a new business for them. They brought a competitively priced product with significantly improved safety features. They were attacking a large and entrenched market. A limited number of large competitors with a huge investment in the existing technology owned the market. For them, change was not welcome given the installed base of equipment and the profitability of the business. Their defensive strategy was to reduce prices and tough it out. The strategy worked and the competitors returned to sharing a very profitable business without being forced to change their basic technology.

For other organizations, creation of change is an explicit business strategy and the organization is designed to make change happen. These organizations invest heavily in becoming leaders and staying there. Their strategy is to define the competitive agenda and to force others to respond to the changes they introduce. Their strategy is based on creating more uncertainty in their competitors' environments. The competitors observe the products or services being offered and the ability of the leader to realize premium pricing from the added value they are providing. This makes the business very attractive. Then, while the competition is scurrying to catch the leader or innovator, that leader continues to drive itself forward, reinvesting the earnings from their leadership products or services in more advanced products and services or technology. And, when others are about to match the leader, the leader takes steps to create even more uncertainty. First, they reduce prices. At the lower prices they continue to operate profitably while the entering competitor struggles to compete. Second, they introduce another generation of product or an improved technology that enhances performance and maintains a leading position the others must again pursue.

For these organizations, being in a position to drive the competitive thrust is a critical part of their business strategy. Unless they can achieve and maintain a leading position in their markets, e.g., being first or second, they will divest the business or leave the market. Hewlett Packard's product strategy requires new products to clearly surpass the performance of available products and make a specific technical contribution. 3M has created an environment that promotes *intrapreneurial* behavior, persistence and the development of "new" and "useful" ideas into innovative businesses where they lead. Those who would compete with 3M have little choice but to invest energy in following their lead and scrambling to becoming an alternate source. Intel has used this strategy with incredible success since the founding of the company in the late 1960s. The HP, 3M, and Intel strategies are built on the basic values of those organizations and the creation of uncertainty for competitors is a result. These organizations are managed FOR change and change that leads is clearly a part of the business strategy.

Declaring change to be part of a business strategy, however, is insufficient to make the organization strong in managing FOR change. The stabilizing base of the organization needs to place high value on change, learning, and improvement and to trust the people of the organization to behave responsibly in contributing to the change and innovation required for leading. The operational processes of the organization must also be aligned with the strategies for change and the values. For example, where change is an important business strategy, it is important that structures like small and independent divisions or temporary multifunctional development teams are created to foster change, and innovation in products or services.

Changes or innovations in the way customers experience a product or service is another way to make change part of a business strategy. Disney's obsession with cleanliness and the training of its people as members of the cast of the ongoing show at its theme parks were leading changes that continue to create a standard for would-be competitors to chase. Continuing changes produce an ongoing challenge for competitors to match the experience of customers (guests) at Disney attractions.

Motorola has used change in product and service quality as a key business strategy. Winning one of the early Malcolm Baldrige National Quality Awards put pressures on competitors as well as suppliers to respond. Continuing to move forward with the Six-Sigma target for product defects and errors and institutionalizing their quality process throughout the company around the world has maintained change and improvement as part of their business strategy and the creation of uncertainty and the need for competitors to respond.

In general, as business uncertainty increases, the value of change as a business strategy grows — not only to support operating at the change-friendly or change-seeking level of advanced ECOs, but as a driving and proactive strategy that forces others to consume resources while the change leader moves further ahead.

VII. Adaptive Leadership

The capacity to manage FOR change is heavily dependent on the adaptability of the leaders of the organization. In some situations, the inability to adapt to conditions requiring change may result in a life-or-death situation for the organization. In other situations, the absence of needed flexibility in leaders does not threaten survival but can have a serious blocking effect on the overall capacity of the organization for change.

A. Adaptation of Organizational Direction or Strategy

Many case studies have been written about the failure of organizational leaders to recognize and adapt to changing conditions in their markets and environment. Rather than shift direction or change strategy, the leaders have maintained the course despite indications of impending trouble. Some have stubbornly held onto strategies because of their personal ownership of them. Consider the time and market share losses that occurred before American automobile manufacturers modified the strategy of building large cars for the U.S. market or tackled the challenge of continuous quality improvement.

Other leaders have been insulated from trouble signals by their people due to an unwillingness to deal with bad news or a propensity to "shoot messengers." They may disclaim the threat of new technology or feel locked into older technology. The slowness or refusal to adapt has left many organizations vulnerable and on the road to failure. The loss of long-established positions in steel making or television or audio systems stemmed, at least in part, from denial of what was happening with foreign competitors. Instead of adapting, attempts were make to make the problem go away and seek protection from "predatory" practices through the government.

Adaptive leaders set their sensors on "receive," and stay sensitive to signals that change is needed or would provide new opportunities. Mike Hackworth, former CEO of Cirrus Logic, described a major shift in product direction and market strategy in the company's 1997 annual report. He commented to us that he had felt the need to reexamine his direction and, as a result of intense personal deliberations, confronted a threat to the organization from continuing to pursue the existing product strategy. This meant leaving some markets where the company had at one time had real strength. It meant potentially losing some key development resources with expertise in the areas being abandoned. Yet he knew that the adaptation was critical to the long-term health of the company. He prepared and proposed new direction to his board after discussing his plans with key executives. Extended discussions led to board support for the new direction despite significant costs associated with the change.

Systron-Donner Inertial is a division of BEI Sensors and Systems Company that has been a supplier of specialized motion sensors to the defense industry. Sensing the shifts in spending for defense and the reductions of contract opportunities, the executives actively sought new applications for their products. Dr. Asad Madni, President and CEO of BEI, parent of Systron-Donner, described the nature of the adaptations the leaders of the company have made to support a shift from their primary business. A major new opportunity was identified in automobile sensing and control systems. Today, the company is producing products for the auto industry at rates significantly above previous levels while working to expand its product line and customer base. And they are preparing for further adaptation of internal design and operating practices for competing in the commercial, non-defense marketplace. This includes the ability to meet the difficult auto company specifications yet produce a product that sells for less than 10% of previous products.

Leaders who manage FOR change understand that becoming an ECO requires that they, too, remain flexible and adaptive. This need applies to the direction and strategies they pursue as well as to their personal style. They recognize that whether or not the organization creates greater capability as an ECO is heavily dependent on its behavior and the messages it sends regarding the importance and value of change.

B. Adaptability and Leadership Styles

Fixed and inflexible styles of leadership are not characteristic of ECOs. Nor do they allow an organization to manage FOR change. Emphasis is on treating people consistently. Variation in leader behavior based on the experience and abilities of the individuals involved is believed to be inappropriate. The same belief applies to the idea of modifying a leader's approach based on the nature of the task or the conditions existing when the task is being planned or executed. People are assumed to be incapable of understanding the idea of "different strokes for different folks." Or, in some situations, the leaders have simply evolved a limited range of options for how they manage.

One executive we worked with saw the world very clearly as black or white. Shades of gray or subtly different options were a nuisance, only muddying the water. This characteristic created frequent either-or and win-lose situations which, with his managerial style, he always won. People soon learned not to disagree and the executive lost the benefit of many contributions his people could make. Consulting efforts with this executive focused on helping him identify and explore a wider range of options leading to improved decision making and win-win outcomes. Continuing his or anyone else's inflexible leadership style always works to limit change and creativity.

Extensive work with the Blake and Mouton "Managerial Grid"[20] a number of years ago provided us with insights into the assumptions and beliefs of leaders that influence the flexibility of their behavior. The research base behind the Managerial Grid had identified two independent dimensions of management behavior. The first was labeled "concern for production" and the second "concern for people" (see Figure 4.3). The dimensions are scaled from 1 to 9 to represent low, moderate, and high levels of concern. Managers whose style, i.e., behavior, effectively integrated their concerns for people and production at a very high level (9,9) were found by the research to be more effective, producing high levels of teamwork and achieving better results. The styles that are high on one concern and low on the other are often referred to as autocratic (9,1) and human relations (1,9) styles. The research found that those styles produced poorer results. The midrange style (5,5) attempts to balance and trade off the concerns and yields mediocre outcomes. The low-low style (1,1) is a nondescript, laissez-faire style that neither produces results nor energizes people.

Team-oriented managers (9,9) work from a different set of beliefs about how concern for production and concern for people fit together. They believe that the best results are achieved by appropriately involving the people doing the work in creating common goals and in the planning and managing of

THE MANAGERIAL GRID®

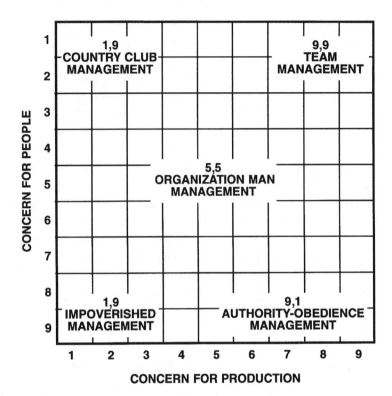

Figure 4.3 The Managerial Grid ®*. Highlights five managerial styles that vary in the magnitude of "concern for people" and "concern for production" and how these concerns are integrated. Team management (9,9) is an adaptive leadership style. (*Registered trademark of Scientific Methods, Inc. Adapted from Blake, R. and Mouton, J., *The New Managerial Grid III*, 1964, 1978, 1985, reproduced by permission from Gulf Publishing Co., Houston, TX, 800-231-6275, all rights reserved.)

the work. They further believe that people receive the greatest satisfaction at work from the achievement of targeted results. High-level managers' concern for people and concern for production generates synergy. The synergy results from effective teamwork and the results obtained are more satisfying for those involved and for the organization.

Failure to integrate concern for production and concern for people at a high level is built on an underlying belief that there is a zero-sum relationship between the concerns. That is, using the numbering of the managerial grid scales, the total of the two values must equal ten. You cannot increase concern for people without reducing concern for production and vice-versa. As a result managers with these styles find it difficult to change and tend to be inflexible in their behavior.

On the other hand, a managerial style that integrates people and production concerns at a high level is characterized by adaptability. It is a participative style but one that uses participation in the most productive ways for the people and the organization. Involvement of one or more or all of the group of people reporting to the manager is determined via consideration of a set of criteria the manager uses that are known to his or her people. For example, when time is not available for a group discussion, the manager will either make the decision or empower someone else to do so and inform the group later. If the subject to be dealt with requires acceptance from the entire group, he or she will involve the entire group in producing a consensus. If only one or two of several people are affected by a decision or the only ones who have the information needed, they may be the only ones involved. In other situations, the manager may elect to involve someone because of the opportunity for learning that exists, not because they have a specific contribution to make.

The style of an adaptive leader does not require that all people be dealt with in the same manner. Differences in role, in experience, in need, in the nature of the task itself, and so on guide the choice of how the manager approaches a situation. The people in the manager's group understand the criteria for the choices and also know they will be involved and informed when appropriate. These managers do not experience the difficulty of managing their people's expectations discussed above because they have been clarified, discussed, and understood in advance.

Increased teamwork and efficiency in groups with more adaptive leaders also supports dealing with change more effectively. The managers are more proactive and stay informed through open communication with their people. When change appears or is imposed, high levels of trust and established communication and decision processes address the need more efficiently. Less resistance and wasted effort disrupt the ongoing work of the group, and the team pulls together to minimize the effects on achievement of established objectives.

Organizations high in managing FOR change encourage adaptive leadership. Opportunities to learn the skills involved and to build one's competency are made available. Positive human values support trust and participation by all. Systematic reviews and critiques of how changes are managed produce learning that highlights the benefit of adaptive and team-oriented styles of managing.

VIII. Change Orientation of Policies, Procedures, and Controls

Classical listings of the functions of a manager include planning, organizing, leading, directing, and controlling. Many years of observation of organizational behavior has convinced us that "control" is the least understood of these functions. Disturbingly large proportions of organizations we have seen appear to take control to mean something that is done to other people by managers.

In these organizations, policy and procedure manuals spell out how things are to be accomplished. Often the steps defined to get something done are helpful in that they provide guidance on what to do, assure consistency, and keep everyone from having to figure out what to do on their own. But the overall procedures don't stop with guidance on what to do to get the task accomplished. They add a variety of levels of review and approval requirements that are intended to achieve control but, in fact, are designed to limit people's ability to act and/or to protect the territory of those who must approve. The continual hue and cry we have heard about the need to rid organizations of hierarchy and bureaucracy are really aimed at these restrictive policies, procedures, and controls.

A. Restricting Change with Policies, Procedures, and Controls

Organizations that are not being managed FOR change are filled with rules and procedures that limit the ability to act. Instead of designing the policies to facilitate getting things done, the written materials add steps and road-blocks that increase the time required to act and severely test the persistence of the people who need to act. Two, three, or more levels of signature approval or "sign-off" by administrative people in other functional areas create frustration and delays, often in situations where the person seeking to get something done clearly knows that the approval signatures are virtually automatic.

We observed such a control and people's reaction to it in a manufacturing plant. Employees doing installation of equipment or maintenance work were provided tools from a tool crib. To assure the need for the tool and to reduce instances of theft, the procedure for getting a tool involved filling out a form and getting the supervisor's signature. Workers complained that the procedure frequently led to delays in getting jobs done because they could not find their supervisor and the needed tools would not be released to them without the signed form. The result was that the supervisors, with great pressure to keep things running and not wanting to be the source of delays, elected to presign piles of the forms and leave them in their desks. Everyone was made aware of this. They could pick up several forms at any time, fill them out as needed (for work or home) and obtain tools without delay. This action helped meet the objective of keeping the operation up and running, but also resulted in an increased flow of tools from the crib beyond what would be expected from normal wear or from lost or misplaced tools.

Increased control was achieved by a simple change that allowed each person who needed a tool to sign for it on his or her own signature. No artificial delays were created by the new procedure. And the organization gained the ability to identify the users and consumers of the tools resulting in reduced theft. The changed procedure now facilitated getting the work of the organization done instead of blocking it.

As the example demonstrates, one of the effects of restrictive and dysfunctional controls is to release creative energy. People create ways to get the job done despite what they perceive as attempts to thwart them in achieving their objectives. In organizations that grant very limited signature authority for purchase requisitions, which many readers are sure to have experienced in the early stages of their careers, one of the first things people learn is to split requisitions into portions where additional signatures are not required. Peers willingly communicate the strategy to newcomers: "If you need ten items and the total value exceeds your signature authority, simply write two or more requisitions, each of which is within the range of your authority," Knowing that their supervisor will approve the requisitions anyway, why waste the time. Of course the "work around" of the established limits increases the cost to the organization of processing additional requisitions and the cost of processing multiple invoices and checks through accounts payable. Yet we have observed this as common practice in many organizations. And the organizations continue such policies because to change them would lead to "loss of control." They fail to consider the idea that creating the conditions to maximize the exercise of responsible self-control would, in fact, lead to greater control and eliminate barriers to the rapid change or improvement required in the faster moving world of today.

Another example of wasted time, effort, and financial resources is to be found in the process of applying for approval of capital spending. Most organizations operate with a highly controlled procedure in this arena and this makes good financial sense. Yet the processes end up severely flawed. Appropriation requests, or whatever the organization chooses to call them, are written by the party with the need to spend the capital. Written explanations of the reasons for the expenditure are required with financial justification. Calculations of internal rates of return (IRR) or payback periods are developed for testing against the organization's internal criteria. We have observed the process of writing, submission, recalculation, and rewriting of capital proposals that have gone through multiple iterations at each level of approval authority. Eventually the hurdles are passed and the proposal approved many months after its original development.

The flaw in the process is not in the desire to invest in projects that are based on a real business need with a reasonable financial return. The problem comes from the gyrations and game playing the process produces, to no real end. Numbers are inflated and manipulated to meet certain criteria, whether or not the end numbers represent reality or simply what must be shown to pass the final approval hurdle. Often these gyrations take place on investments that everyone knows will be approved from the beginning. And the irony is that nearly all of the organizations where the process works as described have no formal, post-project review process to assess performance to projections or, at a minimum, to provide learning that might make future submissions more accurate. Yet these organizations continue to use such processes with the feeling that somehow they are exercising appropriate financial control. They are not managing FOR change.

Another characteristic of organizations with restrictive controls is that they do not impose controls or set policies on who is legitimized to establish policies and who must review and approve policy statements. Embedded in these organizations seems to be a significant concern for control and a set of assumptions about people that predicts they will run amok unless their behavior is controlled by others. People in almost any area are allowed to develop and distribute policies that apply to their own area. In one organization we worked with, the facilities department inserted itself in the signature approval loop for all purchases of equipment, whether a PC or postage meter or an entire new set of office furnishings. When asked why, the explanation was that they had been uninformed of some purchases in the past that required facilities changes. To prevent that problem they demanded to be informed via approval authority on purchase requisitions for all equipment when, in fact, the same purpose would have been served by providing them copies of all of the requisitions. But in this organization that was low in managing FOR change, they were allowed to place themselves in the loop with no need for approval or review of the impact.

Administrative groups are given a dual responsibility to support others and to administer controls. The dual responsibilities frequently are in direct conflict. And the concern of these groups with maintaining power and control is generally the winner. Human resources administrators are often perceived as roadblocks for their tendency to rely on written policies rather than seek solutions for the individual or manager they are asked to support. Similar perceptions are not unusual for people in such functions as facilities, purchasing, expense reimbursements, information systems, travel departments, industrial engineering, and so on. Instead of providing the support function they are assigned, these groups learn to rely on documented policies and procedures and their particular interpretation of their meaning in any situation. Where this condition exists, the policies unleash the creative energies of people for getting things done. The organization often ends up with less control as a direct result of the policies. Such organizations put themselves at the change-averse or change-resistant level of orientation to change.

B. Policies, Procedures, and Controls That Build ECO Capability

Organizations that are strong in managing FOR change work to create policies and controls that help people get things done. Their stabilizing base conveys trust in people. Emphasis is on creating conditions that maximize the ability of individuals to act freely but responsibly. Nordstrom is revered for its intensity and the extent to which its people will go to service and satisfy a customer. Yet those people are guided by a single rule which tells them to use their best judgment in all situations. No rigid set of policies and procedures are in place or approvals required before acting. Do what your good sense and judgment tells you is right.

A fundamental difference exists between organizations whose policies and controls free people to act vs. those that are restrictive. They understand that people behave more responsibly when they are trusted to be responsible. They know that they strive to live up to positive expectations but might also live down to minimal or negative expectation. This is sometimes referred to as the self-fulfilling prophecy. If a manager and one's colleagues believe in and trust someone, that person will do everything in his/her power to avoid letting them down and to live up to their expectations.

An organization's policies, procedures, and controls send clear and unmistakable messages about what the organization believes about its people. Positive beliefs reflected in such documents are energizing and uplifting for members of the organization. Instead of finding ways to work around any rules or procedures, people use them to guide their actions. HP is commonly referenced when discussing organizations with a positive set of beliefs and values. A former colleague who recently retired from HP provided a clear example of how those values affected him as he retired. Previous employers had required that he sign formal documents pledging to protect proprietary information and not to enter into situations which directly competed with them. When leaving HP, he inquired about whether signing such a statement was required. He was told that it was not and that the company trusted that he would use his knowledge discretely and professionally. His comment to us was that he felt a significantly greater commitment to avoid disclosure of information than had been true with any previous employer as a result of the trust the company placed in him and his judgment.

Organizations like HP and Nordstrom's also help people to behave responsibly by being open with data and information about the organization, its direction and goals, and both the organization's and the individual's performance. With this information a person can be confident of the appropriateness of his or her actions. Organizations at the other extreme hoard data under the guise of sharing only what people "need to know," assuming that the organization is better able to make that determination than the people themselves. The lack of information forces people to make guesses about what is needed or appropriate and to be limiting and conservative in their willingness to change or take risk. These organizations have limited their capacity for change, knowingly or not.

With positive policies and control processes, people feel free to act and to improvise, as needed, knowing that their actions will not be second-guessed. They do not feel the need to check and get approvals, because it is unnecessary. Where negative policies and control processes exist, however, action is often delayed and not innovative. The policies and controls signal that risk taking is not valued and decisions that go wrong are likely to be refuted or punished. These are limiting practices for organizations needing to increase capability as an ECO.

C. Challenging Embedded Policies, Procedures, and Controls

Many of an organization's policies and controls are deeply enmeshed in its history and operating practices. They have existed unchallenged and unchanged for long periods of time, often without being updated and beyond their useful life. They have, in many ways, become so much a part of the organization's way of functioning that they either are not questioned or are known by all to be sacred cows and not to be attacked.

This is one area in the managing FOR change section, therefore, that is particularly important for an organization to examine. Actions that challenge the appropriateness of controls might be perceived as questioning a fundamental function required for managing the organization. Yet this is also an area in which the growth of restrictive actions is common and one that exerts great influence on people's effectiveness.

The ABC model discussed earlier may be a useful tool for assessing the underlying beliefs and assumptions of the organization's controls. Beginning with a restatement and examination of the desired results of specific policies or controls, an analysis can be made of whether or not those results are happening or if the policies are being worked around or avoided. Making the assumptions behind the policy or control explicit will lead to an understanding of the positive or more negative nature of those beliefs. Where greater capacity to operate as an Ever-Changing Organization exists, creating a more positive set of assumptions will allow redesign of the policy or control to facilitate the work of the people of the organization and to increase its capacity for change.

IX. Work Design

Does the design of people's work support or discourage ongoing change? Where organizations are strong in managing FOR change, everyone's work includes responsibility for change. Carrying out the work processes of the job and achieving the desired results is always a major responsibility. But it is not the full job. Everyone is also charged with the responsibility to examine his or her work and seek to improve performance on an ongoing basis.

What happens that wastes time and resources and how can that waste be eliminated? If an error or defect occurs, what caused the problem? How can the cause be eliminated and prevented from occurring again? Do all of us doing the same work do it in the same way or has someone developed a better way we can all use? Do we have the information we need for performing at our best? What else do we need? Are there ways to complete our work that will make things better for whoever has the next step in the process? Is the output of our work inconsistent? — If so, how can we reduce its variability? What would need to change for our work output to improve? And so on.

People are not just told that change and improvement are part of their responsibility. They are provided needed time for this activity to make the work legitimate. They participate in planning their own work including setting goals and agreeing on work assignments. They help plan changes in their areas and contribute ideas for how to make the changes successful. They measure their performance and get feedback about the results achieved so that opportunities or needs for improvement can be identified. Supervisors are responsible for identifying and eliminating obstacles to improvement and making it easier for their people to identify and implement change.

A. Managing Your Own Work

People find their work meaningful and satisfying when they are involved in managing it. They have responsibility for carrying out the work task, and the work design also includes responsibility for the planning and control functions of the work.[21] On the other hand, work designs that involve retention of the planning and control aspects of the work by the supervisor have little meaning. People are relegated to simply doing assigned tasks and achieving targets determined by the supervisor. They experience little meaning and satisfaction from the work and withdraw their energy. The work becomes just a job where time is spent in exchange for money and benefits. Lack of information and performance feedback prevents people from making changes aimed at improvement. Concern with finding ways to change or improve is minimal since those tasks are reserved for others. Change, in fact, is likely to produce a flood of resistance and to have negative impact on performance.

A CEO client became aware of the difference when his secretary invited him to an amateur auto race where she and her husband were competing. Upon returning he described the amazing efforts and excitement of the competitors in the race. He observed that no one was paid for their effort, but everyone worked constantly and intensely throughout the weekend of the race. He asked, "What do we do that keeps the company from getting that kind of motivation and energy from our people?" It was pointed out to him that the participants were engaged in managing all aspects of their work, i.e., they planned, organized, controlled, and "did it." Most nonmanagerial jobs in the organizations only involved "doing it." The improvement process this CEO implemented shortly thereafter was designed to add planning and control responsibility to the work of all employees.

B. Autonomous or Semi-Autonomous Work Teams

As the rate of change in the world has increased, more traditional, boss-centered forms of work design have become less functional except in highly stable environments. Not only is the work less meaningful and acceptable to newer generations, such work designs fail to utilize the resources available. Ideas for change are limited or withheld. Opportunities for improvement are not sought or expected.

What has emerged in more uncertain environments is the use of work teams that link people involved in an overall process or component of a process into a single work unit. When these units are provided with targeted outputs or objectives, they are sometimes referred to as a "semiautonomous" work team. Given the targets, the team members are trained and given the autonomy to manage the work of the team. This includes things such as work assignments, break schedules, cross-training of members to increase flexibility, measurement and tracking of performance, quality assurance, workplace layout, and so on. Supervisor's roles shift to providing direction on objectives and to managing the boundaries around the team to optimize their opportunity for success. Gerald Pieters was involved with an early implementation of these ideas at the Orem, Utah plant of Signetics Corporation in the mid-1970s. In that process, supervisory titles were changed to "team advisor" to reflect the new role.

The concept of autonomous work teams (vs. semiautonomous) is very similar. The primary difference is in the freedom of the teams to establish their own specific goals. They are provided data on what is needed and when it is to be delivered to a customer as well as information regarding backlogs and inventory. In both situations the level of involvement of team members in managing their own work is very high. Ideas for change and improvement come from the group or via help the group might request from other functions such as process or industrial engineering, quality, or training. While resistance to change will still be a part of the teams' responses to imposed change, other changes and improvements are much more common. And they are implemented with the ownership of the team. These concepts have become more and more useful in organizations in more rapidly changing environments that need increased ECO capability. A valuable reference for those seeking more information in this area is the book *Work Redesign* by Hackman and Oldham.[22]

X. Use of Change Agents

In the face of increasing change the use of people with specific training and skills in the area of change is also increasing. Many organizations today employ people as change agents to provide support to managers and groups dealing with needs for change, improvement, and learning. The function of these specialists is not to manage change but to support others in the execution of their responsibilities for planning and implementing change.

Pieters[23] argued in the early 1980s that the emergence of specialists in fields such as organization development (OD) was a natural progression of the way other functional specialties evolved. Each evolved to a function that moved beyond the capacity of owners or managers as organizations grew in size and complexity from one-person businesses to much larger institutions. The individual craftsman would hire someone to take examples of his wares to show to others and bring back orders so he could continue to use his specialized talents. Thus the emergence of a sales function. The history of the Dutch multinational, N. V. Philips, relates that one Philips brother started the original business of producing light bulbs. However, for the business to grow, he decided to bring his brother in to handle the selling and delivery of the products, a task for which he was better suited.

Another example would be the hiring and training of apprentice craftsmen to take on the task of producing the wares to free up the owner to procure materials (before the specialization of purchasing was developed) or to deliver completed work to customers (before specialists in shipping and distribution were used). In more recent times, more advanced specialist functions have developed in areas like information processing and services and software development.

None of the specialists took the manager/owner's responsibilities away. Rather they were brought into existence when the need for the function developed and the skills required to handle it effectively moved beyond the reach of people in existing roles. The same has happened with the emergence of specialized roles as change agents. When change was an occasional thing the manager handled the task. As the rate of change accelerated and more specialized tools and processes developed to assist the process of change, managers began to use specialists to assist them. In today's world it is not uncommon to see the existence of departments staffed with OD specialists or others charged with operating as agents of change.

Recognition of this trend can be seen in the consulting practices of the major public accounting firms. All have hired or developed people to operate as change management specialists. Some, such as PricewaterhouseCoopers, have invested in centers where study and analysis has produced systematic consulting models and tools to aid clients with major change or reengineering projects. Professional organizations have evolved such as the Organization Development Network and the OD Division of the American Society of Training and Development. Many thousands of people who specialize in the area of change are members of these associations.

Advanced degrees are offered by an increasing number of universities and institutes in the field of organizational effectiveness and change. As the quality and continuous improvement movement has continued, many institutions are offering specialized degrees or certifications in that area. And a substantial portion of the training of these specialists involves training related to many of the areas of managing FOR change we have been discussing and the development of the consulting and interpersonal skills needed for effectiveness as a change agent.

Organizations that recognize the importance of building their capacity for change employ change agents in a variety of ways. They might assist executives and management teams with analyses of their capacity for change and in the implementation of initiatives to increase that capacity, i.e., in becoming more of an ECO. They might be assigned to support and coach individual managers or team leaders in making changes to their leadership practices to a more change-friendly or change-seeking style. Some may be assigned to a full-time role in support of the management of a business unit or key function to support ongoing improvement of effectiveness and results.

Our experience as an internal change agent included 13 years as a member of a top management team. Consulting and change-agent support covered a wide range of key corporate agendas. Improving the capital assets planning and allocation process, the design of more humane and effective processes for managing downsizing, improvement of product development and introduction processes to reduce time-to-market, corporate restructuring, support to the design and implementation of a corporate-wide quality improvement process, and so on. These are just a few of the areas where our work as a change agent took us.

A more limited change-agent role involves the use of part- or full-time group facilitators. Their specific training and skills are focused on team dynamics and meeting effectiveness. They might be available on an as-needed basis to facilitate modification of group processes that are inhibiting results. Or, they might be assigned the task of assisting a team leader in planning and managing meetings to assure continued growth of his or her team and the output it produces. In many of the client organizations supported by The Quality Improvement Company, the people trained as internal trainers were also assigned an ongoing facilitation task. They were available to team leaders or their improvement teams when either felt bogged down or unsure of how to move ahead with their tasks. The help provided might involve identifying sources of confusion or conflict. They might clarify a planned process for problem solving or process improvement or refresh the team's skills and use of tools. Their involvement in some cases would require only a few minutes of observation and discussion. In others a more extensive assessment of issues and planning of changes was required to help the group back on track.

Organizations that do not manage FOR change do not make use of change agents. They are seen as a frill, or the costs involved are considered non-value-added costs. Many continue to think of the field of OD, if they are aware of it, in terms of the reputation developed 40 years ago as a "touchy-feely" thing only concerned with making people feel good. Being locked into that perception prevents change in their willingness to use OD specialists or other change agents. They remain unaware of the ongoing evolution in the field and the increasing capacity of change agents to support the improvement of business performance and results.

The use of change agents in organizations managed FOR change is not built on softness but on the requirement for measurable improvements in business results. There is a strong expectation that what is learned in the change process will be captured to support continued improvement and results. These organizations know that they have a right to expect change agents to do whatever they can to transfer their tools and skills to others who will use them for similar change efforts in the future. This not only benefits the organization, it frees up the change agents from repeatedly doing the same work. The organization can then employ them for support with the continuing onslaught of issues needing change or for moving to higher levels of change capacity.

XI. Managing FOR Change Summary

As you reflect on the issues raised in this chapter, consider the great range of capacity as an ECO represented by organizations that would be assessed a high or strong in each of the areas covered. These organizations understand and use change instead of fighting or ignoring it and considering change the enemy. They comprehend the human dynamics of change and the importance of communication and participation as part of effective change processes. Change is a legitimate part of everyone's life and is supported to make that life at work more satisfying and meaningful. Obstacles to change have been removed and processes are in place to identify and eliminate others that might appear. The organization has been designed or modified to make change easy and valued as a strategic weapon.

At the other end of these issues are organizations with a dire lack of built-in capacity for change. Frustration with change is undoubtedly high, and it is treated as something that the organization hopes will stop happening. Resources are continually diverted to deal with problems or external forces for change that were not anticipated or put off. There is a strong probability that the design of these organizations is misaligned with the capacity for change required for success and survival.

Determining the extent to which your organization is managing FOR change is one of the important parts of assessing your current status as an Ever-Changing Organization. Assessment of the stabilizing base that has been created and the extent to which you have developed and are using needed processes for continuous improvement and continuous learning provide the other pieces of the puzzle. These assessments, placed in the context of the demand for change capacity that arises, or will arise, from your business environment, point to areas needing change to reach the level of ECO capacity you require.

5 | Continuous Improvement

I. Introduction

The focus of this chapter will be on features of continuous improvement (CI) efforts and their relationship to the process of becoming an Ever-Changing Organization. Our intention in not to prescribe a continuous improvement process or to evaluate and compare processes that are available. Instead, we highlight ten characteristics of continuous improvement methodologies that influence the organization's capacity as an ECO. Where little has been done to establish these features, the organization has failed to create a viable continuous improvement process and unable to address needed growth in ECO capability. As the features become an integral part of continuous improvement processes, ECO capability is increased and the organization becomes more change friendly or change seeking in nature.

A key premise of this chapter is that no organization with intentions to increase ECO capacity can hope to do so without a well-designed and managed continuous improvement process. And, the process must be organization-wide and actively managed from the top. It cannot be simply an annual approach to setting targets for lower costs or more inventory turns. Nor can it be a limited set of projects that involve a small percentage of the people of the organization and still be considered a continuous improvement effort we associate with becoming an ECO.

Charles Harwood, when he was president of Signetics Corporation, initiated a very successful, organization-wide quality and continuous improvement effort that produced savings equal to the organization's pre-tax earnings in its first four years. He later became a founder of The Quality Improvement

Company and recently authored the book *Kick Down the Door of Complacency*[24] relating to his experiences. His decision to drive such an effort came after he recognized that doing so was his obligation as the CEO of the organization. It wasn't just a nice thing to do or another new initiative derived from reading the latest books. It became clear to him that he was underutilizing the resources of the organization and not fulfilling his responsibilities to the owners of the business. Unless he assigned everyone responsibility for relentless improvement of their work output and processes, he would not be fulfilling his obligation. In fact, Chuck felt that boards of directors should hold all CEOs accountable for making continuous improvement happen throughout the organization. The representatives of the organization's owners should remove a CEO who fails to fulfill this responsibility.

A. Roots of Continuous Improvement

Much of the thrust for current continuous improvement efforts was triggered by events in the 1950s and 1960s. As the world was rebuilding after World War II, Japan in particular chose to focus on quality for its reentry into world markets. Competing on the basis of productivity was not a logical strategy with the highly entrenched and productive Western businesses. Yet a great opportunity remained for competing effectively by learning to deliver products that worked as intended. Involving the people of their organizations in continuously improving how they worked and what they produced was key to the success of their quality improvement strategies.

The Japanese were strongly influenced by American quality specialists, Dr. W. Edwards Deming and Dr. Joseph Juran. The Japanese Union of Scientists and Engineers (JUSE) drew on the work of these men and the work of behavioral scientists such as McGregor, Lewin, and others, to integrate technical and human strategies into processes for managing and improving quality. Many businesses previously dominated by American companies lost market position, or failed, as customers learned that they did not have to accept products or services that did not meet their needs or expectations. And American organizations that were established and change averse or resistant countered primarily with claims of unfair business practices. They sought relief through government action and avoided coming to grips with the real problem, often until it was too late.

Eventually quality improvement became a thrust of many American companies in response to growing pressures from foreign competitors. Originally focused primarily on the reduction of product defects, the movement rapidly broadened to include quality in all of an organization's functions and services. The term total quality management (TQM) was applied to the broader efforts. And, as TQM grew in its applications, emphasis increased on the importance of improving business and work processes as a primary strategy for sustainable improvement.

B. Range of Continuous Improvement Models

Recognition of the importance of these activities for competing effectively in global markets led to establishment of a national quality award in the U.S., the Malcolm Baldrige National Quality Award.[25] The award was named for the late U.S. Secretary of Commerce under President Ronald Reagan. Organizations that choose to compete for the award are evaluated against a set of criteria for determining excellence in quality and continuous improvement. The number of formal winners of the Baldrige Award is few by the design of the competition. However, thousands of organizations use the award criteria for self-assessment purposes and for guiding their improvement efforts. Others go through the full process of applying for the award. Many of these organizations feel that they win simply by competing for the award. In addition to the insights and learning derived from completing the application, they receive the benefits of an external assessment and written feedback from the panel of examiners for the Baldrige Award. This feedback has been described by some as the best "free" consulting available.

The Baldrige Award is one of many models and strategies available for CI. Today, it almost certainly represents the model in widest use. Our work with The Quality Improvement Company and its continuous improvement system is another available model. That process utilizes the management system model discussed in the Managing FOR Change chapter as the basis for management planning and implementation of a CI effort. Other approaches include those designed around the teachings of a range of people in the quality and CI field. The approaches share much in common in terms of purpose and the actions involved. At the same time there are variations built on the biases of the designers, which would make one approach or another more suitable for a particular organization. Whatever choice an organization makes, a systematic and systems-oriented process is critical.

C. CI Features and ECO Development

An organization needing to select or reenergize a CI effort can use the features covered in this chapter as a guide, particularly if the organization has also decided that increased capacity as an ECO is required. CI processes without the features discussed will restrict development of a change orientation suitable for conditions of increasing change. Creating a change-seeking level of orientation to change is important in highly uncertain environments. CI processes that fail to provide legitimate time and structures for that work will not take organizations to the change-seeking level. Nor will CI processes that rely on voluntary participation vs. requiring involvement as a component of everyone's job responsibility. We urge you to consider these features and the issues outlined for each as you explore your needs for change and increased ECO capability.

II. Direction and Goals
for Continuous Improvement

Experience teaches a simple truth about creating effective continuous improvement capability in an organization: If you want continuous improvement, you must require it from everyone and provide them with clear goals expressing what management wants to accomplish. The pace of business in general is so fast that people must set priorities and make choices about where to put their effort. The need for priorities and choices is only exaggerated as the rate of change and uncertainty in an organization's environment increases.

Statements about the importance of continuous improvement, by themselves, are inadequate to make it happen. Specific goals that meet the SMART criteria outlined in the chapter on the stabilizing base are also required, i.e., they must be specific, measurable, agreed upon, realistic, and timed. Without such goals the direction remains ambiguous and can be taken as intended for others or not applicable to a particular person or group. In addition, management must convey the specific roles it will play in the continuous improvement process. It must be able to articulate how it will operate differently in identifying and implementing improvements. And it needs to communicate how its behavior will change to enable and support the CI work of everyone in the organization. Without this the validity of the effort will be questioned.

A. *Linking CI Direction to the Organization and Its Needs*

What about current performance suggests that continuous improvement is needed? What is going on in the organization's marketplace and competitive environment that drives the need for continuous improvements? How will CI support accomplishing the organization's vision and business strategies? How will the CI effort add to the ability to cope with the additional forces for change? A thorough assessment of the internal and external environments and development of the organization's stabilizing base will provide answers to these questions. Management must know the answers to these questions, not just as a "gut-feel," but in terms of facts and data when setting the organization on the path of continuous improvement. Sharing that information with the people of the organization makes the need for CI realistic and compelling. Without the information the direction for CI is perceived as little more than "smoke and mirrors" and another change initiative that will also pass quickly.

B. *Focusing the Direction for Continuous Improvement*

Becoming an ECO implies increasing the ability to deal with change. Yet not everything can be changed within the time frame of the organization's normal planning horizons. SMART goals provide focus. But how many should be set at any time? Experience suggests up to five annual goals should be selected for the CI effort. Too many goals give the impression that management is not focused and has not prioritized where energy should be applied to produce the greatest return. The CI direction should be applied to getting the biggest bang for the buck in any time frame by applying the 80/20 rule, i.e., the idea that solving 20% (or fewer) of the issues will produce 80% (or more) of the improvement possible at any point in time.

Providing focus on issues with large potential for improvement is important for the people of the organization. Unfortunately, we have observed many management teams agonizing over which four or five issues to select. Instead of accepting that setting priorities is not an exact science and that the improvement effort will be continuous, they struggle with being correct and precise. The impact can be limiting to the organization's attempt to add ECO capability while those at other levels wait for direction. Our counsel to these teams remains: (1) pick a limited number of issues, (2) set SMART goals, and (3) maintain a list of issues for future focus as improvements reduce the original list.

C. Goal Selection at Lower Levels

Setting direction and goals at the top allows those at lower levels to identify improvement opportunities that support the overall direction. Again, picking a limited number of goals to focus on is important. They should be relevant to the level and group involved and aligned with higher level goals. Two factors are likely to impact a CI effort that the management of ECOs will take into account when setting direction from the top. Other organizations will probably be unaware of, or ignore, these issues.

First, groups at lower levels may not be in a position to contribute directly to achieving all of the organization's CI goals. Where this situation exists, the management of ECOs gives the groups options. They may be told to identify and select goals that will support their customer's or supplier's goals that do fit with the overall CI goals, i.e., the direction would be to find areas for improvement that indirectly support the organization's goals. Or they may be given the freedom to select one or two goals that are relevant and high priority for improved performance in their own area. This option is based on the belief that all improvement is valuable.

Second, there may be improvement opportunities within a department that need high-priority attention. However, these would not be included in the group's goals if only the top-level direction could be considered in setting the CI goals. This condition could conceivably continue through several cycles of goal setting for CI. Inflexibility in the goal-setting process for such groups inhibits both the CI effort and the ongoing development of ECO capacity. The groups involved end up frustrated. They recognize the value of contributing to the organization's overall CI goal achievement. Yet they feel limited when not allowed to work on at least a few of the issues where they know there can be positive impact on their own performance. Effective management of this dilemma may include giving groups the freedom to select one or two improvement opportunities for their own area. At the same time they remain on the hook for contributions to the organization's overall goals for continuous improvement. Contributions occur that are relevant to both the organization and the specific unit. The flexibility demonstrated by management under the conditions described strengthens the CI process and moves the organization to higher levels of ECO capability.

III. Improvement Challenge

The improvement challenge to people in change-averse organizations is clear: "If it ain't broke, don't fix it!" At the other extreme is the change-seeking organization. There the challenge is, "However it works now, make it better than anything else currently known." At the center of the range is the challenge, "Make things as good as the competition." These are very different challenges that generate very different behaviors. People withhold ideas and avoid change at the low end, aim for average or typical performance in the middle, and stretch and innovate to improve to new heights at the high end. At this end the organization is using change as a strategic weapon, improving its performance, raising havoc for competitors, and providing products and services to customers that allow them to lead also. These organizations play in a different arena and are well into becoming an ECO. They are not satisfied with being as good as the best. Rather they challenge their organizations to exceed in all aspects of their business whether it is products or services, quality, timeliness, costs, or other key areas.

A. Challenge to All

ECOs issue their improvement challenge to every member of the organization. It is not confined to certain levels of management or to people-specific improvement roles. Excelling in all work activities is deemed important. Seeking to excel in ECOs means achieving "world class" results that match or exceed the performance of the "best in class." It does not mean to do so with more resources or lower quality or using more time or with higher costs. Such expectations drive organizations and their people to avoid changes and improvements. To excel means being the best in all of these areas.

Challenging all to seek improvement obligates the organization to provide everyone with needed skills and resources, whether those resources involve time, money, people, and/or training. Roger Milliken, owner of early Baldrige Award winner Milliken Corporation, has said, "The height of managerial stupidity is to demand that people improve results and not be willing to change the process." ECOs recognize the validity of this statement and are willing to provide the resources needed as well as to encourage changing processes. Without such support the improvement challenge is shallow and will not encourage change-seeking actions. ECO capacity will be lost.

B. Challenge Is Ongoing and the Work Never Done

Establishing a continuous improvement process implies belief that improvement is always possible and that the work is never finished. ECOs at higher levels of capacity display this belief in their words and actions. At lower levels the idea that change is always possible may be expressed but not acted upon. These organization appear to be committed to "pick the low hanging fruit" and presume that once the easy picking is over the work is done.

In the mid-1980s to early 1990s large numbers of organizations initiated continuous improvement processes and professed belief in the never-ending nature of the improvement challenge. Yet, within relatively brief periods of time, and often with solid improvement results, many of these same organizations pulled back to focus on the breakthrough gains promised by business process reengineering. They clearly abandoned the idea of the continuing challenge to all and moved back towards strategies focused on the "big, quick fix" promised by reengineering. Efforts in that arena typically involved only a few organizational members and hordes of consultants. Others were left to return to "business as usual" as far as continuous improvement was concerned. Now the drive was for discontinuous change and improvement and CI no longer offered sufficient, short-term gains. (See the section of this chapter, "Size of Improvements Expected," for more of this discussion.)

Under similar circumstances of solid gains from a CI process, ECOs take a different approach. They experience reduced defects and improvements in customer satisfaction with quality and service. Costs have been reduced and time saved through the efforts across the full range of the organization's functions. But there is no assumption that this work is done. It is at this point that ECOs realize that the work of continuous improvement has just begun. Not only that but the hard work has yet to be done. Digging in to identify additional opportunities means the ongoing need to make CI a key focus of the organization. Processes have been improved to levels where quality performance measurement has progressed from "acceptable quality levels" measured in percentages or fractions of a percent, e.g., 1% or .065% defective, down to the more difficult to measure level of parts per million, e.g., 50 ppm or the 3.4 ppm of Six-Sigma. Some organizations pursue the often maligned and misunderstood standard of zero defects. Sometimes mistaken to mean "no variation," zero defects is defined as a standard used as a basis of comparison by common agreement. The comparison, in the case of quality, is with the standard of no deviations from agreed-upon customer requirements.

At these quality levels organizations with strong ECO capability believe that the learning and benefits to be gained from even further improvement will clearly outweigh the benefits already realized. This does not mean that they do not embrace ideas like reengineering as part of the overall challenge of continuous improvement. Instead processes such as reengineering are added to the tool set of ECOs as they become available. ECOs make use of any tool or process that will aid in pursuit of the continuous improvement challenge to continually seek performance at and beyond currently known capabilities.

C. Benchmarking and Best Practices

It is difficult for people to see the opportunities for significant change or improvement when they are only aware of how things have been done in their own environment. Often they have made previous attempts to improve performance only to be blocked by the narrow perspective they have regarding options for getting the same tasks accomplished. Their historical perspective limits their ability to look at the problem in innovative ways and break out of the constraints imposed by the limits of their exposure.

Studying and sharing "best practices" among groups doing the same work is one strategy for increasing awareness that other processes are not only possible but are capable of producing better results. These studies may involve appointing groups to visit and compare work processes of different groups doing the same work. The group might look at other groups doing the same tasks on different shifts, in different parts of the same facility, or in different geographic locations. The groups studied may represent any function whether administrative, service, technical, or operations. Observations are made of how the work is done, the work area laid out, tasks assigned, or other differences among the groups. The search is for best practices as indicated by differences in performance. The groups compared all have access to the outcome of the study, become aware of new possibilities for improvements in their own area, and are expected to make use of the findings.

What is commonly referred to as "benchmarking" is a variation on studies of best practices. It was established as an effective tool for use in quality and continuous improvement by reports of its value at Xerox Corporation.[26] Benchmarking became part of the Xerox process that aided their recovery from a loss of market share to foreign competitors. It also was a key element of their successful pursuit of the Baldrige Award.

"Benchmarking" typically involves identifying an organization that excels in a particular business process, whether or not that organization is in the same business. Agreements are made that allow in-depth study of the process producing "best in class" performance for learning and potential adaptation by the studying organization. The organization agreeing to serve as a benchmark is offered reciprocity for the study and analysis of processes in the organization conducting the benchmarking study. Benchmarking and "best practices" studies help organizations move beyond their current capabilities. They develop a new perspective on "what's possible" and how it is done. Use of these processes strengthens their continuous improvement processes. They increase capacity to respond to the change-seeking ECO's improvement challenge, i.e., to match and make things better than anything currently known.

IV. Size of Improvements Expected

Organizations with a high level of ECO capacity recognize that improvements come in all sizes, from all levels and functions of the organization, have broader or narrower effects, and so on. People in these organizations know that continuous improvement of all kinds is important and that this is part of everyone's job responsibility.

A. Incremental or Breakthrough Improvement?

An argument that sometimes bounces around in discussions of improvement efforts concerns whether the organization should target many small, incremental improvements or shoot for discontinuous, breakthrough improvements. Incremental improvements as the focus, according to those who question the strategy, distract people from looking at the big picture and deflect their creative energies away from the greatest opportunities. The effort and costs invested in breakthrough improvements, on the other hand, are said to restrict improvement efforts to one or a few projects at a time and to sadly underutilize the great asset that the people of the organization represent. Further, once a breakthrough is made there will always be opportunities for additional incremental improvements until the process involved requires another breakthrough effort.

Hearing these arguments from proponents or sellers of one approach or the other would not be surprising. Consultants who believe in the concept of incremental improvement, called "kaizen" by the Japanese, would be expected to argue for such methods. Consulting firms selling major business process reengineering or redesign projects would be expected to argue for breakthrough strategies using their methods and tools. Each has a vested interest in seeing their preferred approach selected by a client organization, i.e., business contracts and revenues.

What we find difficult to understand are situations in which executives and internal improvement resources allow themselves to be trapped into the same arguments. They are prisoners of "the tyranny of the OR".[6] We have encountered many situations in the introduction of quality and continuous improvement efforts where the question is asked of management, "What do you want, quantity OR quality?" And the answer to this question must always be "Yes." Implicit in the question is the belief that you cannot have both, when evidence clearly shows that improving quality leads to improvements in volume. The same answer and reasoning apply to arguments about whether incremental or breakthrough improvements are desired. By virtue of their inability to see that both incremental and breakthrough improvements are important for successful continuous improvement, people place limits and restrictions on their ECO capability.

An example of the impact of placing primary emphasis on large gains occurred in a product division of a microelectronics company. People throughout the division were asked to submit ideas for improvement. Some would be assigned by the management team as projects for cross-functional corrective action teams. Others would be referred to a specific department for action. In the initial stages of the process large numbers of ideas were submitted for consideration. Management developed a recognition process to reinforce people's efforts at identifying improvement opportunities. Shortly after the recognition process was introduced the flow of ideas slowed dramatically. When asked about the cause, members of the division reported that they understood that management only wanted "big" ideas. The system was designed to recognize the one idea each month with the greatest impact. As a result people stopped submitting ideas with limited impact. Immediately after receiving the feedback the management team changed the system to make each idea submitted eligible for a drawing for a meal for two. Now the recognition process was refocused on the idea that all ideas and improvements are important. The flow of ideas resumed at previous levels.

B. How Big Is Big?

The word "big" is a relative word. Comedian Henny Youngman, old time king of the "one-liner," would always answer the question, "How's your wife?" with another question, "Compared to what?" It's all relative! The same "compared-to-what?" issue applies to a discussion of the size of improvements expected as part of a CI process. Throughout organizations people at different levels or in different functions have broader or narrower perspectives on the overall work of the organization. The opportunities for improvements they encounter will vary in size, scope, impact, or ease of resolution. No one would be excluded from the work of CI in ECOs because the opportunities they might find are smaller or easier to fix.

What is important where ECO capability is high is that all opportunities are identified. The only place where the size of the potential improvement comes into play will normally be in the process of prioritizing the sequence in which the opportunities are addressed. Whether the criteria for prioritization is dollar savings potential, reduction of errors reaching a customer, frequency of occurrence of the problem, or reduced cycle time, people are encouraged to give highest priority to items that will produce the greatest effect upon the criteria used to set the priorities. As higher impact issues are resolved, lower priority items move up the list and get addressed.

ECOs are never trapped into the either–or question. They maintain a both–and orientation that recognizes the value of all sizes and forms of improvement. If the either–or argument becomes an issue vs. seeking improvement wherever it appears and in whatever size package, the organization needs to seriously consider whether it is building or restricting its capacity as an ECO. It is hard to see this discussion as anything but restricting.

V. Common Language and Definitions

As our model indicates, an effective CI process is a required component of an ECO. An effective CI process requires, among other things, that the organization adopt a common language and set of definitions for communicating about continuous improvement and quality. Communication is hindered when terms are used without agreement on their meaning. Fuzzy or implied definitions leave room for argument and different interpretations of terms. Clarifying language saves time and eliminates arguments about meaning. People focus on the real task of improving results by finding and working through opportunities for improvement. The experience of hundreds of companies and thousands of people suggests keeping definitions simple and unambiguous for best results. ECOs create a common language to maximize the energy available for the improvement task. Other organizations behave as if this issue is not important or they simply do not recognize it.

A. Meaning of Quality

The word *quality* is part of all CI efforts. The definition of the word also varies widely. Some use the term to define quality as in the eye of the beholder, i.e., "I'll know it when I see it!" Others tie the definition to issues like "meeting or exceeding customer expectations" or "delighting customers." Still others link the meaning of quality to the issue of requirements, i.e., meeting a set of agreed upon and objectively measurable requirements. And then there are the off-the-wall uses of the word quality often seen in the names of organizations like "Joe's Quality Used Cars" or "Sally's Diner: Quality Food." Not all of these are useful in an organization-wide CI process.

The criteria we recommend for the definition is that it must be simple and measurable. The person who produces a piece of work should know the definition of quality and be able to determine objectively whether or not they have produced a quality result. Each person should be able to agree with their customer or supplier, without subjective judgments or hassling over meanings, that what was produced either met or did not meet what was agreed upon and, therefore, whether or not quality had been produced. Jeff Miller of Documentum sometimes says to customers, "I expect my people to be rigorous about understanding your requirements, Mr. Customer. We are lousy mind readers. If we agree on your requirements, then we are on a path to perform quality work for you."

Some of the definitions above are clearly subjective and open to personal interpretation. Others sound good but are missing out on the requirement for measurability. For example, consider the implications of the definition of quality as meeting or exceeding customer expectations. If the definition applies to the external customer, "expectations" are often subjective and unspecified. Without direct contact and negotiation with the customer, people are unable to know whether or not they have met or exceeded expectations. If the definition is applied to internal customers additional issues arise, in particular with the idea of "exceeding" expectations. An accountant preparing monthly financial documents, for example, might know that he or she could exceed customers expectations by having the documents printed in color and bound instead of being prepared in the normal black and white, stapled form. Is this the behavior expected with this definition of quality? Probably not, given that the "exceeds" solution means increased time and expense.

B. Mixing Quality and Customer Delight

Then how do organizations deal with the important concept of going the extra mile for a customer? The best solution is probably not to confuse the concept of quality with the idea of doing extra to meet or exceed customers' needs. Viking Freight System has an expression that guides its entire employee population in this area. The expression is "EZTDBW" and stands for "Easy to do business with." It appears everywhere in the organization as a constant reminder. EZTDBW signs are on people's desks, on identification badges, in freight terminals, lobbies, and so on. Yet the definition of quality used in the Viking Improvement Process is "meeting the requirements." People deal with customers, internally and externally, by being sure to understand and agree to the customer's requirement. Yet, they also know they are free to act in any way they believe necessary to make Viking EZTDBW. These are two different issues and people are not confused about either. Quality has been produced when the requirements are met and extra effort is legitimized as needed to assure customer satisfaction and loyalty.

Another important reason for using a simple and unambiguous definition of the word quality was highlighted by a story we were told in work with a major soft-goods manufacturer. The story was about what was called "the healing truck" and related to the definition of quality as meeting the requirements. Truckloads of finished garments were shipped from factories to inventories in major distribution centers from which customer orders were filled. Incoming quality inspection at the distribution center occasionally rejected an entire load for return to the factory. Yet all of these were not returned to the manufacturing location. Instead, the trailer of material remained in a storage lot for a period of time. People attributed magical and healing properties to the trucks when, at the end of months in which the rejected materials were needed to meet shipment forecasts, reinspections led to acceptance of the material as meeting the requirements. In this situation, the product specifications, i.e., the requirements, were subjective or sufficiently nonspecific to allow different interpretations at different times. The impact on the people of the organization was that the definition "meeting the requirements" was confusing. Since nothing was done to the product while in the truck, the requirements must have changed or the real definition was "meeting the requirements unless we need questionable material to make financial goals." They had learned from observation that quality was subjective and subject to negotiation. What resulted was predictable — arguments and negotiations about the definition of quality and the absence of actions to eliminate defect causes or to improve the control of manufacturing processes. These behaviors were not those of an organization working to become an ECO.

C. Quality Standards

Our work with clients of The Quality Improvement Company provided another demonstration of how failure to establish common definitions produces arguments and confusion that detracts from continuous improvement. We had adopted the concept of zero defects as the performance standard for quality as discussed by Crosby.[27] This definition, it turns out, generates significant emotional response. Some scoff and say that this is an unrealistic goal. Never generating a defect is impossible because "people are human" and subject to errors. Others work the technical side of the street with the argument that the concept of zero denies the fact that all processes and their output exhibit variation but zero defects implies no variation. These discussions were generally unproductive and distracting.

After many such discussions we realized that people were applying different meaning to the terms in the definition. There was a need to provide clarification of the meaning of the word "defect." With quality defined as "meeting the requirements" a defect becomes "a failure to meet a requirement" as opposed to something subjective. In addition, the word "standard" was taken by some to mean a goal that might change such as with engineered "standards" for productivity or time. The resolution of this issue came by reference to the dictionary definition of standard as "anything taken by general consent as a basis for comparison; an approved model." In the quality area it is the agreed upon requirements that constitute the basis for comparison and the approved model. Therefore, the meaning of zero defects is "no deviations from agreed upon requirements." With the additional clarification and definition of terms, a more useful common language was created and clients were able to focus more on the task of CI than on the semantics of the terms involved.

An interesting discussion of quality standards took place in a workshop for the CEO and other members of the executive team of a hospital. One of the workshop leaders had told the hypothetical story of bringing his mother for admission for surgery. At the conclusion of the admitting process the admitting officer in this story used a green marking pen to place an "X" on the mother's hand. The explanation given was that the hospital's standard for post-operative infections was 1% and, since they were under that standard and it was late in the month, the mother would get an infection to assure meeting the standard. Later in the workshop, the CEO commented that he would hate to have outsiders listening to discussion regarding performance to standards in his staff meetings. He had recognized that what were called standards were in fact goals. The standard against which they actually measured performance was zero, i.e., no post-operative infections. The target of their improvement efforts was to meet their current goals, e.g., 1% or fewer post operative infections per month, as they drove improvement efforts to meet the zero defects standard.

The discussion in this section has been on developing a common language in the area of quality and continuous improvement. Clarifying relevant terms and definitions is an important part of any change or improvement effort. The action builds ECO capacity.

VI. Customer–Supplier Relationships

Continuous improvement focuses on improving output to customers and includes the concept of work as a process. Processes involve inputs, processes, and outputs. At the organizational level are overall processes that begin with inputs from external suppliers, extend through a series of processing steps that convert the inputs to products or services, and end with outputs delivered to external customers. The overall process concept is useful for helping members of the organization understand their role in CI efforts. Organizations concerned with adding ECO capability will use the idea of work processes and customer–supplier relationships in their CI efforts to give visibility to opportunities for improvement and change.

A. Horizontal Customer–Supplier Connections

The concept of work as a process applies at all levels of detail, down to and including the work of each individual. Each step in any process can be looked at in the same way, i.e., as receiving inputs, acting on the input received, and converting it to output delivered to the next step in the process. The process activities may occur within a major functional area, e.g., operations, finance, information technology. It may happen within a specific department or geographic work area. Or, at the lowest level, the process ends up being the work of an individual.

A very useful effect of the process model of inputs → processes → outputs is to demonstrate and clarify the need for communication, problem solving, cooperation, feedback, and continuous improvement activities horizontally within organizations. Difficulty with these issues across departmental or functional boundaries is common. This is attributable to the fact that our most common structural models involve organizing vertically, by function, as opposed to horizontally. Yet almost all work flows horizontally through organizations and across the artificially created boundaries of departments and functions. And the measurement, reporting, goal setting, and reward systems of most organizations are primarily functional. The vertical organization and its supporting infrastructure creates what some call a "silo" effect. Vertical units maintain an internal focus that often puts them in conflict with units that execute earlier or later steps in a process. The inability to penetrate the sides of the silo blocks the collaboration needed to make processes operate effectively. People are forced to rely on the organizational hierarchy. Time and energy are wasted and collaboration and change become even more difficult. The process concept and the customer–supplier model are ways to break the rigidity of silo thinking and legitimately align work and improvement efforts along the horizontal paths they naturally follow.

B. Customer–Supplier Model

The customer–supplier model (Figure 5.1) is a representation of the process model as it applies at any level and relates to issues of quality and continuous improvement.[23] ECOs build effective CI processes using such a model to guide the actions of all of their people. People learn a number of key points related to this model, as follows:

- Customers and suppliers are external as well as internal to an organization.
- Everyone is a customer, a producer, and a supplier in the work they do.
- We are "customers" of those who supply us with what we need to do our jobs; we are "suppliers" to those who receive the output of our work; and we are "producers" when we perform the tasks that make up our work.

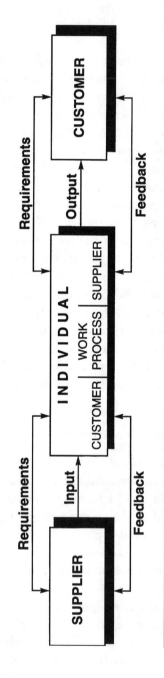

Figure 5.1 Customer–supplier model. Clarifying and getting feedback on performance to requirements is necessary for quality and continuous improvement across all links in the steps of a process.

- To do quality work for customers we must first understand and agree on their requirements, we must receive inputs from our suppliers that meet our needs, and work processes must be capable of meeting the requirements.
- If requirements are not being met, we must work with suppliers to improve the input we receive or improve the process and our ability to use it.
- Unless customers measure and provide feedback to suppliers about what they receive vs. their requirements, improvement cannot and will not occur.
- When customers and suppliers agree on requirements and how they are to be measured, feedback can be given in objective and factual ways and be received as part of a business exchange, not as blame or personal attack.

C. No Requirements, No Feedback, No Improvement

The last of the bullet points above addresses a key value of effective customer–supplier relationships based on the model. The major obstacles to improvement we have observed in most situations stem from failure of organizations to recognize the importance of the customer–supplier model and to insist on its use across units or steps in a process.

First of all, quality, when defined as meeting the requirements, obviously cannot be determined in the absence of requirements. People need to learn that up-front discussion and agreement on requirements is critical to doing quality work or to the ability to improve. Without requirements there can be no measurement and the capacity to use objective facts and data for improvement purposes is lost.

The management of a division of Raychem Corporation supplying parts to airplane manufacturers accepted the importance of understanding requirements up-front and took action to support making that happen. People were empowered to insist on up-front definition requirements to prevent the occurrence of defects or the need for rework. Members of the management team accepted personal responsibility for clarifying requirements when assigning work. Previous behavior in the organization had included managerial responses such as "Oh, you know what I mean" or "Do this like you've done other assignments" when asked for more specific requirements, leaving their expectations unclear.

Second, without requirements feedback is subjective and judgmental and lacking in facts. Attempts to get feedback are avoided. The subjective nature of the feedback makes it feel like a personal attack and not a description of defects. The ability to give and receive objective and nonevaluative feedback changes dramatically with clear and up-front requirements. Suppliers seek facts and data on performance vs. requirements because they are unable to improve without the data. Customers readily agree to provide feedback because it can be specific and objective, creates the opportunity for improvement, and because they too need feedback if they are to improve what is delivered to their customers.

The greater openness and sharing of data and feedback that results from common understanding and use of the customer–supplier model is a sometimes subtle but very powerful effect of using the model. Highly capable ECOs make use of the model, or their own version of the model, as a fundamental piece of their quality and continuous improvement processes.

VII. Prevention Orientation

There are two widely observable strategies applied to the task of quality and continuous improvement. The first, and historically preferred strategy, is inspection. The second, and primary strategy of today's improvement efforts, is prevention. ECOs build increased capacity for change, improvement, and learning via prevention.

A. Prevention vs. Inspection and Impact on Quality and Cost

For 15 years we have been asking workshop participants to discuss inspection and prevention as improvement strategies and the impact of each on quality and costs. The focus of the discussions always surrounds the impact of inspection on quality. Several key points emerge consistently from the discussions. Initially someone supports the idea that inspection improves quality. After all, without inspection a higher level of defects would be delivered to customers. So the quality of what the customer receives is improved. But is quality really improved by the inspection or does it simply remove defective materials that have already been produced? After all, inspection is an after-the-fact activity. It has no effect on the quality of what has been produced. And then someone else wonders whether or not inspection, in fact, could have a negative impact on quality. Sometimes the act of inspection might create defects. Or, does inspection negatively impact people's work? Generally people are being pressed to get a particular volume of work done for delivery at a particular time and to keep costs in line. If someone inspects their work, other than themselves, isn't the organization telling them that the inspectors are responsible for quality while they are responsible for volume, costs, and meeting the schedule? Isn't the focus on quantity and, thus, the quality of their work is reduced?

The overall answer is that the impact of inspection on quality is complex. It may be necessary to keep the customer from receiving defects, especially if the cause of the defects is not yet known. Or, inspection data may be needed to determine whether or not the producing process is "under control." Yet inspection, by itself, does not improve the quality of what is produced. Inspection can contribute to improved quality, but only if the results of the inspection are used to eliminate defect causes or to improve processes, i.e., for prevention.

In the other parts of the discussion, groups readily conclude that inspection processes increase costs and that prevention strategies lead to improvements in quality as well as reduced costs. When defects or errors are prevented from recurring, there is no need for the continuing costs of inspections, except to assure processes are in control, and scrap or rework become unnecessary. Material and labor costs are lower, just-in-case inventory is no longer needed to make up for missed or partial deliveries to customers, and on and on. And, finally, it becomes clear to people that inspection is a non-value-added activity from the perspective of the customer. Expense was added but had no effect on the quality of the organization's products or services.

B. The Limiting Effect of Inspection on ECO Capacity

In our discussion of the stabilizing base of ECOs we emphasized the restrictive nature of organizational policies and controls built on distrust of people. Externally imposed inspections are often an example of control processes built on the assumption that people cannot be trusted.

At Signetics Corporation in the early 1970's we toured a manufacturing area with the President of the company, Chuck Harwood. We observed a woman operating a machine that printed information such as the product number, date produced, and the company logo on circuits ready for shipment to customers. She first went to a holding area to pick up the packages to be marked. She was provided a slip of paper identifying the specification for the marking. She proceeded to the specification files, determined the required marking, and recorded the data. Stopping, she called to the quality inspector. After a few minutes, the inspector came to her, read the information she had recorded, compared it with the specification, and initialed the paper giving her the OK to proceed.

The operator then returned and set up her machine for the specified marking. Then she turned on the machine and ran it to mark five parts. At that point she turned off the machine and again waved to the inspector. A few minutes later the inspector examined the five parts, determined that the machine was properly set up, and again initialed the paper giving permission to proceed.

Leaving the area, we speculated with Mr. Harwood that somehow, at some time in the past, an error had occurred in the marking of products at this operation. Since one person had committed an error it was now assumed that all people might make such an error. A new quality control procedure had been introduced to make the process "idiot-proof." QC inspectors now inspected the work of the unreliable and untrustworthy a minimum of two times for each setup of the equipment. Mr. Harwood commented, "It's no wonder we have high turnover rates in this position. We treat everyone as if they are stupid and can't be trusted to do their work to the specification. Why would anyone doing this work care about quality? All of their work is double-checked and they clearly aren't trusted to do anything right. I personally couldn't work under such conditions for one shift let alone for weeks on end. This is intolerable and must be changed." This experience clearly influenced Mr. Harwood's subsequent leadership of the organization's CI process and its focus on prevention.

C. Proactive and Reactive Prevention

Strong ECOs apply prevention in proactive as well as reactive ways. In the early stages of CI, prevention activities tend to be more reactive. Defects and errors are more frequent. Causes must be found and corrective actions taken to remove the cause and prevent recurrence. As defects are reduced less effort is required for detecting and eliminating them. The energy freed up becomes available for more proactive pursuits. Proactive prevention examines work processes to identify areas where defects may occur. Process modifications are implemented to prevent potential defects. Proactive prevention also seeks to anticipate changes in customers' requirements that are beyond current process capabilities. For example, customers seeking tighter tolerances in physical dimensions or more rapid delivery may require process improvements. Tackling improvement needs proactively reduces the need to fire fight and consume energy reactively. Improved process capabilities may also allow the organization to offer improved performance to customers and lead the competition. Competitors are then forced to react to the lead of the more proactive organization.

In a world of more rapid change people are always faced with the problem of having too much to do. Time is not available or invested in improvement activities and prevention. And being in a reactive mode only adds to the problem. Therefore, it is incumbent on organizations needing to increase their ECO capabilities to develop an effective continuous improvement process. The payoff will be in the availability of time and other resources for anticipatory and proactive efforts that will never be available to reactive organizations with limited ECO capacity.

VIII. Systematic Problem-Solving Processes

Heeding our own admonition to keep definitions simple, we use the term "problem" to mean any condition in which there is a discrepancy between what happens vs. what was expected to happen and the cause of the discrepancy is unknown. The discrepancy could appear in many forms. Defects occur, customers provide feedback about dissatisfaction with service, a process or piece of equipment fails or operates out of control, and on and on. The organization's need under these conditions is to isolate and verify the cause(s) of the discrepancy and to take action that prevents recurrence. Strong or emerging ECOs use common and systematic processes for problem solving.

Problem-solving processes aimed at eliminating discrepancies and preventing recurrence share common characteristics. Many such processes are available. Probably the granddaddy of them all is the process developed by Kepner and Tregoe.[28] In addition, many organizations utilize the plan — do — check — act (PDCA) cycle outlined by Deming.[29] At the Quality Improvement Company, we designed the cycle of continuous improvement with four overall steps[28] labeled identification — monitoring — analysis — corrective Action (IMAC). Many companies have developed a version of a systematic problem-solving process they prefer. Which process fits best should be determined by the organization that will use it. Arguing for one or another process is not what is important.

A certified problem-solving trainer explained that to us what is most important is agreeing on a systematic process, whichever it might be. The people of the organization who will be involved in problem solving must learn the process and be required to use it as their methodology. Since most of the available processes are variations of the scientific method, all can lead to the desired result when used in a disciplined way. Without a systematic process attempts to solve problems wander fruitlessly, consuming significant amounts of effort in trying to get agreement about what steps to take and when. And the probability of reaching a conclusion that eliminates the problem and prevents recurrence is minimal.

A. Problem Definition

A common claim about problem-solving processes is that reaching a clear and agreed upon definition of the problem is 50% of what is required for resolution. Unless the problem is precisely defined, the subsequent steps of the process degrade to speculation related to interpretation of what problem is being addressed. Measurement and data collection are inhibited. Potential causes can be identified but not verified as related to the nonspecifically defined problem.

Most of us have a tendency to state a problem initially in general terms, e.g., "too many late arrivals" or "inadequate communication." Or our initial definitions are descriptions of presumed causes or solutions, e.g., "need for more training" or "outdated equipment." Problem definition needs to start from a description of the observed discrepancy and proceed to provide as specific and narrow a definition as possible.

Some processes involve answering a rigorous and comprehensive set of questions to produce a detailed specification of the problem,[29] covering what the problem IS as well as what it IS NOT. These highly disciplined processes require dedication to the use of facts and data and rejection of guesses and hypotheses. Although frustrating to some because of the discipline required, the precise specification of the problem not only narrows the range of possible causes, it provides a factual base which can be used later to assess the likelihood that a suggested cause is a root cause of the problem. With facts and data in place, hypothesized causes that do not explain the data can be rejected. No time is wasted pursuing them further or making changes that will not solve the problem.

Other approaches to problem definition are simplified versions of the more structured approaches described above. We have worked with a process for problem solving in quality improvement efforts that requires an initial statement of the problem, factual response to several questions, and then a more precise restatement of the problem based on the answers. The questions are the following (or a variation thereof):

- State the problem
- What product or service or process is defective?
- What requirement is not being met?
- What is the deviation from the requirement?
- When and where does the deviation occur?
- How big is the problem (number or percentage of defects)?
- Restate the problem based on factual answers to the questions.

This process requires somewhat less discipline but can also be very helpful producing a precise statement of the problem and focusing the remaining steps of the problem-solving process on the real issue. In a workshop introducing an overall continuous improvement effort and, more specifically, the problem-solving process selected by the organization, a marketing manager made a significant discovery using these questions. His original statement of the problem was "inadequate order entry system." After spending about fifteen minutes recording factual answers to the questions, he restated the problem as "Order entry system cannot handle seasonal orders for X (a specific category of products)." He was amazed by what he had learned. Instead of facing what he originally thought of as a major system overhaul at an expense of multiple millions of dollars, he now recognized the specific nature of the problem and the potential of correction with significantly less effort and money. This experience has been observed in virtually all workshops where the process has been taught and in continuous improvement teams around the world. The importance of using a disciplined process for defining problems cannot be overestimated in the design of CI processes.

B. Data and Fact Orientation

The importance of quantifiable data and facts for achieving permanent problem resolution is well established. Use of data and facts as part of a systematic process eliminates many of the obstacles to effective problem solving. Facts and data are objective, observable, and cannot be denied. Obstructions like bulldozing by people with strong opinions that are not supported by the facts can be dealt with if not eliminated all together. Disagreement that stems from an absence of data or facts can be resolved by getting what is needed instead of being turned into an issue of personal or position power. Testing of possible defect or error causes against the facts avoids wasted time and resources that might otherwise be spent chasing the wrong causes up blind alleys.

C. Tools Support

Training in the problem-solving methodology of the organization is a part of implementing all quality and continuous improvement efforts we have seen. Most organizations provide some level of this training to everyone. Organizations working to increase ECO capacity certainly recognize the need for such training. They insist that it is provided to everyone since continuous improvement is part of everyone's responsibility.

Many tools exist to support the needs of problem-solving processes. These include tools for identification and idea generation (such as brainstorming), definition, measurement, data collection and analysis, prioritization, identification and testing of root causes, planning for implementation and prevention of further problems, and so on. The simplest and easiest to understand tools are the most widely used. Tools relevant to specific problem-solving processes are covered in the training people receive, and they are expected to use them in their continuous improvement work. But the training, by itself, is insufficient to assure effective use of problem-solving methodologies.

1. Post Training Support Required

Our experience with clients' use of designated problem-solving processes and tools has provided insights into the support system needed after training. Involvement in actual problem-solving activities, whether individually or as a member of a team, typically occurs from a few weeks to a few months after training. And it is known that the retention of what is learned in most training is subject to the "three stoplight rule," i.e., no more than 50% of what is learned is retained by the student longer than it takes them to pass through three stoplights on the way home. Something must be provided to keep what was learned alive and available to people in their work environments. And the training should focus more on where and how to use the tools than on expectations of full retention after returning to the job.

In the early days of The Quality Improvement Company we created workshops to provide members of client organizations with a common language and set of terms and also to acquaint them with problem-solving tools and skills. Using feedback collected from our workshops and from internal trainers, we soon realized that people needed something more to take with them from the training. Their comments indicated that they needed more guidance on where to use the tools in the process. They also felt a need for an overall picture of the process to see how the whole thing fit together. A process flow diagram of the problem-solving process was developed with identifiers on the diagram to indicate where the various tools could be used. This solution seemed to satisfy the needs expressed by the users of the process.

Later we learned that we needed to move even further in providing post-training support for the problem-solving process. Two additional support tools were developed through collaboration with internal quality improvement and training resources from Ball InCon Glass Packaging Company (today called Ball-Foster). The first is the *Continuous Improvement Workbook.* The book leads groups step-by-step through the problem-solving process. For each major step a flow chart is provided, each relevant tool and its uses is spelled out, sample forms are provided, and the detailed steps of the process for applying the tool are spelled out. The second tool is a large "storyboard" that problem-solving teams use for tracking and reporting their progress. Copies of completed pages from the workbook are taped to the storyboard and provide a visual display of status. This overall picture keeps the team oriented to where it is and where it is going and also serves as a vehicle for project reviews with internal customers and suppliers or management.

2. *Inexperience and Immaturity with Problem Solving Requires More Support*

People are inexperienced and uncomfortable with the problem-solving process in their early uses of it. In addition, the frequency with which particular tools or steps in the process are used is low enough that support tools are needed to refresh people's learning. They provide the structure needed to use the tools and process as intended. Improving ECO capability requires this level of support. Observation has confirmed that prior failure of clients to use the process or to fully solve problems was not a result of people's resistance or unwillingness to do the work. Instead, people had been left adrift and without needed guidance. The problem was ours, not theirs.

The conclusion from this is that giving people tools training and skills for problem solving and CI is necessary but not sufficient. Additional tools are required to support on-the-job application of what is learned. As use of the tools and experience with the process grows, there will be less reliance on the tools. Yet their availability has a comforting and stabilizing effect, particularly in the face of accelerating change.

IX. Process Improvement Methods

Selecting a common problem-solving process, training people in its use, and providing support tools for use of the process is critical to development of an effective CI process and adding to ECO capacity. The primary focus of these activities is the reduction or elimination of causes and prevention of recurrence. As gains are made via problem solving and prevention, a shift in emphasis occurs that addresses the never-ending task of process improvement. As mentioned previously, an underlying assumption of CI efforts is that improvement of processes is ALWAYS possible. The opportunity never ends and continuous improvement processes must be designed on this belief.

A. Process Mapping

The basic tool of process improvement is process mapping,[30] often called process flow diagramming (PFD). The output of PFD is a visual representation of all of the operating steps, decision points, movements, delay points, control or inspection points, and other activities in a process from initial inputs at the start to the eventual outputs at the end. This tool can be applied to processes ranging from overall business processes such as order fulfillment or product development to subprocesses consisting of the steps in the task of an individual worker. Process mapping and PFDs have been used for many years by industrial engineers and have also been widely used in the work of systems analysts and programmers in the field of information and data processing.

Process flow diagrams serve a number of useful purposes, including the following:

- To create a visual picture of how a process works;
- To assure a thorough knowledge of the existing process and the relationship among the steps of the process;
- To identify differences in how people use the process;
- To see previously unknown problems or opportunities;
- To guide decisions about what to measure;
- To provide documentation of the existing process for use in ongoing process improvement activities; and
- To orient and train new people in the overall process and their place in it.

As with problem-solving processes, effective process improvement processes begin by clarifying and defining the specific process to be mapped and its boundaries. With common focus established a PFD is created of the existing process. In developing the PFD differences in use of the process are identified and resolved before proceeding. Attempts to improve a process that is not commonly accepted as the existing process are not productive.

Simply developing a map of the current process frequently leads to improvement. A few examples illustrate this point. First, a team of five people who trained sewing machine operators in a Levi-Strauss factory developed a PFD of the training process. They discovered that each of them was using a different process. Before proceeding they examined the work records of the people trained by each person and identified performance differences related to the training process used. From this data they made a determination of "best practices" and were able to agree on the training process they would all use. Subsequent process improvements were based on the agreed-upon process.

The second example occurred at a freight terminal of Viking Freight System. It involved a team of dockworkers and their "dock mentor" (a dockworker assigned to orient and train new workers in their jobs). The team developed a process flow diagram for unloading freight from incoming trailers and distributing it to other trailers from which it would be delivered to local customers. The dock mentor found the process particularly useful for his training task, especially when he found that there were parts of the work process that he was either training incompletely or incorrectly. Display of the diagram in the work area made the process available for checking and confirmation of the correct process when questions arose.

The third example occurred in a division of Raychem Corporation. An external consultant assisted in creation of a detailed process flow diagram of the manufacturing process, seeking to locate the greatest opportunities for reduction in cycle time. At the time a key improvement project to reduce the time required for a mechanical operation was consuming process-engineering resources. Achieving this improvement would reduce cycle time by about 0.2 seconds per unit produced. A shift of resources occurred when the process diagram showed that the most significant gains were available by the elimination of bottlenecks that required each unit to spend up to 30 minutes of queue time prior to certain operations. The overall gain in cycle time from a project in this area completely overwhelmed the possible gains from the current improvement project.

B. Improvement Analysis

Armed with an agreed-upon PFD it is possible to proceed to a more detailed analysis of potential improvements. At this stage it is necessary to resist the temptation to jump to conclusions about how to improve the process. Being systematic and disciplined is as important in process improvement as it is in problem solving. Analysis involves measuring relevant parameters of the current process, challenging and testing each step in the process, exploring possible improvements, and then selecting the changes to be implemented.

1. Measurement

If an improvement goal has already been established, selection of the appropriate measure is straightforward. If cycle time reduction is the goal, then measurement of the time taken at each step is relevant. If defect reduction, the number or frequency of defects at various steps is relevant. If improved process control is the issue, measurement of process variation at critical steps is relevant. Whatever the goal, measurement produces the facts and data critical to all successful CI processes. Measurement and data collection require time, but the benefits to the improvement process are such that this step cannot be avoided or truncated. The data identify the greatest opportunities for improvement and serve as a baseline for measuring the gains realized with the improved process.

2. Challenging Process Steps

Several challenges are applied to each process step. They begin with questioning whether or not value is added, from the perspective of the customer, by the step in question. Steps that involve inspection, rework, filing, storage, waiting or travelling to get approvals, or delays are normally non-value-added steps. If the step does not add value, continuing to include it in the process must be justified for conducting the business of the organization or it is a candidate for elimination.

Other tests apply to the time required, i.e., does it appear to take more time than necessary or should alternatives be explored? Is the step overly complex, contributing to the time required or increasing the potential for errors? Do errors or defects occur at the step that increase costs and waste? Is the process step outdated technologically? Again, as these challenges are answered there is a tendency to leap to conclusions about specific improvements to be implemented. This tendency needs to be resisted until the entire picture of the process is in place. Jumping too soon may block even greater potential improvements that appear when all of the pieces of the mosaic are in place.

3. Exploring Improvements

At this point a shift is necessary in the thinking of those pursuing process improvement. Prior steps have required logical and linear thinking and avoidance of the urge to leap to conclusions. Now it is important to release people's creative energies and to focus on developing innovative ways to change and improve the process under consideration. Groundrules like those used in brainstorming and tools that stimulate thinking in new and different ways are helpful. Obstacles to the open flow and exploration of ideas need to be removed. Benchmarking or "best practices" data become useful to open up the flow of ideas and to expand thinking about what's possible. "What if...?" questions legitimize exploration of options beyond existing boundaries. Seeking "what's possible" is the challenge.

Improvement strategies are explored for each step in the process where the answers to the challenges suggest value to be gained from improvement. Should the step be reduced or eliminated all together? Can the step be simplified or modified to improve its effect on the improvement goal? Are there ways to error-proof the step? Can the process be modified to increase process control and reduce variation or the production of defects or errors? Would standardizing the step be helpful and narrow the variety of outcomes it produces? Should the process be upgraded at a particular step to increase the capability of the process? Each of these areas is explored to create ideas for improvement. Ideas are tested for contribution to meeting the established goal, for issues that could effect acceptance or resistance, and put together in a revised PFD to provide an overall picture of the improved process.

C. Implementation

Plans for implementation consider avoidance of additional problems requiring more effort to resolve than would be realized by the new process. Systems thinking forces consideration of the impact of changes on others in the overall process and on up-front agreement to minimize negative consequences. Once the plan is developed and accepted, the new process is documented and implemented, including training and skill development as required. Measurement of the new process is maintained to assess performance improvements vs. expectations and the goal. As the results indicate success, the new flow chart becomes the PFD of the process and serves the purposes discussed above, including its role as a base from which additional and ongoing improvements will be made.

D. Support Tools

Process improvement methodologies take time and involve many tools. Training in the process and the range of available tools must be supplemented with on-the-job support tools for the same reasons necessary with problem-solving processes. Limited experience, tentativeness from lack of experience with the process, delays from the time of learning to the time of application of the learning in the work situation, and so on mean the use of process improvement methods will be hindered without additional support. The Quality Improvement Company includes a detailed and step-by-step *Process Improvement Workbook* for all process-improvement training. The workbook contains all of the tools and forms needed to carry out a process-improvement project on-the-job. Not all are needed for each project, but their availability is comforting to users. As experience is gained, the outline and tools maintain a systematic and data-oriented approach to process improvement even though teams have less need to rely on the back-up materials.

Building ECO capability is enhanced by providing support materials for carrying out complex processes by people with limited experience. The materials must provide for flexibility in their application to avoid the paralyzing effects of rigid structure and infrastructure discussed in Chapter 3 of this book, "Stabilizing Base."

E. Statistical Process Control Methods

All work is a process. This concept is widely accepted in the arena of quality and continuous improvement. Another key concept is that all processes are subject to variation, i.e., they will not produce exactly the same result each time. Statisticians have made great contributions to the areas of quality and continuous improvement by providing methods for understanding variation and achieving improvement in process control and capability. We are not statisticians and have no intention of trying to summarize their thinking. Nor do we feel qualified to evaluate the pros and cons of various approaches to the use of statistical methods for statistical process control (SPC).

What we do feel is important is to emphasize that utilization of SPC methods for continuous improvement and improved control of organizational processes is characteristic of organizations with greater capabilities as an ECO. The effective use of SPC tools increases the efficiency of CI processes. The methods produce the data and facts necessary for efficient CI and avoid the wasted time of improvement attempts based on conjecture and opinion.

Dr. W. Edwards Deming was a revered statistician and philosopher. His writing and teaching made many contributions to quality management and quality improvement in organizations throughout the entire world. His approach to quality improvement has had enormous influence on management thinking in these areas, combining aspects of his philosophy, of management and behavioral science, and of statistics.

One aspect of Deming's work is particularly relevant to the ongoing actions of management and their attempts to improve performance. He emphasized that SPC tools can be applied to any process, including management processes. Among Deming's great contributions for managers building ECO capacity is the distinction between variation in results that is attributable to "common causes" vs. "special causes."[29] Common causes are the result of the normal variation of a process, i.e., the results fall within the range of output to be expected when the process operates normally. Special causes are the result of external influences on the processes that are beyond the normal operation. A critically important feature of this distinction is that different actions are called for when dealing with common cause vs. special cause variation. Common cause variation can only be reduced by changes in the process. Variation due to special causes must be attacked by isolating and removing the cause. When managers fail to understand the differences they tend to treat all variation as due to special causes and end up increasing the variation in their processes as a result.

An example based on management behavior we have observed widely illustrates the point. Nearly all organizations employ processes for forecasting. Then, when the results are in, reviews are held to discuss what happened and the implications. When the results exceed forecast the manager involved is congratulated for his performance and encouraged to keep up the good work. On the other hand, when the results are below the forecast, managers are expected to explain "what caused the miss?" Knowing in advance that this question will be asked, managers often spend incredible amounts of time with their staff and financial people seeking answers to the question. Or, if they haven't done so before the review, they are directed to go back and find out "what happened?"

The effort and energy expended in seeking answers to the question "what happened?" is directed to finding the "special cause" of the variance from forecast. And when an answer is supposedly found, the manager is expected to make changes to fix the problem. Yet no data is collected or analyzed that allows the manager to determine whether special causes were at work or the variation was within what would be expected given the capability of the process to forecast the outcome. If you assume that the forecasting process is capable of predicting the results obtained within plus or minus 5% and that the "miss" was at minus 2%, the time of the manager and of everyone else involved in searching for the cause was wasted. The probability is that there was no special cause since the result was well within the normal variation of the forecasting process. Much greater benefit would have been realized through efforts to understand what influenced variation in the outcome of the forecasting process and improving the process to narrow its variation.

Widespread observation of management behavior indicates that these concepts of variation have had very little influence at the level of business processes employed by senior executives. Whether this criticism is applied to forecasting or budgeting or planning or capital spending processes is immaterial. None of them employs the tools and methods of SPC, and the costs to organizations in terms of wasted and misdirected efforts are large. Managers continue to act as if all variation is due to special causes and, in doing so, actually add to the variation in their processes.

Organizations becoming ECOs recognize the importance of this issue. Management changes behavior so that improvement efforts are directed appropriately whether at the lowest levels or to gaining control of their own processes. More energy will be available for coping with increased rates of change and moving to the change-friendly or change-seeking level of ECO behavior. The diversion of resources associated with the incessant pursuit of special causes will stop.

X. Structures and Time for Continuous Improvement

Strengthening ECO capability means accepting the importance of going beyond setting direction and establishing goals for CI. Management must also create enabling legislation. People have legitimate questions as to how the work is to be done in the context of their current tasks and responsibilities. Is this to be done by individuals or will they work with others? When should the work be done given their already full plates? Is meeting space available and, if so, is it equipped with the tools and materials needed? Will people be provided training and the skills they need? And on and on. Some might take these questions to be indications of resistance. ECOs acknowledge these as legitimate questions and accept management's responsibility to provide answers. Without the answers to these questions the direction and assignment of responsibility is hollow.

A. *Structures for Continuous Improvement*

In most continuous improvement efforts people are told that quality and CI are part of their job. An organizational structure has been created within which they do their jobs. This structure has historically been concerned with (1) producing the desired volume of output at (2) minimum costs and (3) on time. These are three of the four dimensions of work. The fourth dimension is quality. An underlying premise of our work in the fields of quality and continuous improvement has been that quality must not be treated differently from the other dimensions of work when it becomes part of everyone's responsibility.

Quality and CI need to be integrated into people's work primarily within the existing structure of the organization. It should not be done, as some contend, via special structures established specifically for CI. Establishing quality and CI as part of each person's job also means that each employee must be formally and legitimately involved in the CI process.

In excess of a thousand executives have explored the two premises related to the primary structures for quality and CI and the participation of everyone in the process. They were participants in workshops developing implementation plans for their own CI processes. For each premise they were asked to the explore arguments for the premises and the messages and implications of adopting a different strategy. Without exception there was agreement with the premises and recognition that other strategies would create inconsistencies and conflicting messages to the organization. Several issues appeared consistently and the following is a sample:

- Creating special structures would remove quality from the responsibility of people's direct supervisors;
- Placing quality and CI responsibility in special structures takes it away from the current managers and makes it inconsistent with statements about its importance;
- It doesn't make sense to say that everyone is responsible but some only have to participate on a voluntary basis any more than it makes sense to say that carrying out other responsibilities is optional;
- Any who are not involved get the message that they really are not responsible;
- The current organization can deal with quality as well as it deals with other responsibilities;
- People already know the existing organization and do not have to learn to operate in new structures if the current structure is the primary CI vehicle.

The conclusion of most of these management teams is to involve people primarily via their natural work teams. Teams composed of managers and those who report to them are assigned responsibility to meet regularly to work on CI projects. The teams are connected through the hierarchy from top management to the lowest levels. People with supervisory roles play two roles, as member of their supervisor's team and as leader of their own. Temporary, cross-functional teams address improvement projects that cross several groups.

The requirement that all participate was also adopted. How to make this happen is more complex and requires the development of a number of alternatives based on the unique nature of the work involved. Executive secretaries, for example, are sometimes assigned to a common team because they fulfill an individual role yet share many CI issues. Unique ways to participate are needed for some that sell or provide services to customers, but work from their homes or in off-site locations. They are able to contribute by identifying problems or opportunities via paper or e-mail message at any time but cannot participate regularly in improvement projects. Common to all of the approaches developed for these unusual situations is the fact that structures are created for participation in some way as part of each person's job responsibility. ECOs retain the concept of individual responsibility but provide for flexibility in its application.

B. Time for Continuous Improvement

With already full schedules and the need to prioritize their efforts, people express many concerns about where the time for CI work will come from. Change-averse or change-resistant organizations tell people to find the time in their schedules. Those with greater ECO capacity bite the bullet and legitimize the time by specifying a minimum amount of time to be invested in CI by everyone.

Leach, International, for example, sets aside one hour per week for people to meet in their natural work groups and work on CI. Other work stops for that hour and everyone is involved in their quality improvement meeting. The decision to operate this way was sustained through a difficult business cycle, and Leach's Continuous Improvement Manager, Earl Wright, has credited that decision for helping pull the company through its problems.

Many other organizations require a minimum of one hour per week for CI activities. Marmon/Keystone established such a company-wide practice in the late 1980s. The practice remains in effect and has been extended to parts of the organization acquired since the process was initiated. Setting the time requirement conveys management's commitment to the CI process and their belief that the investment will result in returns not otherwise achievable.

As teams mature, those with strong ECO capacity maintain requirements for participation but provide flexibility in how much time is used. In the initial stages of the CI effort at Roadway Services, Inc. teams were required to meet regularly for one hour in continuous improvement meetings other than staff meetings. The purpose was to dedicate the time and learning to becoming proficient with the process and focus on improvement without the distraction of other business. After some time the teams requested that they be allowed to integrate their CI meetings into their regular business meetings and adjust the time committed based on current efforts. Increased autonomy was granted to teams able to meet a set of criteria indicating competence and continued production of results.

Allocating time tests management's belief in the CI process in situations where operating processes are continuous. In glass factories, for example, molten glass is produced and formed 24 hours a day, 7 days a week, and processes only shut down for brief periods of changeover, refurbishing of equipment, or holidays. Regular meetings of intact work groups cannot be held during normal work hours. In these situations organizations pursuing higher level ECO capability have gone as far as to assign projects to teams of people representing the different work positions in the operation and to authorize payment of overtime for their meetings. These organizations develop processes that involve everyone in identifying problems or opportunities for problem solving or process improvements, e.g., forms to be filled out or occasional idea-generating sessions. Not everyone is involved at the same time but all become involved over a period of time. In these ways, no one is "off the hook" for their CI responsibility, but the processes employed are consistent with the nature of the work of the organization.

C. Other Resource Support

People need more than a structure and allocated time to contribute effectively to CI. People must be trained in the process, the skills needed to use the process, and provided with support tools to guide their work. Additional needs include a place to meet that provides a proper environment for the meetings and tools for conducting the meetings. Simple things such as easels and chart pads and masking tape for posting work on the walls and, coincidentally, rooms with wall space are important. Tables and chairs are necessary, as is an environment comfortable for meeting and problem-solving activities. Sound levels that allow communication, temperature and humidity control that is not distracting, proper and continuous lighting, and so on are all necessary. We have observed organizations initiating teams and CI efforts without some or any of these needs met. These organizations are set up for short-term failure. The conditions under which people are expected to operate are so obviously inconsistent with the basic requirements for success that the direction for CI can only be taken as frivolous. Organizations adding to their ECO capacity will certainly not overlook the importance of these issues.

XI. Strategies for Innovation and Creativity

Continuous improvement as a component of increasing ECO capability means tapping into the creative capabilities of everyone in the organization. Several factors that stimulate innovation and open up the search for new possibilities have been discussed previously. These include making people aware of "what's possible" vs. their current situation through "benchmarking" and "best practices" studies.

A. *Stimulating Creativity with CI Goals*

Goals that cannot be realized by "tweaking" or minor changes in a work process force the use of creative thinking and the search for innovative solutions. The head of a large grocery chain described setting goals that represent improvements of multiple orders of magnitude as a part of his strategy to help people break though established ways of doing things. He has been so pleased with many of the innovations that have resulted that he considers them proprietary and prefers not to have them described for his competitors in this book. Collins and Porras[6] describe the positive driving forces for change and innovation derived from BHAGs, i.e., "big, hairy, audacious goals," used by visionary companies. This concept also works at the lowest levels of organizations. Production operators in a semiconductor fabrication area reduced yield losses from 14% to 1.5% in just over one year when they shifted their focus from seeking minor yield improvements to identifying and eliminating all defects, i.e., from 86% "good" to zero yield loss, a target initially considered impossible.

B. *Removing Fear of Failure*

One of the perennial obstacles to innovation and risk taking is fear of failure. Wherever people feel threatened with punishment of some form for failure, they limit the options they will consider to those that reduce their personal risk. As a colleague of many years has often said, "People will not willingly provide their bosses with a club they can use to beat them." Additionally, the importance of this issue is highlighted as one of the basic 14 points of Deming's philosophy, i.e., "drive out fear."[31]

Many organizations talk about innovation and risk taking and stress that people will not be punished for taking risks that fail to produce predicted results. But despite pronouncements about risk, people experience what they consider punishment in many ways. Performance evaluations and salary increases that have been strong become "average." Promotions go to those who have not experienced failure even though they have also not taken any risks. Assignments to exciting projects stop coming and career-oriented discussions stop or indicate more limited possibilities. And, the most negative impacts occur when managers or those at higher levels voice displeasure or frustration with a failure. The occurrence of these experiences is greater in organizations with limited capability as an ECO.

ECO capability is enhanced, on the other hand, when innovation and creativity is given recognition and rewarded, whether or not the outcome was positive. The systems of the organization reward innovation and creativity more than not trying. Performance evaluation, promotion, and salary administration processes accept that all attempts will not succeed and promote the belief that it is better to have tried and failed than not to have tried.

Processes that focus on learning from experience rather than finding someone to blame also strengthen innovation in ECOs. The use of learning-oriented reviews and critiques of the outcomes of CI projects is built on the belief that there is something to be learned from both successful and less successful ventures. Seeking to understand what can be learned from innovative efforts provides a basis for improvement and increases the probability of future success. Jeffrey Miller, CEO of Documentum, says people in his company take great pride in being problem solvers. He described a culture built on a number of key beliefs about how to deal with problems. Open and honest communication is critical. Conditions that support this belief require acceptance that all have problems and that the organization will only succeed when the problems are freely exposed and discussed without fear of retribution. Only by exposing problems to the light of day can they be solved, and people will only expose problems where they are not punished for doing so. Mr. Miller described this approach as a powerful element in the culture of Documentum. Exposure to the success culture of Intel during his employment there contributed to the strength of his personal conviction in this area. (More discussions of open and learning-oriented critique processes can be found in Chapter 6, "Continuous Learning.")

C. Tools to Stimulate Creative Thinking

Benchmarking, challenging goals, practices that value and reward innovation and risk taking, and an open and nonthreatening culture are external factors that support innovation and creativity. Training of individuals in methods that stimulate and encourage the flow of ideas is also helpful. Among the simplest tools available is brainstorming. Establishing groundrules that help make brainstorming effective is always a part of brainstorming processes. Among the groundrules is the statement that the objective of brainstorming is to generate a large volume of ideas and the requirement that evaluative comments are to be avoided since they cut off the flow of ideas. Creation of additional ideas by building on or combining earlier ideas is encouraged, again without negative commentary. Subsequent steps in the process provide additional tools for selecting and testing ideas with the greatest potential. The "nominal group technique" is one tool that allows each person to identify a limited number of ideas they would like to see given further consideration. Some ideas are left behind for later consideration and are unlikely to be used, but none are simply rejected as unworthy. These tools help maintain an environment conducive to creativity and minimize creation of residual effects that would inhibit the contribution of ideas in other situations. While the brainstorming and nominal group technique processes have been around for a long time, it has been surprising to find many organizations or parts of organizations in which it is a totally new concept.

Other processes to stimulate the sharing and emergence of creative ideas or solutions have been developed with very different orientations. Some collect inputs from a variety of sources but without identification of the source. Participants review the inputs and get the benefit of many perspectives on the issue being considered. The intent of these processes is to reduce undue influence on the outcome based on previous contributions or known expertise. Second or third rounds of inputs are collected, again anonymously, and examined for commonalties and trends in the thinking of participants. Innovative strategies or solutions frequently emerge that are influenced by the full range of ideas presented and not primarily by consideration of the source. Technological advances allow creation today of Intranets and allow communication via the Internet or World Wide Web. Availability of these technologies facilitates the use of this type of process.

Alternative strategies have been developed for broadening individuals' perspectives and willingness to accept and work with ideas other than their own. A colleague of ours, Dr. David Cherin, refers to such strategies as "pluralogues." Face-to-face discussions explore the thinking and perspective of all participants with the explicit requirement that the exchanges seek to create understanding and not to reach agreement. The added understanding achieved is available for development of creative solutions as part of subsequent continuous improvement, learning, and change efforts of an ECO. Attempts to agree of necessity involve evaluations and the narrowing of perspective.

Encouraging experimentation adds another tool to the arsenal available to stimulate innovation in the CI efforts of ECOs. Groups are given freedom to experiment with the application of new and creative ideas. Constraints that minimize risks to the business of the organization guide the planning of experiments. But instead of talking ideas to death, people are encouraged to find a way to try them and assess their impact. The data from the experiments may confirm the value of the idea, show it to be untenable, or generate additional ideas for even greater improvement. The attractiveness of experimentation for building ECO capacity is that it produces learning and movement and avoids "paralysis by analysis." Providing support for experimentation with resources and time is another visible indicator of the value the management of ECOs place on innovation and creativity.

Each of the methods and tools discussed builds capability for innovation and creativity. They will be found in the "bag of tricks" associated with higher levels of ECO capability. They are likely to be missing or underutilized where ECO capacity is low.

XII. Summary of Continuous Improvement as an ECO Component

Ten characteristics of the CI processes we associate with high or increasing levels of ECO capacity have been described. A brief summary will be useful before proceeding to the discussion of the continuous learning component of the ECO model.

Direction for continuous improvement has been articulated and clarified with meaningful goals for all. Everyone is challenged to contribute to CI as part of their job responsibility and the challenge is to continually seek to move to and beyond the best of what is currently known to be possible. Any and all improvement is valued and from anywhere in the organization, recognizing that, big or little, the size of available opportunities for improvement varies and is not a relevant issue.

A common set of terms and definitions provides a common basis for communication and avoids wasted efforts arguing about meaning and semantics. Everyone understands his role as a customer, supplier, or producer in his work activities. The "customer–supplier model" guides relationships and the creation of conditions necessary for producing both current results and continuous improvement. The orientation of the organization has shifted away from costly inspections with uncertain effects on quality. It has been replaced with a proactive, prevention strategy that improves quality while reducing costs and improving performance in other areas.

Systematic problem solving and process-improvement processes eliminate root causes of problems or guide the improvement of processes, as appropriate. Participation by all is legitimized by the provision of structures, time, and other resources people need to do the work of CI. And, finally, the conditions, tools, and support processes are in place to encourage and reward creative and unbounded continuous improvement.

Having these conditions in place, or pursuing necessary initiatives to put them in place, moves organizations closer and closer to becoming fully capable as an Ever-Changing Organization. Without such capabilities the growing forces for change are much more likely to lead to the organization's demise.

6 Continuous Learning

I. Introduction

The dictionary defines *learn* to mean "to acquire knowledge or skill by study, instruction, or experience" and *learning* as "the act or process of acquiring skill or knowledge." The **continuous learning** (CL) component of the Ever-Changing Organization model is the subject of this chapter. The focus will be on features of CL processes that build an organization's ECO capacity. Some features emphasize processes that enhance the acquisition of knowledge or skill by individuals, whether via study and instruction or via experience. Others focus on organizational learning processes. These are processes by which individual or group learning is extracted from the organization's experience and becomes part of the organization's collective memory.

Organizations with limited ECO capability have developed few or no processes for either individual or organizational learning. The learning that does occur is a random function of the experiences of individuals and insights they develop. The individual retains the learning or only selectively shares it. The organization has no operating mechanisms for systematically capturing the learning and making it available to others.

Organizations with high levels of ECO capability, on the other hand, build systematic processes for realizing the benefit of learning throughout the organization. They invest in the learning of individuals recognizing that the human resources of the organization are the only assets capable of renewal and appreciation. The features discussed in this chapter are integrated into the organization's strategies for CL and increased ECO capability. They are related to the overall commitment to change, learning, and improvement in a way that builds the organization's stabilizing base (see Chapter 3).

II. Investment in Continuous Learning

Most of the spending on continuous learning is devoted to the area of training. Some commit up to 4% of payroll and as much as 5% of people's time for training. But this level of spending comes from a miniscule portion of the total number of employers in the U.S. Estimates of total spending on training range from 45 to 50 billion dollars annually. Less than 1% of employers spend over 90% of that money. Overall estimates vary but generally suggest that the average organization's spending for training is less than 1% of payroll dollars or of people's time.

These estimates focus on the time and money spent in formal training endeavors whether that be in a classroom, at an educational institution, via computer, or on-the-job. They do not include time spent in more informal or organizational learning processes, e.g., with peers or mentors, in learning-oriented critiques, or in improvement activities with learning and change objectives. If these types of learning were included, the estimates of spending as a percent of time or payroll would increase for many organizations, especially those with significant capacity as an Ever-Changing Organization.

A. *Spending for Training as an Expense*

The estimates of spending for training make no attempt to assess the value received or the return realized from the spending. However, observations suggest that a primary factor in keeping spending levels low is management's very low expectation of a payoff from the spending. Too often the training offered by an organization and the selection process for participation, i.e., how decisions are made regarding who will attend or "get sent to be fixed," is not related to improved achievement of business results. The processes employed are aptly described by a colleague of ours, Jim Bandrowski, as "dip and pray" training. Less purposeful in many ways than "sheep dipping," non-results-oriented training and criteria-less decision making represents little more than an immersion of participants in the training experience accompanied by faint hope that some of the training will take and be useful. In addition, the absence of measurement or efforts to correlate participation to changes in performance leaves evaluation of the impact subjective and without supporting data. Thus, when financial plans are being made training loses out, rightly or wrongly, to spending based on data and with a predictable return.

Unfortunately, the conditions described continue to exist in too many organizations. Spending for training is viewed as an expense. Not only is it seen as an expense, it is viewed as a discretionary expense. Organizations with this perspective do not develop continuous learning processes or capability as an ECO. This is a shortcoming of management and those responsible for the training and development functions. Training is treated as "nice to have when we can afford it." The approach is basically paternalistic and dependent on the good will of a benevolent father, i.e., management. Where training is provided, managers and trainers assume responsibility for deciding what people need, how much they are going to get, and for assessing whether or not learning takes place.

The individual learner is not part of the process except to attend and sit through assigned training and absorb whatever it is that is being taught. No preparation is given and no goals established for on-the-job application of the learning. Managers often do not know what is being presented, how it fits with their own beliefs and style, and may even resent the fact that their people have been assigned to attend. People returning to their jobs find ways to encapsulate what they learn since they know it will not be supported. We have encountered situations where supervisors have explicitly instructed newly trained subordinates to forget what they learned and get back to business. Dr. Tom Hopkins, a former colleague and director of education and career development, described these situations as "sending someone to get religion and then returning them to the pagan environment where practicing the religion is not allowed."

The probability of getting a return from the money and time spent in training is very low under such conditions. If management expects little, they are correct. And their minimal expectations are conveyed to their people. The ultimate effect of all this is another "self-fulfilling prophecy," i.e., we expected little and behaved in ways that proved our expectations to be correct. Unless different sets of beliefs are adopted there is virtually no chance that spending for training will ever be more than an expense. Nor will it contribute to improvements in an organization's ECO capability.

B. Spending for Training as an Investment

Organizations with significant ECO capacity view training and learning activities as an investment in the human capital of the organization. Gary Tooker, CEO of Motorola, says, "If knowledge is becoming antiquated at a faster rate, we have no choice but to spend on education. How can that not be a competitive weapon?"[32] Resources are being applied to the development and appreciation of the organization's only renewable assets, its people. As with any other investment an acceptable return is expected. The outcome of the investment must be related to improvement in individual and business results. When looked at from this perspective the training and development efforts of many organizations would not stand the test and, rightfully, would receive no additional resources.

On the other hand, thinking of CL as an investment and of people as assets capable of appreciation provides a solid basis for changing the organization's approach. Anyone with people reporting to them is seen as responsible for managing a set of assets, both physical and human. The physical assets have required an investment and are expected to produce a return. If those assets are not properly maintained and their processes improved and operated in control, the manager is required to account for the deterioration of the values of the assets involved. Likewise with the human assets, except in this case the investments made are expected to have increased the value of the assets as opposed to maximizing the useful life of depreciating assets.

Consider the following scenario, simplified to cover one supervisor and one subordinate. The subordinate has ten years experience with the company. In that time the total out-of-pocket investment in the person for salary, benefits, training, space and equipment, and so on totals approximately $500,000. The person has held three different positions. The only training received to date, other than on-the-job, involved attendance at a supervisory skills workshop and a workshop to learn tools and skills for participation in the organization's continuous improvement process. She is perceived to have the potential to advance at least one more level in the organization. At the beginning of the year the supervisor is asked about plans to continue this woman's development, to increase her value as a human asset, and to assure an acceptable return on what will then be at least a $550,000 investment. The supervisor is guided by a wide list of actions for developing the person's value as an asset. He is encouraged to consider these and other ideas they might have specific to the person's role and job. The supervisor and employee jointly develop the plan for the year. At the end of the year the supervisor reports what was done and the results of those actions on the value of the woman as a human asset.

Whether or not the numbers reported are correct or defensible is not the critical issue. What is important is that the supervisor is being required to view the person as an asset capable of appreciation and of generating a return on the organization's investment. He is being asked to operate in ways that consider the value of the investment and how to utilize the person and to help her increase her value each year. While some may argue that this perspective dehumanizes the workplace, we believe that just the opposite is true. People are no longer a disposable asset and the organization approaches the management of its people from a much more positive perspective. This model builds ECO capability; the expense model tears it down.

Where spending for training is viewed as an expense, supervisors would never be asked these questions. It is more likely that they would be asked to maintain or reduce budgeting for training or other CL activities. Where CL spending is viewed as an investment the organization will target a specific percentage of payroll and time for training and CL. And that level is likely to be maintained annually by a management that views the spending as a continuing investment in the value of its human assets. But, as with other investments, managers must make the investments wisely, not only from a financial perspective but also in terms of assignments, coaching, competency and developmental planning, and so on. They are required to report on the actions taken and the investment made. They are also expected to offer evidence that wise decisions were made and that the assets under their control appreciated in total value. Helpful to supervisors will be the fact that their managers must address the same issues. The supervisor's value as an asset and what has been done to develop it throughout the year will also be accounted for. Organizations viewing CL as an investment assign the individual responsibility for managing their own development. The organization and the supervisor support the process (see the next section, "Life/Career-Long Learning Support").

The forces on those that design the organization's training offerings will also grow. When seen as an investment with an expected return, selection of subject matter and learning methods must be focused on demonstrable achievement of improved results. There is much that can be done to establish requirements for training and its outcomes and to move away from simply counting numbers of people trained or their responses to post-training questionnaires (sometimes called "happy sheets"). There is a much greater need to consult the customers for the training to identify their needs and not simply offer what is easily available. The customers include supervisors and managers as well as those who participate. They will demand that much greater emphasis be placed on delivery of training on a just-in-time (JIT) basis. Motivation to learn, retention, and on-the-job application of learning increase greatly when learning occurs at the time it is needed and not at the convenience of others.

Overall the focus on training and CL work as an investment is aimed at improving return on human assets (ROHA). Attempts have been made for many years to devise schemes for quantifying ROHA in financial terms. The difficulty is great and much of the problem is attributable to the problem of sorting out cause from effect. If results improved, are the gains attributable to the CL experiences? If not, is it the responsibility of the training design, the trainer, the learner, or the conditions in the work place? The difficulty is partly attributable to managers and financial specialists who prefer to see training as a discretionary expense. Moving it to the category of investment removes a key source of flexible spending and requires that managers and financial people become involved in planning and assessing the impact of CL activities on the organization's results.

Our preference for organization's building ECO capacity is that they begin from the perspective that CL and training are an investment in ROHA and with the strong "commitment to change, learning, and improvement" discussed as part of the stabilizing base of an ECO. Build CL processes on the investment (vs. expense) concept so that thinking, planning, and resource allocation decisions are made on that basis. As the organization moves forward, use the CL processes presented in this chapter to learn which processes improve results and which do not. Continue to learn about results producing CL and in the process add to the organization's ECO capacity.

III. Life/Career-Long Learning Support

Ever-Changing Organizations provide life/career-long support for the learning and developmental needs of their people. This is not simply a "be nice to people" strategy. It is adopted because there are clear win–win outcomes for people and for the organization associated with such a strategy. Among other things this continuing support builds a bond between the person and the organization that meets the needs of both despite the crush of other forces that threaten to drive the two apart.

A. Redefining the Person–Organization Bond

Recent trends in managing excess costs have created a very real dilemma for many organizations. People and jobs have become a major focus of cost reduction. News reports of planned reductions occur almost daily. The dehumanizing nature of many such efforts is revealed by their concentration on ways to eliminate the costs of the longest term, and therefore more expensive, employees. Among the labels that have been used for these processes are lay off, cutback, reduction-in-force (RIF), zero-based budgeting, outplacement, delayering, downsizing (or the more politically correct "rightsizing"), or reengineering. Arguments about the true cost savings or benefits of these actions are common. They are most often won by those with the financial figures and with short-term interests in earnings and stock value, no matter what the one-time "restructuring charges" applied to the balance sheet or the long-term costs of losing valuable assets.

The organizational dilemma arises from people's perception of a unilateral abrogation of a generally implicit, but very powerful, psychological contract based on mutual loyalty. Historically people have committed their entire lives and careers to a particular organization. Many are following in the footsteps of their parents or other family members who devoted their entire work life to the same organization. The implied contract was one of mutual loyalty. People learned to expect that, in return for a good day's work and loyalty to the organization, the organization would be loyal to its employees and be a reliable, career-long source of employment.

With the widespread use of the various methods for terminating people's relationship with the organization, the loyalty paradigm is either dead or severely damaged as a basis for the bond between the organization and its people. And the inclusion of managers and other white-collar employees in these programs has extended the damage to employees who have often felt more secure in their positions than those at lower levels. Many people rue the demise of the implied loyalty contract. But in the increasingly changeable world of today the death of this concept may be overdue. Whether or not the loyalty paradigm is realistic or sustainable in the rapidly changing, knowledge-based, and globally competitive environments of today's organizations is highly questionable.

Yet, organizations and individual employees would still prefer stable and long-term relationships based on mutual loyalty, even in the face of accelerating change. The challenge is to either rebuild or find a meaningful replacement for loyalty as the basis for the person–organization bond. Where ECO capacity is low, little effort and almost no energy is invested in resolving this dilemma. Likewise, there is very little expenditure of money or effort in training or CL. Failure to resolve the dilemma will succeed only if the historical environment of the organization is stable and not subject to the growing uncertainties and forces for change experienced by other organizations. In highly uncertain environments there is no choice but to create an alternative to loyalty as the basis for a meaningful person–organization bond.

Organizations employing the people reduction strategies listed above appear to be unaware of the effects of their actions or convinced that the costs will be less than the savings achieved. Many put more effort into helping the people displaced than those who stay. Very limited effort is made to help the people who remain deal with their uncertainties and fears or with the guilt they feel for having survived while close colleagues did not. In addition to their sense of loss, people feel threatened and out of control. And they have a dilemma. They no longer trust their organization to be what was once a loyal and stable employer. At the same time they really do not want to leave. They feel vulnerable and unprepared to face the change involved if they end up being terminated due to factors beyond their control. Their skills are limited and the organization has probably done little to support development of additional skills or job competencies for other work. It's a scary situation.

B. Life/Career-Long Learning Support as the New Paradigm

There are several features that are integrated into a strategy of life/career-long learning support. Among these are the following;

- Clarity of the psychological contract with the organization. Discomfort may remain but the opportunity to deal with reality is available.
- A partnership between the person and the organization in the continuous learning and development process. The individual assumes responsibility for his or her learning and development. Some will use the processes while others may opt not to participate. The organization assumes responsibility to aid in defining and supporting fulfillment of developmental needs.
- The nature of the partnership as the basis for the person–organization bond is made explicit vs. the implicit loyalty bond.
- The risks associated with expectations of permanent employment are clarified.
- Preparation for alternative employment options, either internal or external, is available to all.
- Fixed percentages of payroll dollars and time are allocated annually. Thus, the process is not on-again, off-again based on current or projected performance.
- A range of learning options is built into the organization, deliverable in a number of ways and adaptable to the needs of the individual and the organization. Many options involve little out-of-pocket spending.

■ Flexibility is built into the processes to maximize accessibility for everyone. Learning via new technologies, as well as with established methods, allows delivery in the manner best suited to the subject and the learner.

C. Win-Win Nature of the New Paradigm

The organization — individual bond created by the life/career-long learning support paradigm may be stronger that the broken bond it replaces. It is based on a "win-win" relationship. The explicit nature of the partnership between the person and the organization and the ongoing ability to test and renew the partnership makes for a stronger relationship. This is like the biological phenomenon that healed bones are stronger at the point of fracture than the original structure.

The "wins" for the organization from this paradigm include:

■ Increasingly more valuable employees.
■ Greater flexibility from availability of a greater number of skilled people with a wider mix of knowledge, skills, and abilities.
■ Rekindled feelings of loyalty via an explicit, realistic, and sustainable psychological contract.
■ Increased employee self-regeneration in response to, or in anticipation of, needs for new or additional competencies.
■ People better equipped to function in the environment of an ECO.
■ Reduced guilt feelings if reductions become necessary since management's actions, while unfortunate, are consistent with the explicit psychological contract.

Employee "wins" with the new paradigm include:

■ Gaining self-control of their ongoing learning and development.
■ Continuing opportunities to grow and advance and to avoid stagnation or obsolescence.
■ Greater insight into needed competencies in current or future positions.
■ Increasing their value to the organization making the person harder to replace and the decision to terminate more difficult.
■ Development of increased value for other employers if the need arises.
■ Explicit awareness of the organization's commitment to support people's needs for growth and development.

In exploring this element of an organization's CL processes it has become very clear that this option will be preferred by organizations building their capacity as an ECO. Win-lose or lose-lose conditions are minimized and the processes developed support proactive creation of increased capacity for change, learning, and improvement.

D. Learning Vehicles

The learning vehicles made available in organizations with strong ECO capabilities go well beyond those available in traditional training departments. While trainer-led seminars, whether internal or external, continue as part of the available vehicles, many other modes of learning are included. Our intention is not to catalog all of the various modalities but to offer a sample, some of which are discussed in this chapter and in the chapter on continuous improvement, e.g., tools and methods for problem solving and process improvement.

Many organizations today have developed corporate learning centers. Others are creating learning capabilities and housing them within "corporate universities." Our colleague Kevin Wheeler, for example, was the founder of National Semiconductor University and was also responsible for Charles Schwab University during his tenure with that organization. He believes that the label "university" should not be used to rename the traditional training function. Rather, the offerings have to be relevant and adaptable to developing needed competencies of individuals as well as those needed for achieving the vision and direction of the organization. Corporate universities should include support to the quality and continuous improvement processes of the organization, to processes for change and organization development, and to the human resource development responsibilities of managers and supervisors.

Processes that provide learning support among peers and across organizational lines and levels are included as key learning vehicles. These are discussed in the section of this chapter called "Structured Developmental Relationships." They represent a trend towards building on the stabilizing base of employees and their knowledge and skill to support others. There is clear evidence that these relationships benefit all parties and can be an important part of the life/career-long learning support for more senior people.

New learning process and technologies also become part of the organization's overall set of learning vehicles. Advancing capabilities in video technology and compact discs make training available to more broadly dispersed sets of employees. Other examples of new and changing technologies would be computer-mediated learning, learning via the Internet or on the organization's own Intranet, distance learning via teleconferencing with remote sites, and continuing education via satellite linkages to private or public universities.

As more learning vehicles are developed and made broadly available the CL processes of the organization are able to provide life/career-long learning support and build increased capacity for change, learning, and improvement in the process.

IV. Competency/Development Planning

Earlier we criticized training delivered without a focus on business results and without processes and criteria for participation, calling it "dip and pray" training. Identifying and developing needed competencies for individuals and for the organization is a critical feature of the CL processes where ECO capabilities are strong. Included are processes for identifying required or anticipated competencies for a specific position. Processes for assessing an individual's competencies are also a must. Armed with the data developed in these processes, supervisors and individual employees work together to identify competency gaps, explore ways to acquire needed competencies, and create meaningful development plans.

A. Identifying Competencies Required for Specific Positions

Competency requirements for a specific position describe the knowledge, skills, and abilities (KSAs) needed for successful job performance. The needs may cover specific technical knowledge, manual skills, supervisory/leadership abilities, interpersonal skills, knowledge gained from prior experiences, and so on.

The process begins with a description of the job, i.e., what is done, where, how frequently, by whom, and so on. More simplified processes involve supervisors and job incumbents in describing the job and the competencies required. Standardized lists of competencies may be provided from which to select those needed for the specific position. Or the KSAs are extracted from the description of the job. More sophisticated approaches have evolved recently based on what is called a "360°" analysis. In addition to incumbents and supervisors these processes involve those who deal with the position from internal or external roles as customers or suppliers, subordinates (as appropriate), competency specialists, and people with prior experience in the position. The purpose is to identify the full range of competencies required as seen from all relevant perspectives, i.e., from the 360 degrees of the sphere surrounding the position.

The position description and its competency requirements serve as tools for assessment and development planning for people already in the position. They can also be made available to people who have a future interest in the position. The data guide individuals and supervisors in creating developmental plans and selecting the most useful vehicles for gaining needed competencies. To be fully effective for development planning the competency analyses also require an inventory of the individual's existing competencies.

B. Inventorying Individual Competencies

Developmental planning focuses on building competencies for current or future positions. Creating an inventory of the person's current set of KSAs is an important step in the planning process. The inventory includes assessment of the set of competencies needed for the individual's present job. It also catalogues KSAs acquired from prior work or life experiences that are current or available for use in other positions.

Individuals contribute data to their personal competency inventory by describing their history and the KSAs acquired. Competencies used in the current position are also included. Reviews and discussions with the immediate supervisor support this process. Valuable additional data are available where a 360° feedback process is in use.

C. Development Planning To Fill Competency Gaps

Competency gaps are identified using information about competencies required in the person's current position and data from the individual's competency inventory. The individual has the responsibility for having a plan and the supervisor is assigned to support the process. The organization also supports the process as described in the section above on life/career-long learning support.

Current competency gaps will need near-term priority while those associated with desirable future positions can be built into a longer term developmental plan. Timing of the developmental plan needs to reflect the urgency and motivation of the individual and the potential availability of the position(s). Annual reviews and updates are required.

Mary Jean Connors, senior VP of Human Resources for Knight-Ridder, is very clear that the responsibility for support to individual development must come from supervisors and managers. "We don't have this little farm at corporate that is growing them." She says that managers need to identify the talent and the skills needed, provide coaching and performance management, do joint developmental planning, and see that the needed training is provided. She describes the insight needed in saying, "Hello, that is not a human resources' job. That is a line manager's job."

D. Building the Organization's Competency Development Plan

Building ECO capabilities requires understanding of the organization's core competencies.[33] Knowing what you have and being able to integrate existing competencies opens up possibilities for creating exciting new products and markets. The organization may also access additional competencies through strategic alliances or acquisitions. Dr. Madni, CEO of BEI Sensors and Systems, described a range of core competencies his company has developed or acquired. Together these "form the basis of any motion sensor system (and allow us to) adapt individual divisional capabilities working with other divisions to generate new business and expand market share and market segments." Building these capabilities becomes more important in rapidly changing environments where organizations seek to lead. Adding to core competency pools or acquiring new competencies does not happen by chance. Management needs systematic competency-planning processes to avoid being caught short.

Analysis of core organizational competencies, competency analyses of existing and future positions, and individual developmental plans provide data for the organization's competency development plan. The planning process involves selection of life/career-long learning support vehicles, design of processes for their delivery, and timing their availability. Management involvement in setting direction and reviewing plans is highly desirable. They will make the resource allocation decisions and need to be aware of how those decisions impact availability of people and competencies to meet current and future needs. Dr. Madni of BEI confirms this:

> When technology starts to change rapidly the external environment changes, the methodology of conducting business changes, and customer needs and expectations change. If the company's knowledge base has not kept up with the external changes and parameters, the knowledgeable people of the company start serving as company historians rather than being leading edge contributors.

Management must stay on top of these issues in a rapidly changing world.

As the rate of change increases, the organization will also have to evolve its processes for acquiring needed competencies. Some advanced technological competencies, for example, actually develop in business organizations before they are taught in colleges or universities. In addition, educational institutions have not been particularly customer oriented or change friendly and may not be turning out people with the competencies needed. This could apply to basic KSAs such as the three R's as well as to competencies associated with advances in technology. When this happens, organizations with strong ECO capability act to find or develop the competencies themselves. Staffing and recruiting practices might be refocused to include new sources. The organization might invest in developing specific competencies internally or contract with educational institutions or private training and development organizations for that service.

The efforts of Knight-Ridder, described by CEO Tony Ridder, include hiring practices in some parts of the organization aimed at people with understanding of new technologies and of the Internet. Competency in these areas has not developed in management ranks dominated by people with many years of industry experience who had no prior need for the competency. At the corporate level, the move of the Knight-Ridder headquarters from Florida to Silicon Valley and the creation of a New Media Group support the strategy of hiring and building these competencies.

Knight-Ridder's New Media Group President, Bob Ingle, and Kathy Yates, VP of Business Development, describe an internal process as a first step to developing awareness of the need for the competencies. It aims to increase the willingness of higher level managers to acquire the competencies and support the changes necessary to compete in the rapidly changing environment of the newspaper industry. The process is called the New Media Fellowship and it has two key components. First, members of the organization deliver an intense series of presentations. They paint a picture of changes in the marketplace due to new forms of competition. Emphasis is placed on how the changes impact the customer and the basis for his or her satisfaction. Participants also tour a number of Silicon Valley companies to observe the differences in the work environment and the thinking of people in those businesses. The result of the process is a group of people opened up and more willing to consider change. And the organization is continuing to learn from the process. One insight, for example, is that "When you get people into a disruptive vision of the old world, you need to be ready to replace it with a vision of the new world." To avoid losing the receptivity to change developed in the process, they have learned that they also need answers to questions about what people are expected to do and specifically where they are going, i.e., it is possible to begin too soon.

Organizations like Knight-Ridder have recognized the need to create competency development and acquisition processes to fill their specific needs. Environmental sensing and internal competency/developmental planning processes are designed to alert them to current or future competency gaps and provide data for proactive steps to fill the gaps. These capabilities help move organizations to change-friendly or change-seeking levels of ECO capability. On the other hand, organizations at the change-managing level of ECO capacity or below will only identify the gaps when it is already too late to be proactive. The organization is then forced into excessive spending or must slow its forward movement while reactive and interim measures are devised. Neither of these options is acceptable in less stable environments that demand proactive and more rapid adaptation to external forces for change.

V. Structured Developmental Relationships

Organizations have been aware of informal relationships that contribute to the development of some individuals for some time. Some of these are called "mentoring" relationships and involve a newer, often younger person whose development benefits from the counsel and guidance of a more experienced person. Similar informal relationships develop when a more experienced peer takes a new person "under his or her wing" to guide them, help them acquire needed knowledge or skills, or to "teach them the ropes" about what is acceptable or not in the organization's culture.

A. Mentors and Protégés

Historically, such informal relationships have benefited the "protégé" and have been satisfying to the "mentor" even though the roles have not been assigned. The relationships have emerged in unplanned ways and often as the result of an introduction or exposure through a special assignment. A positive chemistry has resulted that forms the basis for future contacts. Questioning by the protégé and sharing by the mentor give the protégé access to information not available in other ways and provide an inside track for development of the person's career. Unfortunately, only a few people benefit from these relationships and often in ways that tend to be selectively biased. Many of the connections are developed via the "old boy network" and have systematically been unavailable to those without access to the network, e.g., females and other minorities. But the benefits derived from such relationships are very positive.

As a result, many organizations have developed more formal processes for establishing structured developmental relationships and extending the benefits of such relationships to others in a more equitable and systematic manner.[34] Any or all of the following types of structured developmental relationships may be employed by an organization. Some are more common in larger organizations where the probability of reaping the benefits on an informal basis is constrained by overall size, geographic dispersion, and complexity. Strong capabilities as an ECO are developed via the developmental learning available in these processes.

B. Types of Structured Developmental Relationships

- Supervisor–Subordinate — Virtually all members of an organization have a structured developmental relationship with their direct manager or supervisor. Whether or not the relationship has a healthy developmental component is strongly influenced by the organization's approach to building a life/career-long learning support system. The supervisor/subordinate partnership in the individual's development is supported by the organization's explicit commitment to ongoing development.
- Apprentice — Long known and accepted in trades, this is another type of one-on-one structured developmental relationship. In management situations this involves an assignment to a more senior manager for a period of time.
- Mentor–protégé — Mentioned above, this relationship may extend over a period of years or be limited to a specific period of time and for a specific purpose. It operates outside of normal reporting lines. It may be focused in areas such as management and leadership, technical capabilities, or acculturation of the protégé.

- Peer support systems — These are peer-coaching types of processes that involve the assignment of individuals to assist new people in learning a job and becoming familiar with the work processes and procedures of the department or unit. The "dock-mentor" process used by Viking Freight System to orient and train new dockworkers is a form of this process. Assignment may be to an individual or a team of people who do not report to the assigned coach.
- Trainer assignments — This process involves the preparation of individuals from anywhere in the organization to act as trainers for other people, usually in classroom settings. The role is sometimes extended to serving as a post-training resource regarding the application of what was learned in on-the-job situations. In larger organizations the process might be further extended to include preparation of trainers for the additional task of training other trainers. Clients of The Quality Improvement Company train a range of trainers as do clients of many training organizations.
- Team/group facilitator — This role is focused on helping a group or team leader and the team itself in developing skills and processes for improving their effectiveness.
- Executive coaching — Typically this is a relationship between an executive and an external consultant. It aims at providing support and developing improved executive performance through access to an independent and dispassionate third party.
- Organizational action groups — This process brings together groups of people to work on real-life organizational problems or processes, learning from each other and from the assigned issue. A period of time away from the job is allocated to the learning and problem-resolution process of the group.
- Learning networks — Groups of managers are formed who meet periodically to share and focus on their own issues and developmental needs. These can be established internally or involve groups of executives from different, noncompeting organizations.

C. Mutually Beneficial Relationships

In virtually all of these structured relationships there are developmental payoffs for all parties to the relationship. Managers assigned and trained for roles as trainers almost always comment that the experience confirms the old saying, "The best way to learn a subject is to be required to teach it."

In any of the mentor-like roles there is development and learning associated with the need to coach, listen and support, and challenge the protégé. Mentors are also forced to examine what they know and to become capable of articulating it to another person in a way that withstands the testing and challenges of the protégé. Significant learning and reinforcement occurs via this process. Protégés on the other hand benefit from learning and insights shared by the mentor, from the opportunity to test and challenge the mentor, from explorations of how to apply what they learn, and from the risk-free opportunity for critique and learning in exchanges with the mentor.

The greatest benefit is obtained from structured developmental relationships when the parties involved properly prepare for their roles. Bill Miller, senior VP and Director of the Corporate Learning Center for The Money Store, says the parties involved must have "a clear understanding of what the expectations of a mentor are." An initial attempt at structured developmental relationships did not work as well as expected. Learning from this experience, Mr. Miller now says, "We will not go forward again until we have it clearly structured, have all the competencies of the mentor identified, and know what fits and works for our company. We will have a true mentor process and it will emerge from a leadership discovery process."

Parties involved in structured developmental relationships must be oriented to the process and trained in the nature of the roles. They need training to develop specific new skills required for the role. They need to begin the relationship on common ground and with mutually agreed-upon expectations. This requires investing up-front time in negotiation of roles, groundrules, time commitments, availability, goals, and how to assess and make adjustments to the relationship to better meet the needs of all parties. Relationships built on proper preparation are more meaningful for all parties. Mutually satisfying outcomes cause many of these linkages to become highly valued, long-term relationships extending well beyond the time frame of the developmental assignment.

VI. Learning Critiques

Among the most readily available processes for learning and improvement is the use of critique. The term critique must not be confused with the idea of criticism. Criticism implies some form of negative feedback, usually personal in nature and probably threatening in some way. Critique processes, on the other hand, are used for learning and are not intended as a vehicle for personal attack. The focus of critique is on work processes and results and what can be learned from them. The outcome of a critique may involve decisions to maintain a process as presently practiced, to strengthen the process by adding to it or doing more of what makes the process effective, or to improve the process by reducing or eliminating actions that inhibit the process and diminish results.

The use of learning critiques is a defining characteristic of organizations with a high level of ECO capability. Adding critique processes to an organization's operating practices is among the easiest and most powerful ways to increase ECO capacity in the short run. These processes can be used by everyone in the organization and applied to all work processes. Those who have experienced the process conduct the critique. Preferably the critiques are used when the experience is fresh and not a collection of memories distorted by time.

A. Types of Critique

The three most common forms of critique are retrospective, periodic, and concurrent, i.e., real time. Retrospective critique is often referred to as "post-mortem" and occurs at the completion of an event or project. Our experience in working with hospitals and other health care groups has led us to drop the term "post-mortem." The implication of examination after death denotes a process designed to learn, but sadly the "patient" did not survive. *Retrospective* is a more appropriate term for critique processes that seek learning as a basis for improvement, not as an explanation for failure.

1. Retrospective Critique

This after-the-fact form of critique is probably the most common. It is frequently used as a support to the ongoing efforts of temporary or ongoing work teams to improve the effectiveness of their meetings. Top level executive teams, quality improvement teams, functional work teams, process teams, self-managing work teams, or any other team will find it useful.

In organizations with strong continuous learning processes, the meeting agenda of teams set aside a brief period for critique at the end of each meeting. Since meetings consume significant amounts of time, especially in more complex organizations dealing with rapid change, meeting effectiveness is an important issue. Critique discussions focus on issues the team considers important to its performance. Examples might include advanced availability of a detailed agenda; range and effectiveness of participation; leadership; listening; control; management of conflicts; and many other factors. What should be sustained or changed or eliminated is considered and decisions made for the conduct of future meetings.

Retrospective critique is also used at the completion of the work of project teams. The objective in these cases is on learning that can benefit future teams with similar charters. In some situations the use of critique is extended to the point that the work of the team is not considered complete until the results of the post-project critique have been captured, debriefed, and distributed or placed in an archive for use by future teams. Issues may relate to the process of establishing the team and its charter, selection of members, clarity of goals, planning processes, communications beyond the team, participation, support and resources provided, internal team functioning, interpersonal processes, or other factors inhibiting or facilitating the team and its results.

While common with teams, individuals examining their own work process for potential changes and improvements also conduct retrospective critiques. Sharing the outcomes with supervisors and peers who deal with the same or related processes spreads the learning beyond the person involved.

2. Periodic Critique

This form of critique is really a variation of retrospective critique but it occurs at predetermined intervals. Experienced and ongoing teams may decide to hold a more thorough critique of their working process once a month or every third meeting. More data are available for consideration in discussing potential changes in these situations. Other groups elect to build periodic critiques into an ongoing or lengthy process rather than to wait for completion when change is no longer possible. Trainers will often schedule periodic critiques with participants in the training session, e.g., every half-day or at the end of each day. Consideration of what is working or not working well for participants either confirms continuation of the training design or suggests modifications to improve satisfaction and learning outcomes.

Regularly scheduled reviews and customer feedback are another form of periodic critique. Contractual, weekly customer feedback obtained by Solectron allows the organization to identify and make adjustments that prevent minor issues from becoming full-blown problems.

Signetics Corporation's top management team designed periodic critiques into their quality improvement methodology. Divisional and functional management quality improvement teams (QITs) were scheduled for periodic review and critique meetings with the top management QIT. The process used was designed to promote learning and to facilitate the deployment of the improvement process throughout the corporation. The top team recognized that many of their review meetings had not been conducted as critiques. As teams reviewed their improvement process, goals, and progress, the attention of the top level QIT was focused on what could be learned. What was the team doing that worked well for them and how could this be shared with other teams that might be wrestling with a similar issue? What was the top team doing that facilitated or inhibited the work of the team being reviewed? How else could they be helpful? Had management's expectations and the company plans and goals been clearly communicated? And so on. The process employed clearly represented a critique aimed at learning and away from blame or punishment. Feedback from the teams being reviewed confirmed their experience of the process as learning oriented and helpful.

3. Concurrent Critique

The concurrent critique occurs on a real-time basis. It involves an interruption of the ongoing process to deal with concerns about how the process or group involved is operating. The intention is to test the concern of the person or subgroup that intervenes in the process and, if confirmed, to make midcourse corrections. Typically, something is perceived to be causing reduced effectiveness. Continuation of the process without correction is assumed to mean continuation on a path to failure or inadequate results.

Concurrent critique is most effective when the group involved agrees explicitly that it is desirable and legitimizes its use. A common strategy for making concurrent critique legitimate is the use of a "time-out" signal, either with gestures or verbally. When that occurs, the group agrees to stop what is happening and to take time to understand and eliminate the problem or to adjust the process going forward.

Misuse of concurrent critique can occur when individuals use time-outs in attempting to impose their will on the group. This problem can be minimized by establishing an agreed-upon set of groundrules at the time the group begins its work. Then the criteria for calling a time-out include concerns that the accepted ground rules are being violated and the process needs to be corrected or changed.

In the early stages of a group's life concurrent critique is less likely, even with established ground rules. Familiarity and trust must be built before some will take the risk they perceive in interrupting the work of the group. We have developed a simple, but powerful, process to encourage and legitimize the use of concurrent critique even in newly formed groups or those that will only meet once. The process is called "how to have a lousy meeting!" The meeting begins with a review of the agenda and objectives. The group then brainstorms a list of the things that would be happening if they were involved in a really lousy meeting. In an unfortunate way, but useful for this process, extensive experience with lousy meetings makes development of the list a brief task. The list is then posted where it will be visible throughout the meeting. All participants are asked to commit to two things. First, that they will each manage their own actions to avoid the things on the list. Second, if or when things on the list happen, they will call "time-out" and allow the group to change whatever is needed to move back to a more productive mode. Experience with this process has been very positive. Concurrent critique occurs easily because all have agreed to confront the occurrence of behaviors on the "lousy meeting" list. And confronting the issue is seen to be to everyone's benefit and not a personal attack. The seven or eight minutes needed for this process at the beginning of a meeting appears to eliminate a significant portion of the nagging problems so often experienced in group meetings.

B. Structured vs. Open Critiques

Critique processes vary from open and free-form discussions to highly structured ones. Structured processes provide a framework for the critique discussion. The structure provided varies from a list of subjects to be considered to the use of questionnaires and scales that are completed prior to any discussion.

Some people believe that the use of structure artificially narrows the scope of a critique and should be avoided. Others argue that structure encourages exploring a broad range of effectiveness issues and that the structure assures coverage of the relevant and important issues impacting the group's performance. Our perspective is that there is no one answer.

Figure 6.1 is an example of a structured critique form.[35] The scales are specifically focused on the issue of group communication, an important area of concern but clearly not designed to cover the full range of issues that might be impacting team effectiveness. Several factors to consider in selecting between structured and more open critiques are listed below:

ASSESSING GROUP COMMUNICATION

Rate how you think our team works together in these six areas of communication:

1. We make a point of getting ideas from each other.
   Always   Usually   Sometimes   Rarely
   ☐   ☐   ☐   ☐

2. We listen carefully to what other members have to say.
   Always   Usually   Sometimes   Rarely
   ☐   ☐   ☐   ☐

3. We avoid ignoring anyone during our group discussions.
   Always   Usually   Sometimes   Rarely
   ☐   ☐   ☐   ☐

4. We encourage each other to openly and honestly say what we think.
   Always   Usually   Sometimes   Rarely
   ☐   ☐   ☐   ☐

5. When a member of our group has an especially good idea, we give him/her praise and recognition.
   Always   Usually   Sometimes   Rarely
   ☐   ☐   ☐   ☐

6. We avoid putting other members "down," even in jest.
   Always   Usually   Sometimes   Rarely
   ☐   ☐   ☐   ☐

Figure 6.1   Assessing group communication. Example of a structured critique form for assessing and improving group communication.

- Structured critiques are likely to benefit groups and individuals with limited experience as a group or with critique processes. More mature groups may feel constrained by structure or compelled to cover areas where there is no current need.

- The use of rating scales in structured critiques makes it possible for the information to be collected and summarized anonymously. Sharing reactions in this manner involves less personal risk taking and can help the team through the awkwardness common in the early stages of a team's work.
- Structured critiques using scales allow tracking of the averages and ranges of responses over time. Trends, positively or negatively, provide additional indications of areas for work or where improvement attempts have been beneficial. The caution is to avoid using the scales too frequently. Groups sometimes feel compelled to provide responses indicating improvement in areas previously addressed when there is none.
- Team critiques with respect to ground rules adapted by the group may be either structured or open. Areas for discussion can also be derived by referral to "how to have a lousy meeting" lists. Discussion focuses on whether problem areas were successfully avoided or how to avoid them in subsequent meetings.
- Whether using structured or open forms of critique, the approach used can be altered from time to time to prevent the process from becoming mechanical and inhibiting ongoing change and improvement.

The basic issue, whatever choices are made, is that critiques need to be used regularly and systematically. The outcomes of the processes employed will support learning, change, and improvement and increase the organization's capacity as an ECO.

VII. Identifying Success and Failure Patterns

One way to stimulate learning and change is to find out what makes the organization succeed and fail. Too often learning occurs in a limited area or with respect to a single event. Yet most organizations have extensive experience with their primary business processes and do little to analyze the patterns of success and failure associated with those processes. Building ECO strength requires identifying and learning from these patterns.

A. Applied Materials

Jim Morgan, CEO of Applied Materials, shared a document that is made available and discussed with all members of his company around the world. It is called "10 Ways to be Successful."[36] The introduction tells people that:

Working effectively through change is one of our strongest and most rewarded characteristics. If you are open to change, you will see the challenges as opportunities to succeed. Understand each opportunity in its entirety and complexity, then strive for simplicity to maximize your potential.

In a situation where two thirds of the people had been with the company less than two years, Mr. Morgan felt the need to "go back and restimulate the culture so they would have a better idea of why we are successful and of how to be successful for themselves." He discussed success factors with many others and then produced the document. The importance of open and reliable communication is listed as one of the ways to succeed and is represented in the phrase, "Bad news is good news." These ideas are discussed repeatedly and such phrases have been reestablished as part of the cultural pattern.

B. The Minicase Method

The minicase method represents a tool we feel needs to be integrated into the continuous learning processes of organizations working to increase their CL capability. It was designed and used in work with the top management team of an electronics company. It has since been used with sales organizations, a human resources department, an information services group, quality departments, facilities groups, and with an administrative vice president and his potpourri of functional departments.

The process was developed to avoid the trap of repeating the organization's experiences without learning from them. The consultant and the CEO were planning an offsite retreat for the top team. The consultant commented, "The organization seems to have had one year of experience several times instead of accumulating many years of experience."

Resource and time limitations inhibited preparation of detailed case studies for the study of success and failure. A "minicase method" was created for analyzing success and failure patterns in the organization's experience base. This process combines features of the case study method and force field analysis[11] to seek out patterns of success and failure.

Participants prepared two brief write-ups of situations where they had experienced higher levels of success and two associated with failure. The written descriptions covered the nature of the case, participants, duration of the case, what was done, and the actual results achieved. Copies of each minicase were made for each participant in the meeting.

C. Analysis of Forces Influencing Success or Failure

Subgroups are developed and assigned cases to analyze. The author of the minicase is included in the group doing the analysis. Groups review and analyze an assigned case. About half the time is for developing an understanding of the case. The remaining time is spent producing a force field analysis (see Figure 6.2). Forces are identified that "helped" and "hindered" progress from the starting point of the case to the achievement (or not) of the established goals. Each analysis is captured for use later in the process. Groups analyze two or three cases, take a break, and then are reassigned to different subgroups for analyses of additional cases. At the end of two or three iterations of subgroup work, a large number of cases have been examined and force field charts of each developed.

D. Identifying Patterns

The next step involves examining patterns of forces associated with successes and failures. The task assigned is to "Look for patterns in the force field analyses — what is included or done well when success is realized and, conversely, what is omitted or done poorly when failure occurs."

Each individual reviews all of the assigned cases and writes down his personal observations of the pattern of forces associated with success or failure. The group then discusses and condenses its individual findings into a single force field chart. Clear patterns invariably appear and most variations in success or failure clearly are attributable to the processes employed. When included in the management of the case and done well, success follows. Failure to include the process or poor execution leads to failure.

The initial use of this process involved 15 executives who examined 27 cases. When the charts were presented that summarized the analysis of the patterns observed the collective comment of the group was that all of the summaries addressed the same set of operating processes and practices. Interestingly, the consultant and the CEO had worked to avoid instructions for case writing that might preclude consideration of issues other than the processes used. When the CEO observed the pattern that emerged he smiled at the consultant saying, "You knew that this would be the result from the beginning, didn't you?" The consultant's response was, "I suspected it but wouldn't have bet my fees on it."

FORCE FIELD CHART

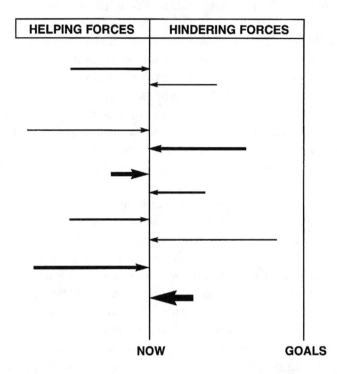

Figure 6.2   Force-field analysis chart. Used to analyze forces helping and hindering progress from where things are to established goals and objectives. A collection of such forms from minicase analyses helps identify patterns of behavior associated with success and failure.

E. Using Outcomes of the Minicase Method

Participants to the analysis seek ways to apply the learning. If these processes and actions are associated with success or failure, how can we assure that they are appropriately included in our work? Among the most common uses of the outcomes is the development of some form of checklist. Checklists provide a tool that can be made available for use by all members of the organization. As people take on assignments or projects, the checklist deals with the first-level issue of whether or not the items and processes on the list are part of how the task will be managed.

The second issue that arises in using the results has to do with whether or not people have the tools and skills needed to use the processes associated with success or failure. If not, how do they get help from those with the requisite skill, first of all, and second, how do they acquire the skills themselves? The answers to these questions are significantly easier if the organization has developed continuous learning processes characteristic of organizations with strong ECO capabilities. Access to training, to skilled managers, to mentors, or to peers who are legitimized to support other's learning and growth all provide avenues for acquiring the needed competence. Such vehicles are not available in organizations with limited ECO capacity and the answers to the questions above are either unavailable or hard to find.

The use of critiques will support learning in specific situations. Extensions of that learning to patterns of success and failure at the organizational level are possible via processes like the minicase method. Learning of this type can be shared and made available across the entire organization.

An example of this came from work with a senior VP of administration and human resources. The VP had expressed concern that he saw very limited opportunities for executives who reported to him to work together as a team. After several discussions with the group it became clear that each of the diverse functions in his organization shared a common and testy issue. Each was charged with dual and often conflicting roles. First, they were charged with administering the policies of the organization, many of which were mandated by external agencies. Administration of the policies imposed limits and controls on the actions of individuals and managers. At the same time, each of the functions, e.g., HR, IS, quality and reliability, facilities, and so on, was also charged with being a support resource to others throughout the organization. In this capacity they were expected to be available to help their internal customers do what they needed to do. It was not uncommon to have to deny support or approval to internal customers in the name of consistent or legal application of established policies.

The minicase process was used to analyze the factors associated with successes or failures in each of the administrative functions. The results of these analyses then became data for a meeting at the VPs' level to consider the keys to success in managing the conflicts inherent in their roles. A number of learning points emerged from this process:

- The success and failure factors identified by each function included common processes.

- Each group identified a tendency, when faced with conflicting responsibilities, to exert their power to control and to rely on the more mechanical and legalistic side of their role, creating tensions and counter-forces.
- Each group found solutions for improved management of their dual and conflicting roles when they accepted the requirement that both responsibilities must be met.
- The group as a whole instituted changes to their work processes that included educating customers about their dual roles, acknowledging the constraints they were forced to administer, and discussions of how to work together most productively without being forced into conflicts neither could control.

The minicase method provided valuable learning across a diverse set of functions in this case. The functions involved become more customer focused and change friendly.

VIII. Archiving and Accessing Organizational Memory

Since an organization is not a living, biological entity, it technically does not have memory. The organization's memory is the collection of the memories of its individual members and whatever has been captured from experience and preserved in some type of archive. Archived historical data and individual memories are valuable sources of information for addressing situations the organization faces. Without access to these memories the organization must approach each issue that emerges as a new issue. Current members cannot learn from the prior experiences of others and are forced to "start from scratch" each time.

Starting from scratch is required when no effort has been made to create an archive of the organization's experience and learning. It also occurs when access to the memories of individuals is lost through transfer, promotion, resignation, retirement, termination, or any form of downsizing and restructuring. Some of the attempts of organizations to downsize in the 1980s, for example, provided incentives for early retirement to people with long service and generally higher wages and salaries. When more people than anticipated accepted the early retirement packages, a severe depletion of the organizational memory occurred. Nothing had been done to capture the memory of those who left and the organizations were forced to work through a painful and costly process of relearning or reacquiring the memory by hiring retirees as consultants.

Significant portions of the knowledge base of organizations is carried around in the memories of employees or is stored somewhere like a file or in a PC where no one can find it or access it. As change accelerates it becomes more important for organizations to find a way to capture the knowledge, make it available to those who would benefit from having it, and use the knowledge to leverage the organization's future success. CL processes for archiving and accessing organizational memory grow in importance and become an important factor for increasing the organization's capacity as an ECO.

A. Lessons Learned

In the mid-1990s we had an opportunity to visit a Texas Instruments assembly factory in Singapore. As in most high-tech manufacturing operations the plant contained a "spec center" where all of their product and process specifications were controlled and maintained. They also employed an innovative approach to their need for continuous learning and for building an organizational memory by creating a "lessons learned" center. Loose-leaf binders were maintained in the center for capturing the organization's experience with each process and each piece of equipment. Maintenance history, process variability, modifications and the reasons for them, unusual operating results, indicators of problems and things to check for, and so on were all captured and made available for anyone dealing with the specific process or equipment. Although the specific people involved with the process changed from time to time, the lessons learned books contained the corporate memory. Experienced people could review the books to refresh or update their personal knowledge base. New people benefit by having access to the experience and learning of those who preceded them.

Simplified, low-tech approaches have been used for recording the occurrence of events in some areas for some time. Ships' logs, appointment books, maintenance logs, sales call reports, phone records, and so on describe what has occurred. Most of these are quite specific, confined to a single location, and are not designed to capture learning. The demands of today's environment of change may not displace these tools, but failure to develop better tools for archiving and retrieving organizational memory could be fatal.

B. Using Advanced Technology

The memory of the organization is contained in the collective memories of its people and archives. Before the development of software technology for archiving and retrieving an organization's memory, we observed a use of technology for accessing the memories of a worldwide set of resources and experiences. Price Waterhouse, LLP (now PricewaterhouseCoopers) designed a way to access all of its human resources using computer networking. People seeking information were able to post questions about specific issues to bulletin boards accessed by all of their counterparts throughout the world. With this system they created the capacity to access, overnight if not sooner, the collective experience of thousands. The information could support a customer proposal by identifying other clients using the services for a specific need or from a particular industry. It might include descriptions of processes used and results obtained in a wide spectrum of client organizations. And so on. Thus, even though a singular memory did not exist and could not be accessed, a process existed to access the collective organizational memories for application to an incredible number of possible needs. Additional advances in technology via the Internet and Intranets continue to make this approach more available to any that need and are willing to invest in it.

More recently, while conducting the research for this book, we had the opportunity to interview Jeffrey Miller, President and CEO, Documentum, Inc. His organization is a rapidly growing software company in the business of "enterprise document management." Their aim is to provide solutions for their customers' growing need to access and manage all of the unstructured information in their organizations. Approximately 80% of the knowledge and information in an organization is unstructured and inaccessible to others. Advances in computer hardware and software technology are now making it possible to archive and retrieve that information as has been possible with quantifiable information for some time.

We had been aware of few tools for archiving and retrieving unstructured information. The challenge of doing this had been beyond the scope of existing technologies. Our contact with Documentum, however, revealed the development of products and technology that now make this possible. Advances by Documentum and its competitors will bring new possibilities to this area. Advancing capabilities will encourage organizations' building CL and ECO capacity to invest in the technology for archiving and accessing their organizational memories. In the future this capability will be a defining characteristic of organizations with high levels of ECO capability.

IX. Identifying and Testing Assumptions

Throughout this book we have referred to the Assumptions — Behaviors — Consequences model and the need for individuals and organizations to identify and test the assumptions driving their behavior (refer to the section of Chapter 1 on the ABC model for more specifics about the model). The ABC model is not a new concept. It happens to be our way of expressing a set of concepts that have existed for a long time. We find this model particularly useful for issues regarding change, learning, and improvement. A basic premise of the model is that it will be impossible to change to behaviors that will produce intended results as long as there are faulty assumptions driving the behavior that is not producing results. For example, anyone whose behavior is built on the assumption that "people really don't care about quality" will be unable to change to other behaviors unless that assumption is made explicit and changed. They will never escape using behaviors that rely on external control of people's work because their assumptions drive them to such actions. Only when inappropriate assumptions are made explicit and exposed to the light of day will they be seen as faulty. And only then will explicit articulation of new assumptions free up the person or organization to adopt behaviors that will produce desired results.

The issues brought into focus with the ABC model are similar in nature to those discussed by many others.[4,20] Each clearly expresses the importance of being able to understand the assumptions underlying the behavior of the organization as a basis for real and sustainable change. Argyris and Schön,[37] for example, talk about the distinction between "espoused theories," i.e., what people or organizations say they believe, and "theories in use," i.e., the actual set of assumptions that influence behavior. Until there is an awareness of the discrepancy between the two the organization will continue to act on its theory in use while deluding itself that it is driven by what it says it believes.

Senge[38] includes "mental models" as one of the five disciplines of a learning organization. Mental models are akin to the concept of underlying assumptions of the ABC model. Organizations need skills for articulating their mental models (assumptions) so they can be learned from and changed where they drive and sustain ineffective behaviors.

A. The Unmotivated Quality Techician

The manager and supervisors of a manufacturing quality control department sought consulting help regarding one of their technicians. They perceived this person as a man with good capabilities and skills but were concerned with a perceived lack of motivation. The description of his behavior was that "he moves around the plant at about half speed all day." Consultation took place in the manager's office and the ABC model guided the process of exploration.

The desired results in this case were that the technician operate up to his capacity and provide a full day's work to the organization. It was also desired that his behavior serve as a role model for other technicians since he was a senior and respected member of the department. What was happening, i.e., the experienced results, included half-paced work not up to the level of the person's capacity and negative effects of the behavior on peers. The supervisors and manager acknowledged that the current behavior represented a change from experience with the person in previous positions. They observed that he worked at full speed outside of work. He was president of the junior chamber of commerce in his hometown and was active with his children's school and sports programs.

Limited attempts to encourage more energetic behavior had been awkward. The only observable effect of these efforts was that the technician had become more difficult to find. He appeared to be staying out of sight so that the slower pace of his movements were less visible. The clearly stated assumptions of the supervisors and manager were that this man had lost interest in his job and the slow pace of his work reflected a lack of motivation to perform.

As the consultation continued the supervisors were asked to describe the technician's task assignments and responsibilities. When this description was completed they were asked, "If he moved at full speed how much time would it take each day to do the job?" The sheepish look of the supervisors was obvious at that point when they responded, "About half a day." They immediately recognized the fallacy of their assumption of lost motivation. They concluded that the more appropriate assumption was that the slower behavior they had observed was simply an adaptive response to only having a half-time set of job assignments and had nothing to do with lack of motivation.

Based on the modified assumptions new supervisory options developed almost immediately. The supervisors explored additional tasks the technician could be assigned. They talked about things they were unable to get to that were within the capabilities of the technician and which ones to assign to him. The new supervisory behavior selected involved testing the revised assumptions by assigning the technician responsibility for planning and coordinating a pending move of the quality control lab from one area of the plant to another, a task they had not found time to do themselves.

Four weeks later another meeting was held with the QC management group. They were ecstatic with the changes in their technician's behavior and with the confirmation of their revised assumptions about his capability to handle significantly more work. He had already developed and had the plan for moving the lab approved and was busily arranging the specifics required for building the new area and for disconnecting, moving, and setting up equipment in the new lab.

This case demonstrates the value of the ABC model for identifying and testing managerial or organizational assumptions. If the managers involved had continued with their assumption of inadequate motivation, there is a high probability that the end result would have been the loss of a capable employee along with his years of experience and value as a resource to other QC technicians. But operating from modified and more appropriate assumptions produced the desired consequences of the managers, a more involved employee getting much greater satisfaction from his work, and an increase of available resources for the QC department equal to about one half of an experienced person.

B. Getting at Underlying Assumptions

Use of the ABC model for solving problems like those in the example above requires understanding the gap between the results wanted and what is actually happening, i.e., between desired and experienced consequences. It also requires a description of the actions and behaviors used in attempting to produce the desired results. From these data it is possible to infer underlying assumptions with some confidence. In the example above, identifying the assumption of lost motivation was easy since it was clearly articulated by the managers involved. This assumption of reduced motivation guided the behavior of the managers. But until the manager's behavior was specified and made part of the picture, including the description of the work assigned to the position, the fallacy of the assumption was not obvious. Improved assumptions and additional options for addressing the problem were unavailable.

The importance of building improvement and actions on facts and data to get at the root causes of problems was emphasized repeatedly in the chapter on continuous improvement. The same concept makes the problem solving or planning that is possible with the ABC model work or not work. Implicit and questionable assumptions lead to a limited set of behavior options that do not produce intended results. Only when all of the facts and data are collected do the pieces fit together that bring faulty assumptions to light. It is our experience that faulty assumptions stand out and are easily discarded when made explicit. The persons or managers with the assumptions recognize the misfits without feeling judged or put down. More appropriate assumptions can then be made. And they guide the selection of alternate behaviors that yield the desired results.

Getting at the underlying assumptions or mental models or theories in use offers a sound basis for learning, change, and improvement. The skills and models involved will be useful to any organization. They will be particularly valuable tools for organizations that must be flexible and adaptive and cannot be trapped into rigid and inflexible behaviors by poor assumptions. Thus, tools such as the ABC model will become an important part of the CL repertoire for creating greater capacity as an Ever-Changing Organization.

C. ABCs of Organizational Alignment

Much of the discussion about the stabilizing base and managing FOR change in this book has emphasized the need for consistency and fit among the components of the organizational system. When the ABC model and its underlying premises are understood it can be used for testing and planning of organizational behaviors. Statements exist about the values of the organization and principles to which it is committed, e.g., continuous change, learning, and improvement or trust in people and so on. The statements represent the beliefs and assumptions of the ABC model. Additional documents present the organization's vision and its goals, direction, and strategies. These represent the consequences or desired results of the model. With these articulated it becomes possible to examine the behavior of the organization for consistency and fit.

Management is able to ask whether the components of the organization's structure and infrastructure, i.e., its behavior, are consistent with its assumptions and the consequences the organization is aiming to achieve. The introduction of new policies or controls can be examined to determine their fit with the concept of trust and individual freedom and the desire that people take responsible independent action. Current organizational systems and practices can be evaluated for their fit and alignment with the underlying values and principles or with expected changes in direction or strategy.

Prior behaviors of those considered for promotion can be examined for consistency with the organization's basic assumptions and desired consequences. It is surprising how often obvious misfits between the values and principles of newly hired executives and those of the organization are ignored. Such a failure wreaks havoc on the organization, especially when this occurs at senior management levels. The costs in terms of time and energy wasted trying to reconcile and deal with the inconsistent behavior of the new person are enormous and preventable. Assessing the organizational fit of potential placements via a tool like the ABC model would guide the organization away from most of these decisions. People with equal capabilities would be hired and placed. Their behavior would not leave a major disaster in their own wake.

The ability to identify and test assumptions and to use tools such as the ABC model is limited in most organizations. This weakness must be addressed by organizations that need to be more facile and must not add to their own instability through inconsistent behaviors and confusing signals to their people. Their capacity as an ECO will be eroded if this capability remains weak.

X. Learning How To Learn

Increasing the capacity of the organization to learn is obviously a critical component of increasing ECO capability. This means increasing its capacity "to acquire knowledge or skill by study, instruction, or experience" on a continuing basis as defined in the first paragraph of this chapter. Many of the features of organizations with greater ECO capability are designed to increase the learning capacity of individuals as well as of the organization. But to realize the payoff available from these features the individual members of the organization must know "how to learn."

A. *Organizational Responsibility*

The organization must not rely on osmosis. It must not assume that everyone has acquired necessary learning skills from prior experience or that previously acquired skills remain available to them. Rather the organization must provide the tools, training, and support needed for individuals to learn. It must also assure that organizational obstacles to learning, e.g., time availability or accessibility and so on, have been removed.

Many have complained about the failure of our basic educational system to prepare people with sufficient skills in the three R's. What is called "social promotion" allows some to graduate without the ability to read and write. Nor have these people acquired skills such as basic study skills or oral communication skills needed for many of the forms of learning offered by the organization. When market conditions require hiring from a pool of people with these limited skills, many employees will be unable to use prepared training materials or to interact with others in a manner that supports their learning and that of others.

In organizations with high ethnic diversity, people may have limited skills in English as a second language. The organization may need to offer basic educational development for these people before they are qualified to participate in the range of developmental offerings available.

Development via newer learning technologies often requires skills that some organizational members have not previously acquired. These people will need to "learn how to learn" before they are able to use the technology. Some may have no experience with computers and may be reluctant to use them. Or the software in use may be unfamiliar and require another level of learning. Investing in training and support resources by the organization becomes necessary when newer technologies are to be used in the learning process. And the purpose of these investments is to help people "learn how to learn." Young[39] has noted that organizations may provide resources and learning support but still be missing a critical part of the equation if individuals being trained do not have the personal learning capability or tools to learn.

Incorporating and supporting the application of CL tools and methods described in this book assures the organization that it has fulfilled much of what it needs to do. There will have been a significant increase in the organization's capacity to learn as well as its capacity for change and continuous improvement. But members of the organization also need to accept responsibility for development of their individual competencies for learning how to learn.

B. Individual Responsibility

Individuals may carry their own obstacles to learning. They must accept responsibility for overcoming those obstacles with the support of their manager and the organization. They must understand where they are vs. where they need to be to become what we earlier described as the Ever-Changing Person (ECP) if they are to succeed and survive in an ECO.

Our personal careers have been guided by a saying on a banner in our offices that says, "When you're through improving yourself, you're through." As the rate of change in our world and in our organizations accelerates, this expression becomes more relevant to all members of organizations. The individual becomes an obstacle to the organization's development of ECO capability unless he or she is also engaged in the process of learning how to continuously change, learn, and improve.

Learning the tools of problem solving and process improvement increase an individual's capacity to learn. Identifying competencies needed to fulfill the learning, change, and improvement requirements of a position provides a basis for determining individual needs. Seeking feedback and assessment of current knowledge, skills, and abilities builds awareness of the gaps in the individual's competency inventory. And actively utilizing the resources that are part of the organization's life/career-long learning support process helps to fill the gaps and improve the individual's capacity to learn.

The personal obstacles to learning may rest in the listening skills and other communication skills of those people. They may lack interpersonal skills for coping with conflict or influence issues. They may need help in developing self-esteem or reducing fear of failure. Or they may have needs in terms of basic knowledge and skills missing from their personal education. Whatever the needs, each person must work to fill their individual gaps and move towards increasing their capacity as an Ever-Changing Person (ECP). Increased skills and abilities for learning how to learn build ECP capability and, in the process, strengthen the organization's continuous learning and overall ECO capability.

XI. Summary of Continuous Learning as an ECO Component

Before proceeding to the discussion of implementation strategies for becoming an ECO, reflect briefly on the CL features described in this chapter as contributors to an organization's capacity for change, learning, and improvement.

- The time and money spent on learning and development are viewed as an investment in the development of human capital. Expecting a return on this investment drives design of more relevant and results-focused learning processes.
- The person–organization bond is based on self-interest and a mutual contract for life/career-long learning support.

- Competency needs are known for the organization, for individuals, and for current or future jobs. Developmental plans are created to fill the gaps.
- Structured developmental relationships of benefit to all parties systematically draw on the knowledge base of the organization and contribute to continuing personal growth.
- Systematic use of critique encourages learning and change based on what works or does not, and what does not work needs to be eliminated, modified, or decreased.
- Patterns associated with success and failure across many situations support ways to assure inclusion of processes that work and avoidance of those that don't.
- Disconnected individual learning or group memories are cumulated, archived, and made retrievable for use in other situations where they will be useful.
- Assumptions that block the use of result-producing behaviors are made explicit and eliminated or changed. What is learned leads to more productive behaviors and results.
- People throughout the organization have developed their learning skills, increased their personal capacity as Ever-Changing Persons (ECP), and built the organization's capacity as an ECO.

Exactly how and when each of these features is designed into a particular organization will be a function of its unique situation and requirements. But there is little doubt that each will contribute to the organization's capacity for continuous learning. The final chapter of this book spells out a general process for building ECO capability, integrating all of the major components of an ECO into what will also be a unique application of the ECO model to the specifics of the organization involved.

7 | Implementation

The purposes of this chapter are multiple. A primary intention is to provide the reader with a description of a viable process for implementation of the ECO model and development of greater ECO capacity. Second, the process has been designed to be consistent with the concepts and tools presented throughout the book. As you are aware by this point this is not about a simplified, quick-change process. The ECO model reflects the complexity of today's organizations and the key issues that build ECO capacity. Careful reading and use of the book will guide you through the process and help you on your way. The resources of The EverChange Institute are also available to support your efforts as needed.

The process outlined in this chapter is only one of many possible approaches to deciding and carrying out the implementation of an ECO-building process. It is offered as a guide and as an option. It is not intended to replace processes an organization has developed that will serve its purposes. Nor is it intended to be a prescription. Consider each of the steps and their fit for your organization. Feel free to take a different set of steps or to vary the process to fit the needs of your organization. We do suggest, however, that you make sure that whatever process is used covers the issues we outline in some way.

I. Deciding to Move to Implementation

As you have read this book and used the "snapshot diagnosis," you have developed a sense of the ECO capability your organization requires (or will require) based on current or predicted environmental conditions. You also have a sense of where your organization is today. As a result you have already begun to consider the question of implementing a process for developing greater ECO capability. Anyone who has gotten to this point in the book, either by reading it all or by skimming the introduction, table of contents, and a sampling of the chapters, has reasons for seriously considering becoming an ECO. Needs to increase capacity for change or improve success with implementation of change efforts are probably among the reasons. The need to cope with the increasing rates of change in the environment is almost certain to be another factor.

The following list includes a number of other reasons. These were previously outlined in a 1996 EverChange Institute "white paper"[40]:

- Need for a living vision that can integrate new initiatives without each being seen as an independent activity or part of a continuing series of "programs of the month."
- Stagnant or deteriorating organizational performance — on an absolute basis, based on competitive comparisons, or vs. the organization's own plans or expectations.
- Increasing external pressures for change from customers, competitors, suppliers, new technology, government regulations, potential employees, or other sources.
- Need to create a new basis for the employee–organization bond where management actions have severed the more traditional bond of mutual loyalty.
- Slow or late delivery of new products and services to customers.
- Failed or ineffective efforts in the area of TQM or continuous improvement where management still sees these as important to their overall long-term strategy.
- Recognition that greater capacity for change is critical for survival. "Riding the wave" of previous success won't work and even successful change processes must improve.
- Inability of the organization to address the needs for competently prepared employees in a timely manner.
- Recognition that the current operating practices of the organization are designed for permanence and have become blocks to dealing with a more rapidly changing world.
- Adoption of a competitive strategy focused on rapid, proactive change and fast cycle times. Wanting to force others to respond to the organization's lead, not vice versa.
- Leader's or the organization's vision includes changing, learning, and improving as aspects of each person's role.

- Desire to appreciate the value of the organization's human capital to maximize return on human assets (ROHA).
- Leader who wants to leave the organization capable of continuous change, learning, and improvement as part of his or her personal legacy.

It is important that the decision to move toward increasing ECO capability is based on sound thinking and analyses and more than a quirky sense of need or a short-term response to the latest management theory. The effort required is not short term. Support for the process cannot wax and wane if success is to be achieved. The environment of all organizations is changing, some more than others. Rapid and accelerating rates of change will continue. The thrust to become an ECO must also continue!

II. Leadership of the Implementation Process

The answer to the question of who should lead any major change effort is almost always "the top person." It is clear that a significant percentage of failed change efforts can be traced to the organization's overall leader. Therefore, the answer to the question "Who should lead the initiation of an ECO process?" must obviously include the leader.

But leaders come and go. And leadership changes are frequently accompanied by changes in direction on initiatives such as becoming an ECO. Therefore, it is important that those who appoint and provide direction to the leader also understand and commit to the decision to implement an ECO strategy. Boards of directors are elected to represent the interests of the owners of the organization. Yet their responsibility often seems to be taken narrowly to mean maximizing the short-term financial performance of the organization. People in these roles need to become aware of the ECO concept and its importance for both the short- and longer-term performance of the organization. Prior to setting out on the ECO course, the Board should be educated about the concept and its implications. It needs to be committed to building ECO capacity as a strategy that must be maintained. Included in its buy-in should be acceptance of the idea that decisions about leadership succession must include selecting people who will continue the direction. The costs of discarding the strategy are unacceptable and incoming executives need to understand the requirement to pursue it. Additionally, shareholders must come to demand accountability of the board as well as the individual leader of the organization for progress in development of ECO capacity.

Does this mean that an ECO initiative should not be undertaken without up-front buy-in from the "board"? No, not necessarily. But it does mean that the issue should be resolved in the early stages or the organization will be faced with another potential "program of the month," a situation to be avoided like the plague. Attaining sustainable success and becoming an ECO are not mutually exclusive. Rather, they are complementary and both are critical to short- and long-term survival. The ECO direction should not be abandoned for short-term financial considerations.

III. Getting Started

Becoming familiar with the Ever-Changing Organization model is one step in the process of getting started. But the decision to begin implementation sets the organization on a long-term path and must be made with that in mind. Organizations are strongly urged to include a full-blown Ever-Changing Organization diagnostic process as part of the decision-making process. The foundation for ECO development will be built on unstable and shifting sands without the complete diagnosis.

A. Preliminary Management Exploration

The scope of work is substantial when the decision is made to proceed. Our hope is that readers will utilize this book and/or other resources familiar with the ECO model to assist with these decisions. Exploration of the model increases awareness of the magnitude of the task. The exploration needs to include discussion of probable resource requirements and anticipated time frames for implementation and results. Consideration of the contribution of previous efforts and the ECO effects of existing practices could make the task seem overwhelming or build confidence that progress to needed levels of ECO capacity has already been substantial. Using the data from a full ECO diagnosis provides a reality check for the management team and needed support to decisions regarding implementation. The payoff vs. the investment required is great.

Failure to engage in sufficient preimplementation exploration led some executives to abandon fledgling TQM efforts when they came face-to-face with the reality of the work involved. They carried high and unrealistic expectations into the process. Despite warnings about the size of the undertaking and the need for continuing effort they plunged in. Perceptions of the time commitment required were minimized and estimates of the speed with which results could be achieved were exaggerated. After all, we are action driven and probably better managers than those who have taken longer, so we will handle the challenge more effectively and expeditiously. The frustration and impatience that resulted made these executives vulnerable to any new program offering greater returns and faster payoff.

B. Selecting and Orienting a Diagnostic Team

The next step in the process involves thoughtful selection and appointment of a team of people to conduct a full ECO diagnosis and report their findings to top management. Members of the team should represent a cross section of the organization. They should be selected from different functions and different managerial and supervisory levels. This does not mean that those at other levels are excluded from the diagnosis. Instructions to the team include the requirement for collection of data from all parts of the organization.

Team members should be perceived to have a continuing commitment to the organization. They should bring a range of perspectives and experience with the behavior of the organization. Team members should also be seen as having the potential for future growth. Being a part of the diagnostic process is an investment by the organization and a developmental experience for the individuals involved. The team is an "organizational action group" and members will be participating in a type of structured developmental relationship described in the "Continuous Learning" chapter. Mutual benefit for the members and the organization will be realized by investing in people who are most likely to profit from the experience and produce a return on the investment.

Orientation of the diagnostic team is an important step in the process. Several issues are covered in the orientation:

- Management shares the outcomes of their exploration of the ECO concept and the thinking behind the decision to proceed with the full ECO diagnosis.
- A member of the top team is identified as a liaison for answering questions and dealing with resource issues and assuring access to people and data as needed.

- The team is given a charter describing management expectations and an indication of the time frame for their work. Included is the stipulation that all data needed are available to the team and the expectation for open and candid feedback.
- Membership on the team is presented as a developmental assignment and the criteria for selection are described (this process should be followed by a one-on-one discussion with each member's immediate supervisor, including steps to be taken to make time available for the assignment).
- How and when the team will be trained in the ECO model and diagnostic methods is described along with confirmation of the availability of resources with "subject matter expertise."
- A copy of *The Ever-Changing Organization* is provided to each member.
- Members are given the opportunity to raise questions or concerns and, at the conclusion, offered congratulations on the assignment and wished great success.

While the diagnostic team is being trained and developing plans for the assessment, top management should also orient other employees to the activities of the team and the reason the process is underway.

C. Training the Diagnostic Team

The suggested approach to training of members of diagnostic teams is designed to make them sophisticated, not naïve, assessors. The outcome of the diagnosis has important implications for the direction of the organization and needs to be as valid as possible. Giving the trainers this book and providing them with standardized questionnaires based on the ECO model does not prepare them for the task. The training they receive must prepare them to conduct a thorough and valid diagnosis designed for the unique nature of their organization.

Diagnostic teams are given intensive training in the ECO model and each of its components. Their task will include assessing how the organization addresses each component and the implication of the data for the overall change orientation of the organization. They also learn to think about organizations as systems, how to examine alignment of the various components of the organizational system as it relates to change, and how the degree of alignment impacts the organization's ECO capability.

They learn the ABC model as a framework for a valid diagnosis. The importance of identifying questionable assumptions that stimulate ineffective behaviors and inadequate results is stressed. The ABC model is also used to help the team plan the diagnosis and the specifics of what to examine vis-à-vis the components of an ECO. Examination of missions and goals and observations of actual behavior surface the assumptions that guide the organization. Also examining results produces awareness of assumptions needing change to increase ECO capability.

Since all organizations are unique, what is appropriate to include in the diagnosis and how it is best collected is an important feature of the training for diagnostic team members. The more specific and relevant the diagnosis for the specific organization, the greater its validity and impact on management. Emphasis is placed on methods of data collection that are objective and behavioral. Members are encouraged to focus on descriptive, nonjudgmental data. They do not rely only on managers' descriptions of what they believe. Methods range from direct observation of work processes or meetings or shadowing of managers to review of written materials such as policy and procedure manuals, historical records, reporting and control processes, and so on. Interviews and focus groups may be included. Customers and suppliers may be contacted. Any process that yields facts and observable behaviors related to the components of the ECO model is legitimate. Methods that call for opinions or guesses and infer motives are avoided. They require interpretation and lead to controversial conclusions.

D. Planning and Conducting Diagnosis

Based on the training provided, the diagnostic team examines the components and subcomponents of the ECO model and designs the data collection processes that will provide the desired data. Issues and questions regarding each of the ECO components are spelled out in the first six chapters of this book. Review of those chapters provides guidance on what to look for and relevant questions to ask. Where the data will be obtained, how, from whom, and who will collect it are all issues resolved in the planning process. How the data will be summarized is also considered. Subgroups may be formed to focus on the various ECO components. If so, plans of the subgroups are shared and compared to avoid redundant diagnostic activities or overemphasis in particular areas of the organization.

In the actual diagnosis of status as an ECO, the team uses a scale for each feature of the components of the ECO model to describe the organization's behavior and its orientation to change. Figure 7.1 is an example of the layout of a scale. The upper portion is used to plan what data to collect, from whom, by whom, and how. The data are not simply summarized as a point on a scale. The team pools specific facts and observations about the behavior of the organization from the diagnostic data before assigning the appropriate rating. The process becomes more difficult when a profile of ECO status cannot be developed from personal biases or unsubstantiated feelings without reference to facts. But it is just this discipline that produces outcomes with greater face validity, greater buy-in from those who receive it, and a greater probability that the data will be acted on.

E. Preparing a Summary Report for Management

Generally the diagnostic data are shared among team members prior to getting together for consolidation, reaching conclusions, and preparing the report to top management. The diagnostic team then meets to review and consolidate the data. If subgroups have focused on the individual components of the ECO model, they will probably meet separately to develop preliminary scoring and data highlights for each scale to review with the overall team.

In the full team meeting relevant data from all of the diagnostic activities are presented and discussed. Decisions are made about the most descriptive point for each scale. The specific facts or observations that influence the team's choice are highlighted for inclusion in the management report. The full team reaches final conclusions on the scale points and data highlights. A profile is produced for the five components of the ECO model. Blank profiles for each component are shown as Figures 7.2 to 7.6.

The environmental scales range from low to moderate to high uncertainty. Scales for elements of the stabilizing base indicate impacts that range from destabilizing to stabilizing to paralyzing. For this ECO component stronger profiles are centered in the scales. For the managing FOR change, continuous improvement, and continuous learning components the five points of the scales cover the range from very limited extent (or little or weak) to very great extent (or much or strong). As these profiles move from left to right the organization increases ECO capacity and moves up on the overall orientation to change scale, i.e., from averse to seeking.

Managing FOR Change Section -- Environmental Sensing Scale

ISSUES TO ANALYZE: (Details in chapter)   DATA COLLECTED: (What, from, how)

ENVIRONMENTAL SENSING: Organizational Behaviors / Data Influencing Choice of Scale Point

To what extent are ENVIRONMENTAL SENSING processes designed and in use for this organization? (Circle the most descriptive point on the Extent Scale below)

:_____:_____:_____:_____:
Very Limited   Limited   Moderate   Great   Very Great

Implications of data for organization's overall orientation to change
(i.e. trend towards Averse, Resistant, Managing, Friendly, Seeking - and why?)

Figure 7.1   Sample diagnostic scale. Form used to plan and carry out diagnostic activity for environmental sensing in the managing FOR change component. Data is accumulated and discussed prior to rating to increase validity of the assessment.

Environment Profile

SCALE	DEGREE OF UNCERTAINTY		
	LOW	MODERATE	HIGH

Rate of Technological Change   :_____:_____:_____:_____:

Product/Service Life Cycles   :_____:_____:_____:_____:

Rate of Market Growth   :_____:_____:_____:_____:

Changing Customer Expectations   :_____:_____:_____:_____:
  and Requirements
Competitive Situation   :_____:_____:_____:_____:

Globalization of Business/Markets   :_____:_____:_____:_____:

Application Base: Products/Market   :_____:_____:_____:_____:

Access to Information   :_____:_____:_____:_____:

Environmental Impact of Business   :_____:_____:_____:_____:

Environment: :_____:_____:_____:_____:

                                  Average (X) and range (I)

Summary of Key Data Points:

Figure 7.2   Profile summarizing diagnosis of the environment component of the ECO model. As the average scale point moves to the right, higher levels of ECO capacity, i.e., change-friendly or change-seeking capabilities, are needed.

Stabilizing Base Profile

SCALE	IMPACT		
	Destabilizing	Stabilizing	Paralyzing
Shared Values	: ____ : ____ : ____ : ____ :
Living Vision	: ____ : ____ : ____ : ____ :
Commitment to Change, Learning and Improvement	: ____ : ____ : ____ : ____ :
Clear Goals and Direction	: ____ : ____ : ____ : ____ :
Belief and Trust in People	: ____ : ____ : ____ : ____ :
Stability of Employee Base	: ____ : ____ : ____ : ____ :
Flexibility of Systems, Structures and Infrastructure	: ____ : ____ : ____ : ____ :
Access to Data and Information	: ____ : ____ : ____ : ____ :
Emphasis on Process and Results	: ____ : ____ : ____ : ____ :
Balance	: ____ : ____ : ____ : ____ :

Stabilizing Base: __   __   __   __   __

(Frequency at Each Point of Scale)

Figure 7.3 Stabilizing base profile. Depicts the distribution of diagnostic ratings on the features of the stabilizing base. Note that the most useful profile for this ECO component is concentrated in the center and away from actions that destabilize or paralyze the organization's ECO capacity.

Managing FOR Change Profile

<u>SCALE</u>   <u>EXTENT</u>

	Very Limited	Limited	Moderate	Great	Very Great
Customer Focus	:	:	:	:	:
Environmental Sensing	:	:	:	:	:
Impetus for Change	:	:	:	:	:
Change Planning/Management	:	:	:	:	:
Systems Model for Change and Alignment	:	:	:	:	:
Change as a Business Strategy	:	:	:	:	:
Adaptive Leadership	:	:	:	:	:
Change Orientation of Policies Procedures, and Controls	:	:	:	:	:
Work Design	:	:	:	:	:
Use of Change Agents	:	:	:	:	:

Managing FOR Change: :_____:_____:_____:_____:

Average (X) and range (I)

Summary of Key Data Points:

Figure 7.4   Managing FOR change profile. Patterns of the profile toward the right of the scales indicate greater ECO capacity. Change-averse and change-resistant organizations demonstrate patterns to the left of the scales. Wide variation results in confusing signals and reduces ECO capability.

Continuous Improvement Profile

SCALE	EXTENT				
	Very Limited	Limited	Moderate	Great	Very Great

Scale	Very Limited	Limited	Moderate	Great	Very Great
Direction and Goals	:	:	:	:	:
Improvement Challenge	:	:	:	:	:
Size of Improvements Expected	:	:	:	:	:
Common Language/Definitions	:	:	:	:	:
Customer-Supplier Relationships	:	:	:	:	:
Prevention Orientation	:	:	:	:	:
Systematic Problem-Solving	:	:	:	:	:
Process Improvement Methods	:	:	:	:	:
Time and Structures for CI	:	:	:	:	:
Innovation/Creativity Strategies	:	:	:	:	:

Continuous Improvement: :_____:_____:_____:_____:

Average (X) and range (I)

Summary of Key Data Points:

Figure 7.5   Continuous improvement profile. Higher levels of ECO capability are exhibited in continuous improvement profiles with averages to the right and with a narrow range of variation. Wider variation suggests more limited ECO capacity and highlights areas needing attention.

Continuous Learning Profile

SCALE	EXTENT				
	Very Limited	Limited	Moderate	Great	Very Great
Investment in CL	:	:	:	:	:
Life/Career-long Learning Support	:	:	:	:	:
Competency/Develop Planning	:	:	:	:	:
Structured Developmental Relationships	:	:	:	:	:
Learning Critiques	:	:	:	:	:
Identify Success/Failure Patterns	:	:	:	:	:
Archiving/Accessing Org. Memory	:	:	:	:	:
Identifying/Testing Assumptions	:	:	:	:	:
Learning How to Learn	:	:	:	:	:

Continuous Learning: :_____:_____:_____:_____:

Average (X) and range (I)

Summary of Key Data Points:

Figure 7.6   Continuous learning profile. Higher levels of ECO capability are exhibited in continuous learning profiles with averages to the right and with a narrow range of variation. Wider variation suggests more limited ECO capacity and highlights areas needing attention.

A report is prepared for management that includes the profiles, the data highlights that influenced the choices of the diagnostic team, and the team's conclusions about the organization's status and needs as an ECO. The profiles provide a visual summary of the organization's position on each ECO component. But the richness of the data in the report comes from the quotes, observations, facts or artifacts of the organization that are collected and highlighted by the team. Management teams receiving reports with both kinds of data are observed in deep study of the written aspects of the report. For this reason a copy of the report is given to the management team for review prior to an off-site management retreat. The report and its conclusions will be discussed in depth at the retreat. Unless the management team is unfamiliar with the ECO model, the retreat is more productive when there has been time to review and absorb the data in advance. Discussions are more focused and the executives are much less distracted by wanting to read the report during the discussions.

IV. Management Retreat

Get into an environment for a management retreat that is conducive to in-depth discussion and planning. Set up the meeting to preclude the press of the day-to-day business from distracting the attention of the participants. For most management teams an off-site location with minimal outside distractions works best. "Business casual" dress is preferred by many to encourage open and informal exchanges. Arrange for the taking and delivery of messages at specified times only and provide time at meals and breaks for dealing with issues that cannot be put off. Many groups do not allow cell phones and pagers in the meeting.

We have a number of biases for the timing and process of the meeting. Plan to stay for two nights at the facility where the meetings will be held. Use a third party resource, i.e., an internal or external consultant, to assist with planning the retreat and to facilitate the meetings. A brief start-up meeting of the management team precedes a group dinner the first evening for both the management and diagnostic teams in order to review the meeting objectives, agenda, and roles. Encourage everyone to complete a thorough review of the diagnostic team report. Agree on how the management team will operate in the next day's meeting with the diagnostic team to get the maximum benefit from their work and learning. Make the evening brief and informal and an opportunity for members of the two teams to become better acquainted, not for discussion of the report.

A. Reviewing and Exploring Diagnostic Results

Allow the first morning for presentation of the diagnostic report. If the team used subgroups for the components of the ECO model, give each subgroup time to share their findings. Be sure that the management team understands how the data was collected, and where or from whom it was obtained. Provide an opportunity for questions and answers designed to increase understanding of the data and conclusions. Disagreeing or arguing at this point is unproductive.

Have the diagnostic team stay through lunch and allow time for informal one-on-one or small subgroup discussions of the report among the executives and the team. When the meeting reconvenes, thank the team for its effort. Let them know that they will be kept informed of the management team's decisions and action plans. Presenting some form of recognition is appropriate at this point. The diagnostic team then departs while the management team continues the retreat.

B. Deciding on ECO Development

Moving to this step presumes that the diagnosis and its conclusions have identified discrepancies between where the organization is and where it needs to be. At a minimum the management team sees value in moving forward with some level of ECO-building effort. The value of the ECO diagnostic process and its summation of the organization's behavior and orientation to change is not in deciding for management how it should be oriented to change. Rather, the value comes from providing executives data about their behavior and a framework for examining both that behavior and its underlying assumptions in the context of results they aim to achieve. Armed with this analysis a path to the desired future can be plotted and initiatives prioritized towards development of the capacity to function as an ECO.

Should an overall effort be launched and based on the ECO model? A specific benefit of such an approach comes from use of the ECO model as a rational framework for change initiatives, in the short term and in the future. The model is presented to the organization as the basis for decisions about change initiatives. New initiatives are tested for relevance to improving components of the ECO model. If they don't fit they are rejected. The latest fad or management theory is not adopted if it cannot pass the test of supporting development of ECO capacity. Prior initiatives can also be evaluated vs. the EOC model and the organization's needs. Where they are useful and relevant they are sustained or revitalized. Where they are not relevant, termination of the effort frees up energy for the effort to increase ECO capability.

A limited set of new initiatives is identified for more detailed planning based on the diagnostic results. Other issues are prioritized for action when the first initiatives have been implemented successfully. Selection criteria might include consideration of which will provide the greatest gains, are easiest to develop and implement, and/or address the issues of greatest concern to the organization as blocks to change, learning, and improvement.

Diagnostic results that indicate little current or future need for increased ECO capacity may lead to the decision to move forward without the need to launch an overall strategy. Recall that in discussing the impact of the environment on needed ECO capability, it was emphasized that too much flexibility could be destabilizing for organizations in more certain environments. Individual initiatives may still be identified and implemented but without the need for placing them into the overall framework of the ECO model. The information in the "Managing FOR Change" chapter will still be helpful for planning and managing individual initiatives where management sees a need and payoff.

Where need for the overall ECO model are minimal, the management team should determine whether there are needs to improve the stabilizing base and the processes for planning and managing specific changes. On the assumption that all environments are changing more rapidly than they have historically, features of the stabilizing base that are destabilizing or paralyzing reduce the capacity for change, learning, and improvement. Adjustments to the features of the stabilizing base that make them more stabilizing will always be useful. Change processes can be made more effective and consume less time and energy. Virtually all organizations can benefit from these improvements.

C. Planning Start-Up and Management of ECO Process

The later part of the management retreat is devoted to planning. A process is needed to take the ECO-building initiatives from concept to implementation. In addition, plans must be made for the introduction and ongoing management of the ECO process. The management team designs these processes to be consistent with the organization's practices and culture. In addition, it is recommended that they reflect on the concepts presented in this book. Reference to the table of contents will assist recall about where ideas are discussed and examples provided of tools and processes associated with higher levels of ECO capacity.

In particular the materials in the chapters "Managing FOR Change" and "Stabilizing Base" will be useful for the management team's planning activities. The subsection "Change Planning and Management" emphasizes minimizing imposed change and maximizing participation. It also suggests focusing the energy released by impending change by involving people in productive activities related to implementing the new processes.

Assigning members of the management team to lead teams in the process of planning the new initiatives is one way to increase participation. Members of their teams could include a sample of those from the diagnostic team as well as people from other levels of the organization. Developing and experimenting with options for the change brings even more people into the process and increases the creativity of the solutions. The teams propose the changes and present implementation plans that include development of change readiness and thinking through the systems impact of the changes for prevention of problems.

Planning for introduction of an overall ECO-building process must include decisions about the role(s) of the management team and how they will manage the ongoing process. The team can use the management system model (refer to the "Systems Model For Change and Alignment" section of the "Managing FOR Change" chapter for details) to look at the fit of the new direction with current practices. Do people have needed skills or will they need training? Where new behaviors are expected will they tie into the existing reward and recognition systems? What measurement, reporting, and tracking will be required and will it fit into existing methods? And so on. Plans are developed and shared with the organization regarding how misalignments will be corrected. Without change the misalignments send mixed signals that cause confusion and raise resistance.

Communication plans are developed for introducing the ECO-building process. Presentation of the new direction uses data from the completed diagnostic of ECO status. The findings are shared with members of the organization along with the direction set by management. Consistency of the direction with the organization's values and vision is demonstrated. Discussions to clarify the implications of the direction and expectations for each person's behavior assist people through the phases of change.

Management also defines processes for maintaining awareness of initiatives and progress. Timing of the introduction is scheduled when proper preparations have been completed. There may be concerns that too much of a delay is involved because expectations have developed that "management is up to something" in their retreat. If so, provide a simple communication that a report will be given to everyone within a specified period of time and that there is no need to fear what is coming. Assure people that additional time is being used to prepare for the meeting and that they can expect a positive message. People can cope with the delay when they understand what is happening. It is the unknown that they fear. As a close colleague has said frequently, "When all else fails, tell the truth!"

V. Renewing the Process

An ECO-building process is like any other business process. It can always be improved. Organizations with strong ECO capability will apply the components of the ECO model to the continuous improvement of their capability.

Among the steps in making the ECO process self-renewing is a periodic reassessment and critique of the process. The learning that results is applied to improve the ability of the process to meet the shifting needs of the organization for continuous change, learning, and improvement.

Conducting periodic follow-up diagnoses of ECO status will indicate whether there is a greater need for ECO capacity from changes in the environment. They will also show progress or decline in the status of ECO components and indicate areas needing further development. The development of greater perspective and managerial potential will result from training additional people as ECO diagnosticians. These people develop greater awareness and sensitivity to the ECO practices of the organization. They use the tools and methods of managing FOR change, continuous improvement, and continuous learning in their own units and are happy to share their knowledge and skills with others.

The gains in ECO capability will grow as the process grows and is sustained. Without renewal the process will deteriorate. Continuing to build the ECO process is the only way to go! Improved results will confirm the wisdom of that statement.

References

1. Miles, R. E., Human relations or human resources?, *Harv. Bus. Rev.*, July/August, 1965.
2. Moore, G., *Crossing the Chasm: Marketing and Selling Technology Products to Mainstream Customers*, Harper Business, New York, 1995.
3. Pieters, G. R., The A–B–C Model, Unpublished internal paper, Signetics Corporation, Sunnyvale, CA, 1976.
4. McGregor, D., *The Human Side of Enterprise*, McGraw-Hill, New York, 1960.
5. Lawrence, P. and Lorsch, J., *Organization and Environment: Managing Differentiation and Integration*, Harvard University Press, Boston, 1967.
6. Collins, J. and Porras, J., *Built to Last: Successful Habits of Visionary Companies*, Harper Business, New York, 1994.
7. Christensen, C., *The Innovator's Dilemma: When New Technologies Cause Great Firms to Fail*, Harvard Business School Press, Boston, 1997.
8. Peters, T. and Waterman, R., *In Search of Excellence*, Warner, New York, 1988.
9. Harvey, J., The Abilene paradox: Managing agreement in organizations, *Organ. Dyn.*, Summer, 1974.
10. Livingstone, J., Pygmalion in management, *Harv. Bus. Rev.*, July/August, 1969.
11. Lewin, K., *Field Theory in Social Sciences: Selected Theoretical Papers*, Harper and Row, New York, 1951.
12. Levinson, H., Appraisal of what performance, *Harv. Bus. Rev.*, July/August, 1956.
13. Kennedy, T. and Allen, R., Solectron Corporation internal paper, 1994.
14. Jaffe, D., Scott, C., and Tobe, G., *Rekindling Commitment*, Jossey-Bass, San Francisco, CA, 1994.
15. Bridges, W., *Transitions: Making Sense of Life's Changes*, Addison Wesley, Reading, MA, 1980.
16. Marrow, A., *Management by Participation: Creating a Climate for Personal and Organizational Development*, Harper and Row, New York, 1967.
17. Waterman, R., Peters, T., and Phillips, J., Structure is not organization, *Bus. Horiz.*, June, 1980.
18. Weisbord, M., *Organizational Diagnosis: A Workbook of Theory and Practice*, Perseus Books, Reading, MA, 1978.

19. Pieters, G., *Quality Improvement Team Reference Manual*, The Quality Improvement Company, Cupertino, CA, 1989.

20. Blake, R. and Mouton, J., *The New Managerial Grid*, Gulf Publishing Company, Houston, TX, 1978.

21. Myers, S., Every employee a manager, *Calif. Manage. Rev.*, Vol. X, No. 3, Berkley, CA, Spring, 1968, pp. 9-20.

22. Hackman, R. and Oldham, G., *Work Redesign*, Addison Wesley, Reading, MA, 1980.

23. Pieters, G., OD: Not if, but how?, *Vision/Action: The Journal of The Bay Area Organization Development Network*, Vol. 2, No. 3, San Francisco, CA, 1982.

24. Harwood, C., *Kick Down the Door of Complacency*, St. Lucie Press, Boca Raton, FL, 1998.

25. *1999 Criteria for Performance Excellence*, Malcolm Baldrige National Quality Award, Gaithersburg, MD, 1999.

26. Ramcharamdas, E., Xerox creates a continuous learning environment for business transformation, *Planning Rev.*, March/April, 1994.

27. Crosby, P., *Quality is Free: The Art of Making Quality Certain*, Mentor Books, New York, 1978.

28. Kepner, C. and Tregoe, B., *The New Rational Manager*, Princeton Research Press, Princeton, NJ, 1981.

29. Gabor, A., *The Man Who Discovered Quality*, Penguin Books, New York, 1990.

30. Rummler, G. and Brache, A., *Improving Performance*, Jossey-Bass, San Francisco, CA, 1990.

31. Walton, M. and Deming, W. E., *The Deming Management Method*, Perigree Publishing, New York, 1988.

32. Motorola, Training for the millenium, *Bus. Week*, March 28, 1994, p. 158.

33. Prahalad, C. and Hamel, G., The core competencies of the corporation, *Harv. Bus. Rev.*, May/June, 1990.

34. Douglas, C. and McCauley, C., A survey on the use of formal developmental relationships in organizations, *Issues Observ.*, Vol. 17, No. 1-2, Center for Creative Leadership, 1997.

35. Neri, T., *Continuous Improvement Workbook I*, The Quality Improvement Company, Cupertino, CA, 1995.

36. Applied Materials, Inc., 10 Ways to be Successful, Internal document, 1997.

37. Argyris, C. and Schön, D., *Organizational Learning II: Theory, Method and Practice*, Addison-Wesley, Reading, MA, 1996.

38. Senge, P., *The Fifth Discipline: The Art and Practice of The Learning Organization*, Doubleday/Currency, New York, 1990.

39. Young, D., "Closing the Skills Gap in American Business," *The Personnel News*, San Jose, CA, 1990, pp. 21–24.

40 Pieters, G. and Young, D., The Changing, Learning and Improving Organization, Unpublished EverChange Institute paper, 1996.

Index

A

ABC model
    getting started in ECO, 241
    identification/testing assumptions,
        226–228
    organizational control assessment and
        managing FOR change, 144
    problem solving, 17–21
    results and stabilizing base, 102
Abilene Paradox, 46, 81
Acceptable quality levels (AQLs), 47
Accountability, 127, 129, *see also*
        Management Systems Model
Adaptability, organizations, 15
Adaptations, 37, *see also* Uncertainty
Advocacy groups, 56–57
Agreed upon goals, *see* Goals
Alignment
    goal and stabilizing base, 80–82
    organizational and ABC model, 229–230
Amazon.com, 50–51
Ann Taylor, 64, 68
Application base, 54–55
Applied Materials, 218–219
Apprentice, 210, *see also* Continuous
        learning
AQLs, *see* Acceptable quality levels
Assumptions
    ABC model, 18, 19
    testing/identification and continuous
        learning, 226–230

Attitude, changes with information access,
        99–100
Autodesk, 52, 86
Automobile industry, 47
Autonomous work teams, 146–147
Awareness, 127, 128, *see also* Management
        Systems Model

B

Balance, 103–106, *see also* Stabilizing base
Banks, 109
Barriers, change, 15
Behavior, 18, 19, 84–86, *see also* ABC model;
        Stabilizing base
BEI Sensors and Systems, 39, 135, 207–208
Benchmarking, 114, 159–160
Best practices, 159
BHAGS, *see* Big, hairy, audacious goals
Bias, 249
Big, hairy, audacious goals (BHAGS), 189
Board of Directors, 237
Boundaries, knowledge of, 90
Brainstorming, 190–191
Breakthrough change, 118–119
Breakthrough improvement, 160–161, *see
        also* Continuous improvement
Business, change as strategy, 132–134

C